ANGLISTIK UND ENGLISCHUNTERRICHT

Herausgegeben von
Gabriele Linke
Holger Rossow
Merle Tönnies

Band 87

SARAH HERBE
GABRIELE LINKE (Eds.)

British Autobiography in the 20th and 21st Centuries

Universitätsverlag
WINTER
Heidelberg

Bibliografische Information der Deutschen Nationalbibliothek

Die Deutsche Nationalbibliothek verzeichnet diese Publikation
in der Deutschen Nationalbibliografie;
detaillierte bibliografische Daten sind im Internet
über *http://dnb.d-nb.de* abrufbar.

Herausgeber:

Prof. Dr. Gabriele Linke
PD Dr. Holger Rossow
Prof. Dr. Merle Tönnies

ISBN 978-3-8253-6848-7
ISSN 0344-8266

Imprimé en Allemagne · Printed in Germany
Druck: Memminger MedienCentrum, 87700 Memmingen

Gedruckt auf umweltfreundlichem, chlorfrei gebleichtem
und alterungsbeständigem Papier

Den Verlag erreichen Sie im Internet unter:
www.winter-verlag.de

Contents

Sarah Herbe (Salzburg) and Gabriele Linke (Rostock)

Introduction

Autobiographies are among the bestselling books in Britain, and other forms of autobiographical expression outside the book format flourish as well. In the book market alone, the published life narratives reflect the richness and diversity of the human experience, of which John Sutherland's memoir *Blue* about police work, Gordon Smith's *Autobiography of the World's Greatest Living Medium* and Laura James' autobiographical narrative of *An Autistic Woman in a Neurotypical World* are just a few if characteristic examples. In the digital world, vlogging and blogging, for example, have become major means of re-constructing and representing lives. With regard to scholarly responses, a glance at the activities of the *International Auto/Biography Association* (IABA) and at academic publications reveals that the study of life writing has developed into a vibrant field of research. It has moved towards recognition as a discipline in its own right, for example with the publication of Ricia Anne Chansky and Emily Hipchen's *Routledge Autobiography Studies Reader*, as such *Readers* represent sure signs of a field taking shape through the dynamic canonisation[1] of theoretical approaches. However, while a number of publications dedicated to the study of American autobiography have recently come out, such as *Reading African American Autobiography: Twenty-First-Century Contexts and Criticism* (Lamore 2017), *American Autobiography after 9/11* (Brown 2016) or *Words of Witness: Black Women's Autobiography in the Post-Brown Era* (Ards 2016), monographs and collections of critical perspectives on twentieth and twenty-first century British autobiography have been rare, and most of them already date back several years.

There is, however, a tradition of British scholarship on autobiography. In *English Autobiography: Its Emergence, Materials and Form,* published in 1954, Wayne Shumaker (an American scholar) claimed that the conventions of British autobiography still dominant by the mid-twentieth century were already in place in the eighteenth century, arguing that "[t]he whole body of English autobiography from 1796 to the present is thus recognizably one genre".[2] Though Shumaker's study focuses on an almost exclusively British corpus of texts, its avowed ahistorical approach means that the cultural and historical particularities of these texts are largely neglected.

Roy Pascal's *Design and Truth in Autobiography* (1960) is an example of an early British contribution to the field but Pascal considers autobiography to be a European phenomenon, less determined by nation though with each culture having produced its own treasures. Therefore, he employs a wide range of European examples rather than focusing on British ones. The recent *Cambridge Companion to Autobiography* follows a similar line, privileging British works only in chapters on Romantic and Victorian autobiography.[3] There are, however, a few more comprehensive studies with a British focus, such as Brian Finney's *The Inner I: British Literary Autobiography of the Twentieth Century*, which was published in 1985. In his introduction, Finney addresses the lack of critical material on British autobiography, as opposed to American autobiography, in general, and a dearth of studies on the twentieth century in particular. In his own study, Finney focuses on the autobiographies of British writers in the twentieth century, thus remaining within the boundaries of literary studies. An issue of *Prose Studies* dedicated to *Modern British and American Autobiography* also dates back to 1985.

Although the 1990s brought a further elaboration of concepts and theories in autobiography studies with British contributions such as Liz Stanley's *The Autobiographical I* and Harold Rosen's *Speaking from Memory: A Guide to Autobiographical Acts and Practices*, the study of contemporary British autobiography in particular evolved mainly through individual articles in collections and journals. Such individual chapters and essays dedicated to the study of British autobiography are, for example, Wendy Webster's "Our Life: Working-Class Women's Autobiography in Britain" (1992), or Nicola King's "Uses of the Past: Hindsight and the Representation of Childhood in some Recent British Academic Autobiography" (2009), but a collection that introduces the variety of British autobiographical writing in the twentieth and twenty-first centuries is still missing.

To our knowledge, there is no British equivalent for studies like Barbara Prys-Williams' *Twentieth-Century Autobiography* (2004) for Wales, or Claire Lynch's *Irish Autobiography: Stories of the Self in the Narrative of a Nation* (2009) for Ireland. The volume presented here, though, cannot close that gap and provide a coherent and conclusive overview on twentieth-century British autobiography as the field is too vast; it will, however, bring together exemplary studies of different media, forms and issues of British autobiographical writing in the twentieth and twenty-first centuries, testifying to the creativity and diversity of both autobiographical texts and analytical angles.

British autobiography itself has, by and large, followed international trends, with the continuation of traditional (exemplary lives) life narratives by statesmen and -women, or authors and artists, while it has also participated in the rise of popular autobiography and the genre's democratization, as exemplified at the beginning of this introduction, as well as the diversification of subgenres and forms, including genres that have developed with the new opportunities social media offer. The essays collected here give an insight into the variety of forms of autobiographical expression in Britain.

Defining issues of British society such as class are immanently present in most contributions to this volume, as for example in Simone Herrmann's, Gabriele Linke's and Cyprian Piskurek's essays. The construction of Britishness through encounters with an Other is present in some graphic memoirs but the complexity and inner contradictions of lives in Britain prevail. More generally, questions of identity are addressed in almost all of the contributions collected here, ranging from national identities in the essays by Herrmann, Linke and Sarah Herbe through how identity is affected by one's football fandom to the multiple identities the authors of disability autobiographies create for themselves in their work.

Since all of the essays collected here address questions of genre, they are not just relevant as case studies of texts which have often not yet attracted much scholarly attention, but present an introduction to some of the most popular contemporary autobiographical genres, such as autobiographical comics, fan autobiographies or blogs.

Furthermore, this volume is intended to contribute to the growing field of 'teaching life writing studies', which, initiated by the collection *Teaching Life Writing Texts* edited by Miriam Fuchs and Craig Howes in 2008, has become increasingly popular over the past decade as evident in, for example, the recent special issue of *a/b: Auto/biography Studies* on "Teaching Lives" (32.1, 2017) or the envisaged teaching section in the *European Journal of Life Writing*. While only Markus Oppolzer and Ralf Schneider provide explicit didactic recommendations in their contributions, the other articles also offer material for various teaching contexts, particularly for university settings. Football fan autobiographies (Piskurek), life narratives from rural Scotland (Linke) and the anthology of women's disability narratives (Röder) can provide the basis for explorations of (British) identity in cultural studies as well as literature classes, while a discussion of Jeanette Winterson's blog can serve to create awareness of students' own online life writing activities as well as an introduction to the subject and methods of the digital humanities.

In a collection on twentieth and twenty-first century British autobiography assembled at the time of the centenary of the First World War, an article on autobiographical writing of the Great War seems more than appropriate. Ralf Schneider argues that these autobiographies provided a forum for the communication of individual experience and memory on the one hand, and, on the other hand, contributed to a diversification of the autobiographical genre and the subgenre of the war autobiography in particular. In support of his major thesis of the diversity of autobiographical writing about the First World War, Schneider inspects examples along various axes such as canonical and non-canonical texts, texts written and published at different times from 1918 to the 1990s, autobiographies by persons from different ranks and branches of the military and women's war autobiographies from different times and perspectives.

In the second part of his argument, that is, his discussion of the subgenre of the war autobiography, Schneider succeeds in determining several defining features of these texts, such as a concern with the gap between those who experienced the war and those who did not, with authentication and the difficulties of communicating the uncommunicable. In the description of both the diversity of the genre and its peculiarities, Schneider achieves a high degree of systematicity, elucidating main features of a large body of texts. Furthermore, he suggests teaching strategies that make use of and establish links between diverse texts to highlight certain features of the Great War, war experiences and memorialisation.

The title of James Fenwick's contribution, "'Freddie, Can You Talk?' The Ethics of Betrayal in Frederic Raphael's Memoir *Eyes Wide Open* (1999)", indicates already that ethical questions involved in auto/biographical writing are being addressed here. Raphael had collaborated with Kubrick on the screenplay for *Eyes Wide Shut*, being fully aware of Kubrick's trust and intense need for privacy, but later he published his memories of their numerous conversations, which evoked protests from the Kubrick estate. Fenwick uses this case to raise the question to what extent Kubrick's trust was betrayed by Raphael and how the particular stylistic qualities of Raphael's text make it a literary work in its own right and justify the breach of trust.

In some ways, Sarah Herbe's "Self-Presentation and -Promotion in Jeanette Winterson's Online Column (2000–2014)" also deals with ethical issues though in the context of a different medium and genre. From a description of the contents and form of Winterson's blog, Herbe moves on to questions of genre, detecting elements of the conversion story, scriptotherapy and self-help instructions for readers. On this basis, she problematises Winterson's uses of her blog space, arguing that the dissolving of the boundaries between private and public and the creation of an intimate public are not only a form of self-expression but also of advertising, self-promotion and binding readers as customers, which involves ethical questions. Winterson's frustration with blogging and subsequent shift to twitter for more immediacy are also discussed critically.

Online self-presentation is among the most widespread forms of autobiographical expression in the twenty-first century; another form that has become increasingly popular since the 1980s are autobiographical comics. In "Graphic Isolation? Imagining Contemporary Britain in Graphic Memoirs", the first of two contributions on autobiographical comics, Simone Herrmann argues that graphic memoirs are particularly suitable for expressing questions of identity formation in a historical context. Based on a reading of four graphic memoirs published between 1998 and 2012, she explores how Britishness is negotiated with the help of visual and verbal strategies. She shows how the depiction of intergenerational conflicts expresses changing notions of class consciousness and explores the relationships between personal and historical memory in both Raymond Briggs' *Ethel & Ernest – A True Story* (1998) and Mary M. and Bryan Talbot's *Dotter of her Father's Eye* (2012). Her reading of Marc Ellerby's *Ellerbisms* (2012) and James Harvey's *A Long Day of Mr. James-Teacher* (2011) shows how Britishness as a cultural identity emerges particularly when the author-protagonists find themselves confronted with European and other international settings.

Markus Oppolzer, then, gives an overview of sources on teaching autobiographical comics in schools and suggests classroom activities for different age groups in his contribution on "Teaching (British) Autobiographical Comics". He starts his article with a profound discussion of the terminological difficulties we are confronted with in debates around both life writing in general and autobiographical comics in particular. He proceeds to outline the importance of paying attention to the language of comics and of considering the cultural context as well as the question of genre when comics are taught in schools in order to train the students' literary and intercultural competences. Based on examples from a variety of British autobiographical comics, Oppolzer argues that it is important to draw the students' attention to the verbal and visual particularities of the comics genre as well as to the generic characteristics of autobiographical writing when one uses autobiographical comics as teaching material. As issues relevant for teaching, he identifies the 'autobiographical I', embodiment as visually presented in comics and autobiographical truth as central for fostering a thorough engagement with autobiographical comics and for developing a critical reading stance.

A rather different angle is taken by Katrin Röder in her article on British women's disability autobiographies. Her starting point is that autobiographical writing functions as an important cultural practice of representing disability because it allows self-representation and challenges popular stereotypes. Röder analyses the accounts by women with disabilities which are assembled in Lois Keith's anthology *Mustn't Grumble* to discuss the connections between femininity, dependence / independence and disability. The texts are by authors of diverse backgrounds and with very different disabilities who, each in their own way, write about their life with disabilities, not conforming to normative expectations but expressing different perceptions of themselves and their environment, different affective responses but a general refusal to see their lives as tragedy and to repress anger. Röder pays special attention to affects such as shame, anger and fear as well as self-love and enjoyment and links the texts to the British – social – model of disability.

Focusing on a different framework of social arrangements, Cyprian Piskurek examines the phenomenon of the football fan autobiography in the context of the changes that have taken place in football culture in the UK since the late 1980s, including the recognition of football fandom as forming part of one's identity. He argues that "[t]his new-found consciousness of self [among football fans] was a prerequisite for the urge to represent those selves in writing" (164). Starting from Nick Hornby's *Fever Pitch* (1992) as a model for later football fan autobiographies, Piskurek discusses the particularities of this genre, showing how fandom and its associated activities emerge as the ordering principle of these texts, and ultimately as defining the identities of the author-protagonists. He pays close attention to the generic labels attached to those texts (for marketing reasons), which highlights the tenuous boundary between autobiographical and fictionalised elements. After addressing the sub-genre of hooligan autobiographies in the final part of his contribution, Piskurek concludes that the emergence of autobiographies by football fans in addition to autobiographies by football players or managers has added to the democratisation of the market for autobiographies, where not only the voices of the famous, but also of the marginalised make themselves heard.

The marketplace is also considered in Gabriele Linke's contribution on "Autobiographical Narratives from Rural Scotland since the Second World War". Linke argues that the titles and labels of the corpus of texts she considers suggest a far more uniform experience of life in the Highlands and islands than a close reading of the nine autobiographies reveals. In these texts, published between 1960 and 2015, perspectives on rural Scotland are provided by both authors who were born there as well as outsiders who chose to start a new life in Scotland in the context of the 'return to nature' movement since the 1950s. What the autobiographies have in common is that they do not only trace the personal experience of the authors, but also document the changes of life and rural labour that have taken place in Scotland since the middle of the twentieth century. They also preserve the memories of a way of living that no longer exists, which turns their narrators into ethnographers. Some of the autobiographies go beyond a merely nostalgic lament for the past in their display of a markedly ecocritical stance, and Linke identifies the "ecological epilogue" as a frequently employed element in these texts.

While the genres and texts discussed in the contributions in this volume cover a broad spectrum, it is of course no complete survey of British autobiographical writing of the twentieth and twenty-first centuries, which would further include, for example, working-class autobiographies and life writing found in archives, as well as fictional autobiographies or autobiographies by celebrities. Transgender autobiographies have recently won great critical acclaim as stage performances with two productions by the National Theatre of Scotland that were presented at the Edinburgh International Festival 2017: *Eve*, in which Jo Clifford speaks about her search for her self, from her childhood as a boy in the 1950s to her present life as a woman, and *Eve*'s companion piece *Adam*, whose script was written by Frances Poet in collaboration with Adam Kashmiri. Kashmiri, born as a girl in Egypt, tells his tale of fleeing from Egypt for Scotland, where he transitions from a woman to a man. Furthermore, memoirs about the diverse experiences of immigrants and ethnic groups have recently come to some prominence with, for example, the publication of Jackie Kay's *Red Dust Road: An Autobiographical Journey* and Hanif Kureishi's *My Ear at His Heart: Reading My Father*, both of which were critically acclaimed. Other autobiographical texts respond rather directly to recent changes in the situation of ethnic groups, such as Zia Chaudhry's *Just Your Average Muslim: The Unheard Voice* or the autobiographical essays collected in *The Good Immigrant*, while there has also been a growing number of memoirs by Eastern Europeans living in Britain, of which Vesna Maric's *Bluebird: A Memoir* may suffice as an example. These, again, could not be considered in our collection, but studies have been published elsewhere.

Contributions on more traditional autobiographies of politicians or authors, which still comprise a big share in the book market, have not been included in order to draw the readers' attention to more marginal texts, and to autobiographies on which there has not been much scholarship so far. More work needs to be done, but we are confident that more studies will follow and continue to reflect the diversity and dynamics of life and its stories.

Notes

1 On the question of the canon of autobiography, see Stelzig, Eugene (1992). "Is There a Canon of Autobiography?" *a/b Auto/Biography Studies* 7.1, 1-13.

2 Shumaker, Wayne (1954). *English Autobiography: Its Emergence, Materials, and Form.* Berkeley and Los Angeles: University of California Press, 30.

3 DiBattista, Maria, and Emily O. Wittman (eds.) (2014). *The Cambridge Companion to Autobiography.* Cambridge: Cambridge University Press.

Bibliography

Ards, Angela D. (2016). *Words of Witness: Black Women's Autobiography in the Post-Brown Era.* Madison, WI: University of Wisconsin Press.

Brown, Megan (2016). *American Autobiography after 9/11.* Wisconsin: University of Wisconsin Press.

Chansky, Ricia Anne, and Emily Hipchen (eds.) (2016). *The Routledge Autobiography Studies Reader.* London & New York: Routledge.

Chaudhry, Zia (2015). *Just Your Average Muslim: The Unheard Voice.* London: Short Books.

Clifford, Jo, and Chris Goode (2017). *Eve.* London: Oberon Books.

DiBattista, Maria, and Emily O. Wittman (eds.) (2014). *The Cambridge Companion to Autobiography.* New York: CUP.

Finney, Brian (1985). *The Inner I: British Literary Autobiography of the Twentieth Century.* London and Boston: Faber & Faber.

Fuchs, Miriam and Craig Howes (eds.) (2008). *Teaching Life Writing Texts.* New York: MLA.

James, Laura (2017). *Odd Girl Out: An Autistic Woman in a Neurotypical World.* London: Bluebird.

Jensen, Meg, and Jane Jordan (eds.) (2009). *Life Writing: The Spirit of the Age and the State of the Art.* Newcastle: Cambridge Scholars.

Kay, Jackie (2010). *Red Dust Road: An Autobiographical Journey.* London: Picador.

King, Nicola (2009). "Uses of the Past: Hindsight and the Representation of Childhood in some Recent British Academic Autobiography." *Rethinking History* 13.1: 95-108.

Kureishi, Hanif (2004). *My Ear at His Heart: Reading My Father.* London: Faber & Faber.

Lamore, Eric D. (2017). *Reading African American Autobiography: Twenty-First-Century Contexts and Criticism.* Chicago: University of Wisconsin Press.

Lynch, Claire (2009). *Irish Autobiography: Stories of Self in the Narrative of a Nation.* Oxford et al.: Peter Lang.

Maric, Vesna (2009). *Bluebird: A Memoir.* London: Granta.

Pascal, Roy (1960). *Design and Truth in Autobiography.* London: Routledge & Kegan Paul.

Poet, Frances (2017). *Adam.* London: Nick Hern Books.

Prys-Williams, Barbara (2004). *Twentieth-century Autobiography.* Cardiff: University of Wales Press.

Rosen, Harold (1998). *Speaking from Memory: A Guide to Autobiographical Acts and Practices.* Stoke on Trent: Trentham.

Shukla, Nikesh (ed.) (2016). *The Good Immigrant.* London: Unbound.

Shumaker, Wayne (1954). *English Autobiography: Its Emergence, Materials, and Form.* Berkeley and Los Angeles: University of California Press.

Smith, Gordon (2014). *The Best of Both Worlds: The Autobiography of the World's Greatest Living Medium.* London: Coronet.

Stanley, Liz (1992). *The Autobiographical I.* Manchester: Manchester University Press.

Stelzig, Eugene (1992). "Is There a Canon of Autobiography?" *a/b Auto/Biography Studies* 7.1, 1-13.

Sutherland, John (2017*). Blue. A Memoir – Keeping the Peace and Falling to Pieces*. London: Weidenfeld & Nicolson

Teaching Lives: Contemporary Pedagogies of Life Narratives (2017). *a/b: Auto/Biography Studies* 32.1.

Webster, Wendy (1992). "*Our life: working class women's autobiography in Britain." Imagining Women: Cultural Representations and Gender.* Ed. Frances Bonner. Issues in Women's Studies. Cambridge: Polity Press, 116-127.

Ralf Schneider (Bielefeld)

The Autobiography of the First World War

1. Introduction

The First World War is generally held to be a cataclysm, an *Ur*-catastrophe of modernity. A plethora of poems, novels and short stories as well as films and also some theatre plays have recorded and evaluated the experience of the 'Great War', or WWI, as it is frequently abbreviated, and they have shaped the ways in which it is remembered.[1] That this war should have an even more prominent position in the cultural memory of Great Britain than the Second World War is partly due to that sprawling field of literary and documentary medialisation. Autobiographies had a significant share in that process, and they are a highly interesting, complex and rather ambiguous genre that deserves deeper study, as I will argue below.[2] In general, the autobiography is a mode of writing in which both the experience and the memory of a person have their place. As far as the First World War is concerned, there is a mutual influence between the genre and the events that find their way into autobiographies. On the one hand, the genre of the autobiography provided a forum for the expression of the experience and memory of WWI of individuals and made them available to a wide audience. On the other, the genre framework of autobiographical writing itself was affected by the impact of the war: While previous autobiographies were usually written at a late phase in life and usually covered either the entire life-span of the author or at least significant phases of considerable length,[3] WWI autobiographies tend to focus on the war years and the years immediately following them, and sometimes they restrict themselves to very short phases within that time frame. For the first time in the history of autobiography, large numbers of texts were written by men and women in their late twenties and thirties.[4] These are some of the characteristics that have significantly shaped the cultural memory of that war on a larger scale, and they have done so over an entire century: Autobiographies centrally concerned with the experience and memory of WWI have been a continuous presence on the British book market. The early ones have been reprinted (often in connection with the anniversaries of the beginning or end of the war), and new texts have kept appearing. Although the corpus is extremely large and varied, as will become clear in what follows, there are some characteristic features that WWI autobiographies share because the trauma of war experience and the concomitant difficulties of remembering shape the way that this particular type of autobiography is written. In this article, I aim at delivering an impression of the variety of First World War autobiographies, at giving insight into the features that characterise the war autobiography as a special subgenre by pointing to some prototypical examples. I will conclude with some considerations concerning the didactic potential of these texts.

2. Selected Memories and the Variety of WWI Autobiographies, or: What Is the Corpus?

Some autobiographies belong to the canon of British First World War literature. Edmund Blunden's *Undertones of War* (1928), Robert Graves' *Goodbye to All That* (1929), Siegfried Sassoon's *Memoirs of an Infantry Officer* (1930) and Vera Brittain's *Testament of Youth* (1933) are among the core texts of that canon. Together with many poems, some novels and very few theatre plays, their representations of the experience of trench warfare at the Western front – with glimpses of the home front, as in Vera Brittain's case – have led to a selection and even narrowing down of images of the WWI symptomatic of the overall emergence of the cultural memory of that war.[5] Until today, the texts of a few highly educated persons, who were writers already before they went to war, who were stationed mostly with the infantry at the Western front, and whose experiences focused on the hardships and horrors of trench warfare in Flanders and France, have dominated the perception of the Great War with the autobiographies they published some ten years after the end of the war. However, the overall autobiographical output on WWI is much more diverse and extensive.

First of all, autobiographies kept appearing as long as there were survivors of the war. The first and most productive phase of war-related autobiographical writing lasted from the end of the war until the late 1930s. These texts presented a number of tensions and ambivalences that are characteristic of the entire genre of WWI autobiography, as I will elaborate further below. The second phase, which lasted roughly from the 1940s until the 1970s, saw the reprinting of some major earlier texts that were already regarded as 'classics' of English Literature.[6] The reprints were certainly prompted by the 50th anniversaries of the beginning and end of the war as well as the later peace movement. That phase also produced a number of new autobiographies of writers who looked back at their war experience from some distance, such as Edgar Norman Gladden's *Ypres, 1917: A Personal Account* (1967 and reprinted in 1977). Some texts now saw the light of the British book market although they had been written or even published elsewhere before: Richard Aldington, the author of an influential novel that fictionalised his war experience (*Death of a Hero*, 1929), had written an autobiography, *Life for Life's Sake*, that was first printed in the USA in 1941 and republished in Britain in 1968; Ernest Parker's *Into Battle* was first published in 1964, but written in the 1930s "when the experiences of early youth were fresh in my mind".[7] In the third phase, the 1980s and 1990s, there were naturally fewer veterans who would be able to write their autobiographies, but not only did many reprints of the earlier texts appear, some elderly authors also returned to their diaries or other documents from the war years to finally put together an autobiographical account, while others retrieved their own accounts which had been written already in the immediate post-war years but had never been published. Some of them add different perspectives to the established perception of WWI, including George Ashurst, whose *My Bit: A Lancashire Fusilier at war 1914-1918* (1983) is the account of a simple worker turned soldier who was present at some major theatres of war (Ypres, the Somme and Gallipoli). Norman Tennant's *A Saturday Night Soldier's War, 1913-1918* (1983) is another example: the text alternates between autobiographical chapters and the reproduction of the author's diary entries from 1916 on. Tennant was a member of the Local Territorial Army, which "differed from the Regular Army in that they consisted of officers and men who knew each other intimately in civilian life",[8] and his war experience was that of a signaller responsible for "laying and maintaining, in impossible conditions, the miles of telephone cables on the Western Front"[9] – a job that fulfilled vital functions for military communication at the front line, but is hardly ever represented in the cultural production of the First World War.

As far as the branches of the military are concerned, autobiographies were written not only by members of the infantry, such as Blunden, Graves and Sassoon, but also by soldiers of other branches, reminding us that the men 'going over the top' of the trenches were not the only ones who fought in the First World War. Some authors belong to the artillery (including Aubrey Wade's *War of the Guns*, of 1936, reprinted in 1959 with the new title *Gunner on the Western Front*), others were pilots (James Byford McCudden's *Flying Fury* of 1918, Duncan Grinnell-Milne's *Wind in the Wires* of 1933, and Cecil Lewis' *Sagittarius Rising* of 1936, to name just a few examples), cavalrymen (Ben Clouting, *Tickled to Death to Go*, 1996) and even members of the navy (Filson Young's *With the Battlecruisers*, 1921, and E. Hilton Young's *By Sea and Land*, 1924). The areas of war experience represented in these texts are naturally rather different from each other, the artillery for instance being concerned with the problem of transporting heavy guns and ammunition across heavily bombarded countryside, while the airmen conjure up a special ethos, and a kind of hero-worship that is reminiscent of earlier types of warfare and evokes notions of fights of man against man, praising individual skills – something rarely to be found in attacks conducted by the infantry.

Feminist literary scholarship has shifted the balance away from the predominantly male perspective to acknowledge the autobiographical output of women beside Vera Brittain.[10] Female war autobiographies include a variety of texts, covering the experience of, and views on, the war by women who worked as nurses or at rest camps behind the lines (Enid Bagnold, *A Diary Without Dates*, 1918; Lesley Smith, *Four Years Out Of Life*, 1931; Irene Rathbone, *We That Were Young*, 1932, a text that can be read as a semi-fictional autobiography or a semi-autobiographical novel),[11] and women campaigning against the war in England (Silvia Pankhurst, *The Home Front*, 1937). Virago Press managed to reprint many of those texts in the 1970s and 1980s, keeping them available to complement the public memory of the war that had been dominated by male voices. Beside the texts written by nurses, there are also some by doctors (e.g., David Rorie, *A Medico's Luck in the War*,

1929). In addition to that, soldiers who never fought at the front but worked in administration (W.N. Nicholson, *Behind the Lines*, 1939) contributed to the genre, as did soldiers who were kept prisoners of war (Alec Waugh, *The Prisoners of Mainz*, 1919; Hugh Durnford, *The Tunnelers of Holzminden*, 1920) or were involved in the war as war reporters (Philip Gibbs, *Now It Can Be Told*, 1920; Basil H. Liddell Hart, *The Memoirs of Captain Liddell Hart*, 1956). What is more, not only highly educated men – who were directly slotted into the position of officers, as were Blunden and Sassoon – wrote their autobiographies, but some simple soldiers did, too (Frank Richards, *Old Soldiers Never Die*, 1933, repr. 1964; W.H.A. Groom, *Poor Bloody Infantry*, 1976). The accounts of the latter frequently centre on the physical hardships of trench life, on the inadequacy of the equipment, on the incomprehensibility of orders and strategies, and the arrogance of the generals, but they also highlight the importance of the spirit of comradeship, so that their accounts, astonishingly perhaps, do not necessarily amount to overall anti-war pamphlets. Less surprisingly, when professional soldiers write their autobiography, particularly if they belonged to the military leaders, the emphasis is usually less on the personal experience, but on the inevitability of war and the opportunities it offers men to demonstrate such laudable dispositions as a sense of duty, courage, and comradeship. Sir Tom Bridges, who published *Alarms and Excursions* in 1930, was a Lieutenant General in the war, and the introduction by Winston Churchill (who was Lord of the Admiralty between 1915 and 1919) focuses on the political significance of the autobiographer. Frank Percy Crozier's *A Brass Hat in No Man's Land* (1930, and republished 1937 and 1987) stresses the necessity of professionalism in the art of warfare, and although he maintains that the sacrifice of a thousand men in half an hour is justified if territory can be gained, he concedes that it is despicable if no land gain can be made – as happened in the Battle of the Somme. He doubts that warfare can be made more 'human': "Far better to eradicate the cause – War itself – than to build up hope that it can be waged in any other way than by brute force and brute means."[12]

3. The War Autobiography – a Special Genre?

We have seen that the autobiography of the First World War is a genre of many voices and perspectives, and one that has had an almost uninterrupted presence on the British book market. In spite of this diversity, there are some aspects that the texts tend to share, and that turn the WWI autobiography into a rather special subgenre of autobiographical writing. The autobiography of the First World War inherits some general features from the overall genre of autobiographical writing, but it displays some special characteristics, too. Hynes claims that war writing is "a genre without a tradition to the men who write it".[13] I do not entirely agree with this because some early war autobiographies make use of other literary traditions as I will point out below, and at least many later autobiographers must have been very much aware of previous contributions to their genre. However, the point Hynes makes that the previous tradition of autobiographical life-writing could hardly provide suitable models for the rendering of war experience, holds true. One important issue in discussions of the genre characteristics of autobiographical writing is the question of veracity. According to Lejeune (1994), there exists a tacit 'autobiographical pact' between the author and the reader of an autobiography, on the basis of which both treat the text in particular ways: the author does not deliberately mislead the reader as to the facts he or she reports, and the reader assumes that he or she is given a truthful account of lived experience. The important thing is that the author will not be held responsible if he utters statements that may deviate slightly from established knowledge, because there is room for the individual experience of the speaker. There is then, an emphasis on the *truthfulness of the experience* rendered, rather than on some kind of objective truth, in the production and reception of autobiographies. Things are a bit more complicated in the case of the war autobiography. Of course, readers may expect the authors not to be lying outright – war is simply a topic you do not mess around with, it is too serious, painful and tragic to allow for much bending of the truth.[14] But then, the war also places a high degree of responsibility on writers, and the authors studied here are all very much aware of that burden. I will argue that this can be seen in the way they situated themselves, and their texts, within four opposing force fields: They stand between non-communicability and the need to talk, between authentication and distancing, between literariness and factuality, and between individual and collective memory. It is also striking that the authors position themselves in rather diverse ways, but conspicuously throughout the entire corpus, both vis-à-vis the younger self that they remember and the general memory discourse of the First World War. I will introduce the term 'meta-mnestic commentary' to describe this self-positioning.

Almost all authors claim in the prefaces, introductions, or first paragraphs of their texts that they feel an unbridgeable gap between those who experienced the war themselves and those who did not; as Charles 'Edmonds' (a pseudonym for Charles Carrington) puts it in *A Subaltern's War* (1929): "Middle-aged men, strenuously as they attempt to deny it, are united by a secret bond and separated by a mental barrier from their fellows who were too young or too old to fight in the war."[15] The problem is that most of the authors thought they would never manage to communicate their experiences. Remarkably, though, such utterances precede the attempts, which are rather lengthy in most cases, to do precisely what ought to be impossible: to communicate the incommunicable. In contrast to other autobiographies, the war autobiography is burdened with the task to give access to ranges of experience for which the writers find it hard to find words – the event was so enormous, so bizarre and unprecedented that none of the war autobiographies is a simple narrative of the speaking self's own life. This difficult position of the autobiographer vis-à-vis his or her own previous experience must affect the treatment of the material. It manifests itself in different modes of writing that I would like to subsume under 'authentication strategies' on the one hand, and 'distancing strategies' on the other.

I regard as authentication strategies all the means that help the reader to envision and visualise the circumstances described in the text and to alert him or her to the presence experienced by the writer in the wartime. One such device is the use of the present tense instead of the usual narrative preterite. Very few war autobiographies are entirely written in the present tense (as, for instance, Charles Yale Harrison's *Generals Die in Bed*, 1930), because thereby the author deprives himself of the opportunity to comment on the younger self or the impressions of that time in retrospect. Individual scenes, however, can easily be rendered in that fashion to highlight the emergency, the intensity of emotion, or the breathlessness of the experience. Another authentication strategy is the use of documentary modes of presentation. Authors can simply claim the factuality of their account by referring to authentic sources. Edmonds'/Carrington's *A Subaltern's War* uses this strategy when he says that in the writing process he was aided by his own "war diaries and other confidential papers" and other material:

> By referring to them, a journal which I kept irregularly at the front, and to letters to my mother, I have been able to substantiate the main facts of the stories, which, to the best of my knowledge, are historically accurate. The rest of this book is composed of fragments from the same sources with a good deal of explanatory matter, which I venture to add for the information of any post-war readers of this book.[16]

Some authors also integrate documentary material, such as a variety of texts and documents, drawings and photos from the immediate wartime into their texts to signal authenticity, either by way of quotation or direct facsimile reproduction. Only a third of Norman Tennant's *A Saturday Night Soldiers' War, 1913-1918* (1983), for instance, actually consists of an autobiographical account; the rest is the reprint of the author's diary of the time after January 1916, on which the autobiography is based. The text is full of Tennant's humoristic drawings, with which he intends to render an impression of the good mood that dominated in his unit. H.S. Clapham's *Mud and Khaki* (1930) features sixteen photographs of the trenches, including one taken "during the attack on June 16th (From a film found on the body of a soldier killed that day)".[17] It is almost impossible to discern anything on this grainy picture taken from a large distance, except for a few tiny soldiers who appear to be running in a crouched position, and some others lying in cover or dead, and some pillars of smoke. The function of this image, then, is not the concrete illustration of any scene described in the surrounding text, but to evoke the thrill of a documentary recording of a battle. The aviators' autobiographies, unsurprisingly, feature many photos of the planes the authors used (e.g. Duncan Grinnell-Milne's *Wind in the Wires*, 1933, and Louis A. Strange's *Recollections of an Airman*, 1933).

Another authentication strategy that many war autobiographies use is to print maps of the front line, the trench system and the (rather few) changes in the possession of territory by the opposing armies. Some also heighten the special appeal of their subject matter that way: Hugh Durnford's *The Tunnelers of Holzminden* (1920) reproduces drawings and maps of the tunnel that a group of British prisoners of war dug to escape from the POW camp in Germany, as well as photos of the later excavation of that tunnel; a peculiar authenticity marker is provided by the reproduction of one of the fake ID cards the prisoners produced, with which the escaped soldiers planned to pass as Germans on their way back to the British lines.[18] Among the texts that are included to highlight authenticity are some private ones, such as letters to and from home, but in some cases we also find official documents, such as the King's commission for an officer, or other military orders. I consider these texts far more than mere embellishments or illustrations because they may comment on the main text in interesting and ambiguous ways: although they help to envision a particular moment in history, and thus serve the authentication function, they can also highlight the distance between the speaker and the historical moment because many authors have realised, by the time they are writing their autobiographies, how naïve they were when they volunteered and how limited their knowledge of the military was back then. The presence of such documents, then, can ultimately even work towards distancing, as far as the author/ speaker is concerned.

In contrast to authentication devices, which aim at creating a closeness between the teller and his story, distancing strategies are modes of representation which highlight the fact that there is a narrative distance between the self as experiencing the events on the one hand, and the self that narrates in retrospect (just like in the autodiegetic novel) on the other. The awareness of this distance is present in almost all of the texts and it is particularly tangible when the autobiographer returns to the old battlefield, as did Henry Williamson, the author of *The Wet Flanders Plain* (1929), who turned a journey to the continent that was supposed to be his honeymoon into a revisiting of the places of his war experience. In one passage, Williamson describes a moment after a walk he has just taken across the ramparts at Ypres; he turns from the rendering of this post-war situation in the past tense to a spontaneous vision of the past, which is given in the historical present to highlight its immediacy:

> I left the ramparts, and sought the café where my foot-weary companion was awaiting me. There was much noise there, and the lights were bright. Men were playing billiards, others talked with animation at the tables; waiters hurried with trays of filled glasses. […] but the café scene fades, and I am a wraith again in the darkness rushing by, yet stagnant

> amid the soundless cries, the viewless white flashes of file guns lighting the broken wall and the scattered rubble; the misery of men marching, laden and sweating through the ruin of Menin Gate. [...] Alas, prayers do not deflect the hissing flight of bullets that rip, or dissolve the shell that scatters trunk and limbs into charred fragments among the upheaved tree-stumps of Polygon Wood.
> I get up and go back to the ramparts. [19]

Williamson sees his younger self as something different, a ghostly presence ("wraith"), but that presence is still very near to him. 'Distance', therefore, does not mean that the autobiographer feels entirely disconnected from his war experience, but refers to the feeling of the difference between the younger and the older self, the war experience and its post-war retrieval. Many writers evoke the concrete moment of writing and thus draw attention to the framework within which the subsequent memory work is going to be performed. At the beginning of his autobiography *Sagittarius Rising* (1936), the pilot Cecil Lewis writes: "Within my study all is quiet and peaceful. The paper on which I write lies in a little pool of light, and my hand moves laboriously, back and cross, back and cross."[20] Lewis does not only indicate that remembering can be hard work, he also contrasts the moment of remembering with the scenes he is going to retrieve from memory, which are of course not "quiet and peaceful" at all. Robert Graves comments on the work of the autobiographer in a special way in *Goodbye to All That*: "In 1916, when on leave in England after being wounded, I began an account of my first few months in France. Having stupidly written it as a novel, I now have to re-translate it into history."[21] Memories are not simply 'there' as stored experience that can simply be transformed into writing; rather, the writer needs to overcome the distance that lies between the experience and the memory, and must then undergo the labour of formulating.

In this context, as far as the relationship between the experience and the memory of war is concerned, another kind of commentary is relevant, which I propose to call 'meta-mnestic' (from the Greek *mnesis* = memory): a commentary that addresses the processes and, in most cases, the difficulties of remembering. This type of commentary is perhaps the most particular feature of war autobiographies, it can be found throughout the corpus from the very first texts to the most recent ones; I consider it a genre marker of this type of autobiographical writing. Lewis continues the above quotation from *Sagittarius Rising* with a meta-mnestic commentary: "It is not easy. I kept no diaries, and memory, that imperfect vista of recorded thought, eludes and deceives. As in distorting mirrors at a fair, I can see myself long or stumpy, lean or fat, at will. Never my true self. Mercifully, no doubt."[22] Many such commentaries are placed in the introductions, so that the entire attempt at re-envisioning the war experience is primed by the awareness of the tricks of memory. Edmund Blunden introduces his *Undertones of War* with the following words: "I know that memory has her little ways, and by now she has concealed precisely that look, that word, that coincidence of nature without and nature within which I long to remember."[23] This, however, does not stop him from trying; on the contrary: "If these things are so, it is now or never for the rendering, however discoloured and lacunary, which I propose." [24] This leads necessarily to some imprecision, but Blunden maintains that there is "no heavy reconstruction anywhere", and highlights the truthfulness of his memories in spite of, or even due to, the minor vaguenesses: "Some uncertainties of time and situation, about which I have been notified, are left, because their character was genuine". [25] Meta-mnestic commentaries do not necessarily establish memory as inferior to experience; they can also signal that some areas of experience are so traumatising that current experience needs to edit them out, as it were. In Edward Liveing's *Attack* (1918), there is a scene in which the moment of remembering reconstructs a piece of information that was not available at the time: "I nearly trod on a motionless form. It lay in a natural position, but the ashen face, fixed fearful eyes told me that the man had just fallen. I did not recognise him then. I remember him now. He was one of my own platoon."[26] The shock of seeing the man so shortly after he died seems to have blurred the vision of the speaker in that moment. This retrospective insight highlights the distance between the experience of the moment in war and the moment in which it is evoked again for the purpose of autobiographical writing. While many meta-mnestic commentaries point to the deficiency of the workings of memory, in this case the memory is superior to the experience.

Finally, there is a kind of distancing that results from the use of rhetorical devices, which at the same time hint at the literariness of the text. Much of the research on the literature of WWI has pointed out that literary modes of expression could be used to render descriptions of experience for which everyday language would not suffice; Edmund

Blunden, who was a poet before he went to war, is particularly well known for his use of elements of pastoral poetry for the description of landscapes that turn out to be the very opposite of the idealised places of the pastoral tradition in *Undertones of War* (1928).[27] Blunden uses many more stylistic devices, however, all of which draw attention to the literariness of the text and create a distance between the speaker and the experience. The apostrophe, for instance, is a device Blunden uses frequently, not only in the autobiography itself, but also in some of the poems which were printed in the same volume. Blunden claims that the poems help to complement the remembering of his war experience:

> Despite some protests, I retain the poems; if they are of no other quality, they supply details and happenings which would have strengthened the prose had I not already been impelled to express them, and are among such keys as I can provide to the fuller memory.[28]

For Blunden, envisioned details and moods that poetry can evoke play a part in the memory of war experience just as much as factual accounts do, the "fuller memory" suggesting that truthful remembering involves all the senses, cognition, and emotion.

Siegfried Sassoon is another poet-autobiographer who uses language lyrically, as the following extract from the last chapter of his *Memoirs of a Fox-Hunting Man* (1928) demonstrates, in which metaphors and personifications, alliterations and assonances pervade the description of the speaker's journey to his unit:

> Dick and I were on our way to the First Battalion. The real war, that big bullying bogey, had stood up and beckoned to us at last; and now the Base Camp was behind us with its overcrowded discomforts that were unmitigated by esprit de corps. Still remote, the sudden shock of being uprooted from the Camp at Clitherland, and the strained twenty-four hours in London before departure. For the first time in our lives we had crossed the Channel. We had crossed it in bright moonlight on a calm sea – Dick and I sitting together on a tarpaulin cover in the bow of the boat, which was happily named "Victoria". Long after midnight we had left Folkstone, [...] had stared at Calais harbour, and seen sleepy French faces in the blear beginnings of November daylight.[29]

One only needs to take a closer look at the repetition of the [k] and [b] sounds in that passage, and expressions such as "big bullying bogey", "bright moonlight on a calm sea" and "seen sleepy French faces in the blear beginnings of November daylight" to get an impression of the lyrical qualities of the language. Sassoon is an interesting case also in other respects: He does not give himself his own name but uses the pseudonym George Sherston – another distancing device. Many areas of Sassoon's life, including of course his homosexuality,[30] but also his career as a poet, are left out of his autobiographical trilogy. He wrote another autobiography using his real name, *Siegfried's Journey* (1945), in which he leaves out the war, however. It seems that, although Sassoon kept writing about the war, he needed to dissociate the memory from his full personality.

Remembering the experience of the war may sometimes be made difficult by the weakness of memory, but it can also be interfered with by the leaving out of aspects. Blunden, for instance, mentions in *Undertones of War* that he went on home leave several times, but he never utters a word about these periods; nor does he mention that he was awarded a medal and that his participation in the war ended by his being wounded in a gas attack.[31] Robert Graves is another master of silence in *Goodbye to All That*, where he sometimes laconically presents factual information but seems to be unwilling to go deeper into own emotional reactions. His very first experience in trench is that a man who had misfired a grenade so that it fell back into the trench, exploded and smashed his face is carried away on a stretcher in front of Graves. The last sentence of that paragraph reads "He died before they got him to the dressing station", and instead of a reflection on a scene that the reader must envision as shocking, the next paragraph opens with a mere "I felt tired out by the time I reached company headquarters".[32] Whether young Graves did not react more powerfully to that event or whether the absurdity of that death is meant to appear in relief by the lack of commentary is an open question. An even more drastic instance of this kind of emotional under-reporting occurs shortly afterwards, when he tries to speak to a man he assumes is sleeping on the floor: "I shook the sleeper by the arm and noticed suddenly the hole in the back of his head"[33] – the man has shot himself after having survived an attack but learned upon his return that his fiancée had betrayed him back home, as someone explains to Graves. Instead of any sort of reaction to this, Graves merely reports: "At stand-to, rum and tea were served out."[34]

As the autobiographies discussed have shown, the motivations for writing war autobiographies are as diverse as the strategies with which the authors try to get access to the original experience, and they sometimes end up evoking it and distancing themselves from it at the same time. All of these examples demonstrate that the war autobiography is never a simple recording of war experiences, but mostly a shaped, selected, or even manipulated account that colours remembered experience by either dragging it into the presence of the reader through authentication strategies or making it appear as blurred, vague and removed through distancing strategies. The urge to remember and the openly admitted difficulties of doing so remain in a state of unresolved tension. The amount of meta-mnestic commentaries tends to increase in the texts written at a greater distance from the war, but some of the later autobiographies were written in the post-war years but not published immediately, and those actually written later make frequent use of material from the war time. This amounts to saying that there is a remarkable uniformity in the corpus over the decades. Some variations, however, are observable: The topos of incommunicability is strongest in the first phase, i.e., the period between the end of the war and the 1940s. The second phase, from the 1940s to the 1970s, saw an increase in commentaries on the fading of memories, and the awareness that the younger generation who did not witness the war was removed from the generation of combatants. Many authors from that phase also refer to other texts and films about the war; they consider themselves contributors to the general media memory of the First World War. While the 1980s and 1990s in particular were characterised by a steady output of prose fiction and film narratives about the war, autobiographical publications did not cease, even if the number of people who actually remembered the war was naturally dwindling. Partly, this is due to new editions of classical war autobiographies, but partly also to oral history projects: many historians went out to interview the last survivors of WWI and then transcribed the interviews. Ben Clouting's *Tickled to Death to Go: Memoirs of a Cavalryman in the First World War* (1996), for instance, is the result of a series of interviews that historian Richard van Emden, who was actually looking for the soldier who fired the first shot in that war, conducted with Clouting. Although Clouting was not the man he was looking for, van Emden did the interviews with the veteran (Clouting was under age when joined the army, but like many others got in faking his age when he enlisted) over two years until the old man died. The interviewer's questions are left out, and the interviewee's answers are edited into coherent texts, which are added to, interrupted, and sometimes corrected, by comments on the historical context, additional facts and explanations. The autobiographical memory discourse is thereby continually embedded in the historiographical one.

4. Didactic Considerations

The didactic considerations are best prefaced by an admission: many of the texts render an impression of the sheer dullness of military life outside the actual phases of combat, and many are rather long, too, so that reading interest, especially in younger readers, may be difficult to trigger. In most cases, it is therefore advisable to work with extracts from war autobiographies rather than full texts. This limitation can be turned into an advantage, however, for it allows teachers to discuss texts contrastively, which can give rise to a number of discussions of central relevance, for instance about different attitudes towards war, and the fact that one event can be experienced in many different ways by individuals. Also, First World War autobiographies are suitable for teaching English in the school and university classroom because they are, obviously, authentic L1-material, and they provide access to one major historical event that has shaped British culture for over a hundred years now. It makes sense to read extracts from autobiographies parallel to the canonical war poems, because they sometimes support the poems' general evaluations, but sometimes they also modify or contradict them. To read war autobiographies in the context of other texts, photos and films, can demonstrate that what a society regards as its history relies on a multimedia archive of sources and narratives. Beyond the predominantly war-related aspects, the genre of the war autobiography, with its complexities and ambiguities, highlights some issues that learners of English language, literature and culture can profitably discuss, because they have a wider relevance.

To read selected extracts from the large corpus of WWI autobiographies side by side can create an awareness of the fact that there is no such thing as an 'objective description'. In the case of WWI autobiographies, the different soldiers' ranks will have a marked influence on their different perceptions, renderings and evaluations of the very same issues, scenes and experiences. The same holds for the writers' function and area of work in the army, and for the question whether they volunteered or were professional soldiers. It is precisely because historical events tend to turn into simplified, iconic representations which tend to elicit increasingly simplified emotions the longer the temporal distance gets, that a look at the diversity and contradictoriness of views on the First World War can teach us about the complexity of events, as they are experienced and remembered. As has been demonstrated, too, the different modes of expression across the corpus can point to the relevance of language choices in the rendering of experience. It may also raise sociolinguistic issues, such as the interdependence of language-use and education: the juxtaposition of, say George Ashurst's, *My Bit: A Lancashire Fusilier at war 1914-1918* (1983) with Blunden's *Undertones of War* (1928) will highlight the fact that the same type of event can be expressed in rather different styles, the lyrical qualities of the latter being highlighted by the matter-of-factness of the former. Generally, First World War autobiographies raise the question what language and modes of narrative have to offer speakers who want to give shape to their personal experience and relate that meaningfully to the general social and cultural contexts in which they live.

Notes

1 On the connection between public conceptions of WWI and its commemoration on the one hand, and British literary and cultural production on the other, see the classic studies by Bergonzi (1965), Fussell (1975), and Hynes (1990); for excellent summaries, see Goetsch (1981) and Barlow (2000). Erll (2003) provides a much more elaborated approach that also informs this article. Cf. Stevenson (2013) for a more recent account. A handbook is in preparation (Schneider/Potter, forthcoming).

2 In what follows, I draw upon and summarize a longer study of more than 120 British WWI autobiographies I conducted some years ago, the results of

which were published in a collaborative volume on autobiographies, novels and films as media of WWI memory, with Barbara Korte and Claudia Sternberg; see Schneider (2005).

3 See Landow (1979) and Fleishman (1983) for the history of autobiographical writing preceding the First World War.

4 Edmund Blunden was 28 years old when he published *Undertones of War* (1928), Robert Graves was 33 when he wrote *Goodbye to All That* (1929). Herbert Read's *In Retreat* (1925) is an example of a very short time span to be treated in autobiographical fashion, but there are some more extreme cases, in which the focus is on single events, such as Edward Liveing's short narrative *Attack* (1918), which comprises only one day, 1st July 1916, i.e. the beginning of the fateful Somme offensive. Another exception from the standard of autobiographical writing is Sidney Rogerson's *Twelve Days* (1933), which deals with a very short period behind the lines in which practically *nothing* happens.

5 The canon of First World War literature includes the war poetry of Siegfried Sassoon, Wilfred Owen, Edmund Blunden, Richard Aldington, among others (see Das 2013) and some early post-war novels such as A.P. Herbert's *The Secret Battle* (1919) and Ernest Raymond's *Tell England* (1922); on the novel and its continuing contribution to the discourse of WWI memory see Korte (2005). The one theatre play that belongs in that group is R.C. Sherriff's *Journey's End* of 1929.

6 Prominent examples are Blunden's *Undertones of War* (1928), which was reprinted and included in the Oxford World Classics series in 1958, and Graves' *Goodbye to All That* (1929), which saw re-issues in 1957 and 1960, but the second phase was generally very active in reprinting the material from the 1920s and 1930s.

7 Parker, Ernest (1964). *Into Battle: 1914-1918.* London: Longmans, xi.

8 Tennant, Norman (1983). *A Saturday Night Soldier's War, 1913-1918.* Waddeson: Kylin Press, 1.

9 *Ibid.*, 2.

10 See in particular the studies by Tylee (1990) and Ouditt (1994) as well as the anthologies by Higonnet (1987 and 1999) and Goldman (1993).

11 Some texts that have been called war books are in fact difficult to place in the categories of either autobiographies or novels, and Broich (1993) has used the terms 'semi-autobiographical novels' and 'semi-fictional autobiographies' to account for that fact.

12 Crozier, Frank Percy (1930). *A Brass Hat in No Man's Land.* London: Jonathan Cape, 51.

13 Hynes, Samuel (1997). *The Soldiers' Tale: Bearing Witness to Modern War.* New York: Allen Lane, 5.

[14] It comes as no surprise, then, that there was a lot of moral outrage when Binjamin Wilkomirski, the author of an autobiography that described his alleged survival of the Holocaust as a child (*Bruchstücke: Aus einer Kindheit 1939-1948*, 1995) was discovered to be fraud.

[15] Edmonds, Charles [Charles Edmund Carrington] (1929). *A Subaltern's War: Being a Memoir of the Great War from the Point of View of a Romantic Young Man, with Candid Accounts of Two Particular Battles, Written Shortly After They Occured, and an Essay on Militarism.* London: Peter Davies, 192.

[16] *Ibid.*, 8.

[17] Unpaginated insert, facing p. 72.

[18] Durnford, Hugh George Edmund (1920). *The Tunnellers of Holzminden.* Cambridge: Cambridge University Press, 175.

[19] Williamson, Henry (1929). *The Wet Flanders Plain.* London: Beaumont, 38f.

[20] Lewis, Cecil (1936). *Sagittarius Rising*. London: Peter Davies, 3.

[21] Graves, Robert (1960 [1929]). *Goodbye to All That.* Harmondsworth: Penguin, 79.

[22] Lewis (1936), 3.

[23] Blunden, Edmund (1930 [1928]). *Undertones of War.* London: Cobden-Sanderson, v-iv.

[24] *Ibid.*

[25] *Ibid.*, vii.

[26] Liveing, Edward George Downing (1918). *Attack: An Infantry Subaltern's Impression of July 1st 1916.* London: Heinemann, 50.

[27] See Fussell (1975), 245; Graham (1984), 80-121; and Erll (2003), 190-203.

[28] Blunden, Edmund (1930 [1928]). *Undertones of War.* London: Cobden-Sanderson, vii-viii.

[29] Quoted from *Complete Memoirs of George Sherston*, 244.

[30] Homosexuality was a criminal offence in Britain until the 1960s and could not have been made public in such a book.

[31] Cf. Fussell (1975), 255.

[32] Graves, Robert (1960 [1929]). *Goodbye to All That.* Harmondsworth: Penguin, 84.

[33] *Ibid.*, 89.

[34] *Ibid.*

A Selection of Autobiographical Writings:

Aldington, Richard (1968 [1941]). *Life for Life's Sake*. London: Cassell.

--- (1929). *Death of a Hero*. London: Chatto and Windus.

Ashurst, George (1987). *My Bit: A Lancashire Fusilier at War 1914-1918*. Ed. Richard Holmes. Marlborough: Crowood in association with Anthony Bird.

Bagnold, Enid (1978 [1918]). *A Diary Without Dates: Thoughts and Impressions of a V.A.D.* London: Virago in association with Heinemann.

Blunden, Edmund (1930 [1928]). *Undertones of War*. London: Cobden-Sanderson.

Bridges, Tom [Sir Tom George Molesworth Bridges] (1938). *Alarms and Excursions: Reminiscences of a Soldier*. With a preface by Winston S. Churchill. London: Longmans.

Brittain, Vera (1978 [1933]). *Testament of Youth: An Autobiographical Study of the Years 1900-1925*. London: Virago.

Clapham, H.S. (1939). *Mud and Khaki: The Memories of an Incomplete Soldier*. London: Hutchinson.

Clouting, Ben (1996). *Tickled to Death to Go: Memoirs of a Cavalryman in the First World War*. Ed. Richard van Emden. Tonbrige: Spellmount.

Crozier, Frank Percy (1930). *A Brass Hat in No Man's Land*. London: Jonathan Cape.

Durnford, Hugh George Edmund (1920). *The Tunnellers of Holzminden*. Cambridge: Cambridge University Press.

Edmonds, Charles [Charles Edmund Carrington] (1929). *A Subaltern's War: Being a Memoir of the Great War from the Point of View of a Romantic Young Man, with Candid Accounts of Two Particular Battles, Written Shortly After They Occured, and an Essay on Militarism*. London: Peter Davies.

Gibbs, Sir Philip Hamilton (1920). *Now it Can be Told*. New York: Harper.

Gladden, Edgar Norman (1967). *Ypres, 1917: A Personal Account*. London: Kimber.

Graves, Robert (1960 [1929]). *Goodbye to All That*. Harmondsworth: Penguin.

Grinnell-Milne, Duncan (1933). *Wind in the Wires*. London: Hurst and Blackett.

Groom, W.H.A. (1976). *Poor Bloody Infantry: A Memoir of the First World War*. London: Kimber.

Harrison, Charles Yale (1930). *Generals Die in Bed*. London: Noel Douglas.

Lewis, Cecil (1936). *Sagittarius Rising*. London: Peter Davies.

Liddell Hart, Basil Henry (1965). *The Memoirs of Captain Liddell Hart*. 2 volumes. London: Cassell.

Liveing, Edward George Downing (1918). *Attack: An Infantry Subaltern's Impression of July 1st 1916*. London: Heinemann.

McCudden, James Byford (1930 [1918]). *Flying Fury*. London: Hamish Hamilton.
Nicholson, W.N. (1939). *Behind the Lines: An Account of Administrative Staffwork in the British Army 1914-1918*. London: Jonathan Cape.
Pankhurst, Sylvia (1987 [1932]). *The Home Front*. London: Hutchinson.
Parker, Ernest (1964). *Into Battle: 1914-1918*. London: Longmans.
Rathbone, Irene (1932). *We That Were Young*. London: Chatto and Windus.
Read, Herbert (1925). *In Retreat*. London: Hogarth.
Richards, Frank (1964 [1933]). *Old Soldiers Never Die*. London: Faber.
Rogerson, Sidney (1933). *Twelve Days*. With a preface by Basil H. Liddell Hart, Illustrationen Stanley Cursiter. London: Baker.
Rorie, David (1929). *A Medico's Luck in the War: Being Reminiscences of R.A.M.C. Work with the 51st (Highland) Division*. Aberdeen: Milne and Hutchinson.
Sassoon, Siegfried (1984 [1937]). *The Complete Memoirs of George Sherston*. London: Faber. [Separate parts published as: *Memoirs of a Fox-Hunting Man*, 1928; *Memoirs of an Infantry Officer*, 1930; *Sherston's Progress*, 1936].
Smith, Lesley (1931). *Four Years Out of Life*. London: Philip Allan.
Strange, Louis A. (1933). *Recollections of an Airman*. London: John Hamilton.
Tennant, Norman (1983). *A Saturday Night Soldier's War, 1913-1918*. Waddeson: Kylin Press.
Wade, Aubrey (1936 [1959]). *The War of the Guns [Gunner on the Western Front]*. London: Batsford.
Waugh, Alec (1919). *The Prisoners of Mainz*. London: Chapman and Hall.
Williamson, Henry (1929). *The Wet Flanders Plain*. London: Beaumont.
Young, Filson (1921). *With the Battlecruisers*. London: Cassell.
Young, Edward Hilton, Baron Kennet (1924 [1920]). *By Sea and Land: Some Naval Doings*. London: Methuen.

Bibliography

Barlow, Adrian (2000). *The Great War in British Literature*. Cambridge: Cambridge University Press.
Bergonzi, Bernard (1965). *Heroes' Twilight: A Study of the Literature of the Great War*. London: Constable.
Broich, Ulrich (1993). "World War I in Semi-Autobiographical Fiction and in Semi-Fictional Autobiography: Robert Graves and Ludwig Renn." *Intimate Enemies: English and German Literary Reactions to the Great*

War 1914-1918. Ed. Franz K. Stanzel and Martin Löschnigg. Heidelberg: Winter, 313-325.

Das, Santanu. (ed.) (2013). *Cambridge Companion to Poetry of the First World War Cambridge: Cambridge University Press.*

Erll, Astrid (2003). *Gedächtnisromane: Literatur über den Ersten Weltkrieg als Medium englischer und deutscher Erinnerungskulturen in den 1920er Jahren.* Trier: WVT.

Fleishman, Avrom (1983). *Figures of Autobiography: The Language of Self-Writing in Victorian and Modern England.* Berkeley, Los Angeles, London: University of California Press.

Fussell, Paul (1975). *The Great War and Modern Memory.* Oxford: Oxford University Press.

Goetsch, Paul (1981). "Literatur im Zeitraum von 1914-1945." *Englische Literatur und Politik im 20. Jahrhundert.* Ed. Paul Goetsch and Heinz-Joachim Müllenbrock. Wiesbaden: Athenaion, 31-59.

Goldman, Dorothy (ed.) (1993). *Women and World War I: The Written Response.* Basingstoke: Macmillan.

Dawson, Graham (1994). *Soldier Heroes: British Adventure, Empire and the Imagining of Masculinities.* London: Routledge.

Higonnet, Margaret R. (ed.) (1999). *Lines of Fire: Women Writers of World War I.* New York: Plume.

---, et al. (eds.) (1987). *Behind the Lines: Gender and the Two World Wars.* New Haven: Yale University Press.

Hynes, Samuel (1990). *A War Imagined: The First World War and English Culture.* London: Bodley Head.

--- (1997). *The Soldiers' Tale: Bearing Witness to Modern War.* New York: Allen Lane.

Korte, Barbara (2005). "Der Erinnerungsdiskurs im Roman." *Der Erste Weltkrieg und die Mediendiskurse der Erinnerung in Großbritannien: Autobiographie – Roman – Film (1919-1999).* Barbara Korte, Ralf Schneider, Claudia Sternberg. Würzburg: Königshausen & Neumann, 143-241.

Korte, Barbara, Ralf Schneider and Claudia Sternberg (2005). *Der Erste Weltkrieg und die Mediendiskurse der Erinnerung in Großbritannien: Autobiographie – Roman – Film (1919-1999).* Würzburg: Königshausen & Neumann.

Landow, George (1979). "Introduction." *Approaches to Victorian Autobiography.* Ed. George Landow. Athens: Ohio University Press, xiii-xlvi.

Lejeune, Philippe (1994 [1975]). *Der autobiographische Pakt.* Übersetzung Wolfram Bayer und Dieter Hornig. Frankfurt am Main: Suhrkamp.

Ouditt, Sharon (1994). *Fighting Forces, Writing Women: Identity and Ideology in the First World War*. London: Routledge.

Raymond, Ernest (1930 [1922]). *Tell England: A Study in a Generation*. London: Cassell.

Schneider, Ralf, and Jane Potter (eds.) (forthcoming). *Handbook of British Literature and Culture of the First World War*. Berlin: De Gruyter.

Schneider, Ralf (2005). "Der Erinnerungsdiskurs in der Autobiographie." *Der Erste Weltkrieg und die Mediendiskurse der Erinnerung in Großbritannien: Autobiographie – Roman – Film (1919-1999)*. Barbara Korte, Ralf Schneider, Claudia Sternberg. Würzburg: Königshausen & Neumann, 33-141.

Sheriff, R.C. (1929). *Journey's End*. New York: Brentano's.

Stevenson, Randall (2013). *Literature and the Great War 1914-1918*. Oxford: Oxford University Press.

Tylee, Claire M (1990). *The Great War and Women's Consciousness: Images of Militarism and Womanhood in Women's Writings, 1914-64*. Iowa City: University of Iowa Press.

Wilkomirski, Binjamin (1995). *Bruchstücke. Aus einer Kindheit 1939-1948*. Frankfurt am Main: Jüdischer Verlag.

James Fenwick (Leicester)

"Freddie, Can You Talk?": The Ethics of Betrayal in Frederic Raphael's Memoir *Eyes Wide Open* (1999)

Film director Stanley Kubrick died on 7 March 1999. Three days later, the biographer, novelist and Oscar-winning screenwriter, Frederic Raphael, had put together a three-page proposal for a prospective memoir he wished to write about his time collaborating with Kubrick on the screenplay for *Eyes Wide Shut,* Kubrick's posthumous final film. Dated 10 March 1999, the proposal explains how, in the wake of Kubrick's unexpected death, public curiosity in the man was insatiable. Kubrick had been an intensely private individual and this, Raphael commented, "lent intimacy to our conversations; we enjoyed a kind of disembodied closeness".[1] Over the course of their two-year collaboration in the early 1990s, the pair engaged in lengthy conversations, often over the telephone for several hours at a time, as well as several occasions when Raphael visited Kubrick's home outside St. Albans. Such an intense relationship was not uncommon between Kubrick and his collaborators. Take the writer Michael Herr who had collaborated with Kubrick; Herr said in the foreword to his own memoir about Kubrick that, "I once described 1980-83 as a single phone call lasting three years, with interruptions".[2]

Raphael's resultant memoir, *Eyes Wide Open*, revealed the nature of the conversations he had with Kubrick, as well as opening the readers' eyes to the disembodied closeness involved in the working relationship between the two men. The memoir was not merely an intimate account of Raphael's time writing *Eyes Wide Shut*, but a chance to write about and expose the reclusive Kubrick to the wider world. His initial proposal for the memoir explained that he intended not to "reinforce the myth of his [Kubrick's] disagreeable, tyrannical, paranoid character", but rather to "put right some of the things said about K"[3] – the more malicious rumours and negative press creations around Kubrick had come to portray him as some modern-day Howard Hughes hermit figure. Whether this was achieved, or whether Raphael instead exploited Kubrick's death to his own advantage, is the focus of this article, which will explore the ethics of Raphael's 'betrayal' of Kubrick in *Eyes Wide Open*.

The memoir is fraught with ethical dilemmas, particularly in its writing style. Raphael disclosed in his proposal that he intended the book to be cinematic, utilising a combination of five differing writing styles: a non-fiction prose form, a screenplay formatted style, a talking-heads dialogue style, journal entries, and letter extracts. Raphael said he could remember well much of the dialogue exchanges he had shared with Kubrick, but his professed ability to remember his exchanges means he is purporting to be writing an accurate account of not only his own time spent working on *Eyes Wide Shut*, but also of another individual – Stanley Kubrick. Such validation is to lend the memoir an authenticity and authority to which Kubrick had no agency. It is a primary ethical concern of life writing that when a writer claims, as Raphael does, to be accurately retelling events and the narrative includes other people beyond himself, "he takes it upon himself to expose others in ways of his choosing".[4] The writer's construction of an individual is interpreted by the reader through the choice of writing style and of the anecdotal evidence selected. This is not to suggest that writers like Raphael are not free to write what they wish, but rather such a right must be balanced with the rights of those being exposed particularly when they "have no control over the way that they are portrayed".[5]

Such ethical considerations were at the crux of the reaction of the Kubrick family, in particular Kubrick's widow, Christiane Kubrick, who issued a response to the publication of Raphael's memoir on her website. The public statement denounced *Eyes Wide Open* and Raphael for violating Kubrick's trust and confidence. "Whilst Mr Raphael knew and confirmed in his book that Stanley valued his privacy", wrote Christiane Kubrick, "he showed, by publishing his book, ostensibly in the interests of art, that he in fact has no respect for that privacy".[6] Conversely, however, Christiane Kubrick heads the statement by claiming that she intended to, "take the opportunity to confirm the truths about Stanley and correct the inaccuracies, at least the gross ones".[7] She would go on to publish a picture memoir of her late husband's life and career with her aim being to "correct the mistaken view of Stanley as some sort of isolationist misanthrope".[8]

It is not the purpose of this article to assert the validity of Raphael's memoir, but rather to consider the ethics of betrayal in self-life writing via a case study of *Eyes Wide Open*. Raphael's variety of writing styles challenges the genre and raises questions as to their unethical utilisation. Memoir is a genre that is "by its very nature, a fallible, subjective, and often deliberately artful representation of the past".[9] A subgenre of autobiography, memoirs burgeoned in the 1990s, James Atlas proclaiming it "the age of the literary memoir".[10] What this flourish of memoirs says about us as avid readers – for their proliferation is on the back of commercial success – is that we are living in a culture where "the very notion of privacy, of a zone beyond the reach of public probing, has become an alien concept".[11] The British tradition of the memoir is evident, from the symbiotic development of the fictitious memoir disguised as truth in the eighteenth-century novel by the likes of Daniel Defoe, with his *Robinson Crusoe* and *Memoirs of a Cavalier*, works that were at the time mistakenly read as non-fiction accounts of real-life events. By the twentieth century, the memoir had become a literary staple, though was often confusingly labelled autobiography due to the view of memoir as inferior and salacious. Whereas autobiography covers the entirety of a life of an individual, memoir is about capturing a moment in that life, or recounting a memory of a particular event. To this end, the likes of Winston Churchill (*My Early Life*) and Siegfried Sassoon (*Memoirs of a Fox-Hunting Man*) produced self-life writing that be deemed as memoir. The British memoir developed into a genre that utilised sardonic wit and irreverent black humour, incorporating novelistic techniques and embellished stories;[12] from Clive James's *Unreliable Memoirs*, to Quentin Crisp's numerous memoirs including *The Naked Civil Servant*.

Considering memoir in a post-modern age, it has seen a turn toward an outpouring of personal testament that depends on the author divulging explicit secrets and being honest about one's discretions, a genre described as being one of "crass sensationalism".[13] Yet, there is a strain of British memoir that has a rhetorical focus and a sarcasm that lends itself to the gentle mocking of its characters by its authors. Raphael's work is part of the British tradition in its use of rhetorical devices and black humour, the author mocking not only himself, but the characters he writes about. But *Eyes Wide Open* is indicative of a turn in British memoir toward post-modern sensationalism, becoming tantalisingly scandalous, gossip mongering and "dwelling on the sordid excesses of oneself".[14]

This article will explore the ethical risks inherent in the "sordid excesses"[15] of Raphael's memoir by exploring the disparate writing styles he utilises. I will first examine the contexts of Raphael's employment by Kubrick and the subsequent publication of *Eyes Wide Open* and then move on to analyse Raphael's character portrayal of Kubrick. I will conclude with an exploration of the reaction to the book by the Kubrick Estate. Raphael justified the memoir's publication as humanising Kubrick and offering a more rounded character portrayal that sanctioned biographies of Kubrick did not. The essay will aim to understand the nature of betrayal within self-life writing and the unspoken code of ethics that binds all writers; after all, "when a writer addresses biographical and historical fact, telling the truth is essential".[16] The need for biographical and historical accuracy is even more imperative when the prose is rendered with imaginative interventions, whereby reality is finessed with fictional flourish.[17]

1. A Contractual Vow of Silence

I want to first look at how Raphael came to be employed by Kubrick and the breach of Kubrick's privacy. I will also examine briefly the use of letters and notes sent by Kubrick to Raphael in the book and the ethical implication.

Frederic Raphael was a noted screenwriter who had won an Academy Award for his screenplay *Darling*, and a nomination for *Two for the Road.* Kubrick's attraction to have Raphael write *Eyes Wide Shut* was obvious given his writing credentials. The film was to be an adaptation of Arthur Schnitzler's *Traumnovelle* and Kubrick approached Raphael in the spring of 1994. As with any Kubrick production, the film was shrouded in secrecy and the director wanted to keep it that way by binding his employees to a contract with strict confidentiality clauses. This was to prevent press speculation that might compromise his financial negotiations with Warner Bros. when the time came to put the script into production. Yet, this confidentiality extended to cover the privacy of Stanley Kubrick himself. The initial contract viewed by Raphael included a clause that required him to concede all "decisions concerning who had written any part of the script and who had conceived any of the ideas contained in it".[18] Raphael managed to eschew such conditions by telling Kubrick he could not work under strict creative bondage. Kubrick relented and had the clause removed.[19] But the clause in question also contained a sub-clause, whereby those employed to work with Kubrick were "bound by a legally composed obligation never to disclose anything about their experiences in his employ".[20] Raphael was fully aware that, in asking to be rid of the main clause, it allowed him – by default – to be exempt from the sub-clause. And this awareness meant he was conscious that Kubrick had invested trust in him, welcoming him in to his inner circle in order to collaborate with the confidence that he would not lay bare his private life to anyone else. Though he was now no longer legally bound to maintain confidentiality about Kubrick's private life, there is an argument that Raphael was ethically aware and had to weigh up the moral judgment of whether to expose the details of Kubrick's private life to the wider world – something which Kubrick had avoided throughout his career – or to remain silent. Raphael seemed to delight in the fact that he was not legally bound by Kubrick's confidentiality clauses. In the aftermath of the publication of *Eyes Wide Open*, he commented that there was nothing the Kubrick Estate could do "to stop me from publishing what was at once the truth about working for Stanley and a tribute to his undeniable genius [...] to have indicated that he was not without flaws [...] was deemed tantamount to blasphemy".[21]

Raphael explicitly knew he was betraying Kubrick's confidence with the publication of *Eyes Wide Open*. Here was an author breaking the implicit confidence of another for creative gain, placing that other as a key protagonist of the memoir. But before one places such ethical guilt solely with Raphael, it is necessary to consider the wider set of complicated ethics at work in this case. Raphael had little concern over exposing others in his autobiographical and memoirist works. He even went on to write the fictionalised memoirs of a retired French diplomat in *A Double Life*. Discussing his ethical approach to life writing, Raphael has commented that, "I am as candid as the libel law allows",[22] clarifying that his writings are validated by the precise keeping of personal notebooks where he impels himself to "accurate observation, of life and of ideas and their derivatives".[23] Kubrick and his staffers were fully aware of Raphael's background as a memoirist and biographer, with research on the author being conducted prior to his recruitment.[24] This is not to suggest that, by being informed of Raphael's tendency for non-fiction writing, Kubrick was complicit in the ethical betrayal of *Eyes Wide Open*, but it may suggest a naivety. The two men clearly differed in their understanding and concern for privacy. Raphael regularly emphasises his inability to understand Kubrick's almost 'paranoid' desire for privacy, when he himself was more than happy to bare himself to the world through his prose, even in *Eyes Wide Open*, where he lays out his own anxieties and inner thoughts alongside those of Kubrick.

These differing ideologies around privacy are evidenced in the way Raphael includes in the memoir extracts of letters sent to him by Kubrick. These extracts are usually incorporated in the non-fiction prose form and are often snippets of sentences. One anecdote in the book shows how these extracts were utilised to construct a particular image of Kubrick as excessively private. After having worked for a number of months on the first draft of the *Eyes Wide Shut* screenplay, Raphael, wishing to be paid, asked the William Morris agency to make copies of the script to be sent to both Kubrick and to his own agent, Ron Mardigan.[25] The agency obliged, wrapping it in a folder headed with the company's logo. This alerted Kubrick to the fact that Raphael had allowed others to see the script. Kubrick responded by sending the script back to Raphael and attaching a letter, which Raphael quotes. Kubrick was too upset at the discovery of the script in the William Morris wrapping to read it, and Raphael quotes him as saying, "I could scarcely believe my eyes",[26] and that he could not bring himself to read the script in a "negative frame of mind".[27]

Despite Kubrick's repeated insistence that Raphael concede to his desire for privacy, it was not being acknowledged; in fact, Raphael goes on to expose Kubrick's protestations by publishing extracts from Kubrick's letter and his own letter in reply, and over the course of the next five pages publishes brief extracts from the heated correspondence that ensues. Kubrick is angered by Raphael referring to his need for confidentially and privacy as being a foible, "'even if you don't understand why this is so', he thought that his credentials *as a producer* entitled him to more than having his concerns being off-handedly dismissed as one of his 'foibles'".[28] Raphael's blatant disregard of Kubrick's wish for privacy raises the issue of the need to even publish *Eyes Wide Open* and intimate details of Kubrick's life; Raphael's insights throughout serve to (purposely) bring Kubrick down to the level of a mere mortal being, of flesh-and-blood, when telling us at one point that "Kubrick went to pee".[29] Such detail serves no advantage to being placed in to the public domain and one must ask,

> on what grounds is it possible to argue that readers can be served, not soiled, by the expansion of the domain subjected to the glare of publicity? What is important for a given community, at a given historical moment, to know?[30]

If Raphael's intentions were to reveal Kubrick as a human being, to deconstruct the myth of the cult-auteur, then it is to the numerous writing styles that he uses that we must turn to understand such a construction.

2. The Ethics of Prose Style

The unique selling point of Raphael's memoir was his ability to, "catch Kubrick's voice as no one else could".[31] Very little was known publicly about Kubrick, with actual imagery and footage of the director being rare. Thus, Raphael's claim to recreate Kubrick's voice in *Eyes Wide Open* is predicated on the very notion of exposing his privacy.[32] The lack of information about Kubrick led to speculation in the press, which Kubrick did little to control, and what resulted was an image of a recluse. Raphael, in part, justified his memoir in terms of an attempt to correct this public image of Kubrick, providing readers with, "a chance to 'hear' the thinking attitudes and methods of a great director".[33] Raphael contended that biographical works to date had pieced together an ugly profile of Kubrick[34] and that his memoir would counter this through an accurate construction of the director.

Raphael's claim to be able to catch Kubrick's voice is demonstrated through the use of several differing styles of writing: a screenplay format, a talking-heads style, the inclusion of journal and letter extracts, and a first-person non-fiction prose form. Taken together, these styles present a significant character portrayal of Kubrick, but it often verges on the caricature and brings into question Raphael's claim to be presenting a more accurate picture of Kubrick. I want to focus on Raphael's use of the screenplay format, the talking-heads format, and the ethical dilemma of his use of journal extracts and letters.

The screenplay format aims to cinematise the infrequent face-to-face encounters Raphael had with Kubrick. During their two-year collaboration, he met Kubrick face-to-face on just four occasions at his stately home. These face-to-face encounters with Kubrick are recalled through the use of a studio-formatted screenplay in which there are scene titles with the location and time of the action, the prose (action) is manifestation-orientated describing what is visible and audible and is authoritative in nature, and the dialogue is centred on the page, with the characters' names capitalised. The use of this style plays up the absurdity Raphael felt about the situation, travelling to meet this legendary figure at his mansion. But the novelty of this writing style in the memoir is outweighed by the form's fictitious origins. The screenplay is associated with the invention of fiction and leaves the reader questioning whether the action taking place in these segments is in itself fictitious. Raphael turns the life of Kubrick – or at least the few moments he was exposed to – into a biographical film. Biographical films dramatise the life of historically grounded figures, but in a generalised, even romanticised manner.[35] One is not expected to take away the explicit truth of an individual when viewing a biographical film, but rather an interpretation of the figure. These screenplay moments ground us in a time and place and urge us to cinematically visualise the characters of Raphael and Kubrick. One such cinematic retelling is when Raphael goes to meet Kubrick to discuss the first forty pages of the screenplay he had written. The scene is headed INT.KUBRICK RESIDENCE – DAY and Kubrick asks Raphael if he would like something to eat because he does not want him to have a migraine. In the action, Raphael writes how Kubrick offers a slight smile of ironic affection and how he, F.R., "smiles too; he feels a certain affection for the man who had once intimidated him".[36]

Raphael refers to himself in the third person, as he does in the talking-heads style, indicated by the use of his initialised proper name. Raphael's intention is not clear, though the use of the third person in autobiographical genres may be a "serious (or humorous) use of biographical presentation, imitation of the psychological novel, indication of the formation of a double".[37] What the use of the third person does allow is for internal distancing,[38] which leads to a "disparity of past and present".[39] The resort to the third person at the same time shows the subject (Raphael) to be admittedly fragmented and undermines traditional notions of the autobiographical self, indication of a "postmodernist defiance of boundaries".[40]

If we are to take these screenplay moments as fictitious representations, with Kubrick and Raphael rendered as characters in a film screenplay, does this momentarily extricate them from the ethical boundaries of the autobiographical prose forms of the rest of the book? If non-fiction has a set of ethical considerations that do not apply to fiction,[41] we can surely alleviate these segments from the same ethical considerations one would apply to the first-person non-fiction prose form. But it is Raphael's recourse to be recreating an accurate picture of Kubrick wherein the ethical dilemmas are present. The writing styles used by Raphael are in the realms of imaginative intervention and these still hold "an obligation to truth".[42] A writer may be inclined to take a leap of imagination and recreate moments that are impossible to verify;[43] the scenes with Kubrick often involved only the two men and no one else, and with the passing of Kubrick, there is only the word of Raphael as to their verifiability. Therefore, what has been written can never wholly be said to be what actually happened, but rather what Raphael remembered and then crafted into a narrative. As Miller has said of such imaginative interventions, "one *might* be truth; the other, a good story".[44]

I want to turn to Raphael's talking-heads writing style, used to reconstruct the telephone calls he had with Kubrick. These segments usually commenced with a variation of Kubrick's asking Raphael, "Freddie, can you talk?", presumably in an attempt to capture Kubrick's 'voice'. This writing style is the most realistic, achieving a level of disembodied-ness that Raphael has said best described his relationship with Kubrick. Removed of metaphorical flourishes, these dialogue exchanges can be read at a more objective level; interactions with others take place through the use of speech and so the recording of exactly what an individual said is to capture the moment more precisely, but only if we can be sure it *is* what someone said and is not a fictional recreation. The first appearance of this style comes when Kubrick phones Raphael to ask him if he would like to work on his new project:

> F.R.: Hello.
> S.K.: Is this Freddie? This is Stanley. How are you?

F.R.: Pretty good.
S.K.: Is this a good time?
F.R.: Absolutely.
S.K.: Good. So listen, are you free to work on something with me?

The telephone conversation continues with Kubrick asking Raphael if he would consider reading the book he wishes to adapt:

S.K.: Will you read something if I send it?
F.R.: Of course. What is it? A book?
S.K.: It's a piece of material. How do I get it to you?
F.R.: Is it, ah, science fiction?
S.K.: Who told you that?
F.R.: (Covers mouthpiece, to SYLVIA) *Christ!* It's science fiction.
S.K.: (Overlapping) Because no, it's not. It's something else.

The use of the parenthesis breaks the disembodied-ness of the style by introducing a visual element. It in effect places us in the position of Raphael's space, listening to the talking head of Kubrick. Distance is placed between the reader and Kubrick, but an intimacy is achieved between the reader and Raphael. The talking-heads conversations build a mystique around Kubrick, a voice with no matching visual cues, in contrast to the visual cues Raphael provides for his own character.

Kubrick's 'voice' also appears within the memoir as snippets of letter extracts or recalled spoken word in Raphael's journal extracts. Raphael goes further in his exposing of the private conversations he had with Kubrick by his inclusion of these journal extracts. The journal entries reflect on the conversations he had with Kubrick and evidence his thoughts on his personality, which he found complex and curious. One such entry, from late May 1995, reveals a disturbing remark. Days after the anniversary of Adolf Hitler's birthday, Kubrick apparently told Raphael that he thought Hitler had been "right about almost everything".[45] Raphael contends that the remark was said to purposely shock, rather than an expression of a genuine belief, but its inclusion, with no context surrounding how it had been raised in conversation, does little to address Raphael's assertion that the memoir would allow the reader to hear the thoughts and attitudes of a great director. If Kubrick uttered the remark about Hitler with the aim to shock and outrage, surely its inclusion in the memoir by Raphael attempts exactly the same. Presented is an image not of a convivial family man, but of an individual that always looked to challenge the boundaries of extremity and deplorability, both in his working collaborations and in his films. It is as if Raphael is saying that he has discovered where the depravity and darkness of human behaviour in Kubrick's films stems from. It is a portrait disputed by the Kubrick family, who talked of Kubrick's "domestic virtues",[46] something that Raphael did not recognise. His memoir is not of Kubrick the family man, but of Kubrick the filmmaker and collaborator and of his "professional conduct".[47] Raphael has since said, in defence of his portrayal of Kubrick, "what did they know of my working relationship [...] I never heard him say a single word about his beloved wife and children".[48]

Raphael does attempt a justification of the inclusion of his own journal entries from the time as being an attempt not to "reveal my real feelings about Stanley", but to evidence how "exasperating" Kubrick was at times.[49] It is also a way of allowing him to describe the writing process and the stress and anxieties a writer goes through, particularly when the collaboration is as intense as it was with Kubrick. Each time Raphael submitted a draft of *Eyes Wide Shut* to Kubrick, there would be days, if not weeks of waiting for a response. The anticipation and desire to meet Kubrick's expectations routinely disturbed Raphael's vacations with his wife or holiday periods spent with family, such as one Christmas. The suspense led Raphael to question the worth of Kubrick, to become angry due to the power he held over him: "Who was Kubrick anyway? He had directed some movies [...] Big deal".[50]

What needs to be understood about *Eyes Wide Open* is that it is a memoir of an extraordinary episode in Raphael's life and he makes remarks throughout the work to this end. He is in awe of the talent of Kubrick and of his work and insists that he would not have worked under such conditions and for such length of time if it had been anyone else. Kubrick's mystique lends almost an air of absurdity to Raphael's account, as he approaches the house of a man who has no equal in the film industry, only to discover that he is not some ethereal, omniscient genius, but a man with "foibles" just like himself. Raphael has stood firm with his ethics and right to include Kubrick in his memoir in the face of objection by the Kubrick Estate; what he is including in the memoir is an authentic character portrayal – as he saw it – disguised in fictional prose. But the recourse of four disparate writing styles complicates how the character of Kubrick is being transmitted to the reader; his use of third person and his cinematising of various scenes place distance between Raphael and the events. He prevents the reader from getting closer to Kubrick, instead – intentional or not – revealing the distance that existed in his own relationship with the director. The use of fictional flourishes, juxtaposed with the 'conventional' non-fiction prose (itself prone to fictional intervention), creates a post-modern ironic effect for the reader. The disparate writing styles ask the reader to question if the memoir should even be read as such, or rather be seen in the vein of black humour that pervaded much of Kubrick's own work. The playfulness of the writing styles treats this extraordinary episode in Raphael's life with a lack of earnestness. The awkward mixture of writing styles mocks the genre of memoir in an acknowledgement of the form's distinctly British tradition. It is not meant to be serious, as in the American memoir, but rather to be read humorously, ironically and satirically.

3. Sanctioned Truth

Raphael has confronted the ethical controversies surrounding *Eyes Wide Open* and its denunciation by the Kubrick Estate in subsequent essays. These polemical defences argued that the Kubrick Estate were constructing a sanctioned biography, whereby a divine image of Kubrick was being presented, of a man without flaws and of a transcendent genius. Raphael highlighted the case of the touring Kubrick Exhibition, in which an accompanying catalogue contained a wholly different perspective of Kubrick to the one Raphael said he knew: "The Gospel according to Harlan and his acolytes depicts a Kubrick without humour and without faults".[51] Raphael saw the exhibition catalogue as an advertisement for the Kubrick 'brand' as opposed to insightful biographical assessment.[52] Rather than a portrait of a human, a construction of Kubrick was instead offered in which his humanity had been 'amputated'.[53] Raphael asserts that his ethical motivations for writing the memoir were to rescue Kubrick's life and personality from such worship. His aim was to position him as a human being first, genius second. His memoir was an attempt at a warts-and-all portrayal, not to disparage Kubrick, but to understand him as something other than a mechanical hermit as seen in press accounts. Raphael viewed his betrayal as not of

Stanley Kubrick, but of the sanctioned biography desired by the Kubrick Estate.

Raphael defended his right "to tell a story from his perspective",[54] regardless of whether this met with the desired perception of those being written about. But these rights must be weighed against the lack of agency of those being written about.[55] By its very title – *Eyes Wide Open* – the memoir is setting us up to have our eyes opened to the private world of a very private man. Therefore, Kubrick's family took it upon themselves to defend and protect Kubrick's reputation. Christiane Kubrick viewed Raphael's exposé as a disregard of a "normal professional duty of confidence".[56] This breach of professional duty occurred on several accounts. Firstly, it would seem that the Kubrick Estate took particular issue with how they believed Raphael had given a false impression to his literary agent that the memoir was "both authorised and welcomed by Stanley's family and friends".[57] The memoir was not sanctioned. Secondly, by exposing Kubrick, writing about him from his own perspective and not receiving the permission to do so from his family, Raphael is said to have caused pain to the family and to have denigrated Kubrick.[58] As a result of these breaches of confidence, Raphael became a pariah during the release of *Eyes Wide Shut*, with Warner Bros. not inviting him to the premiere of the film. Speaking shortly afterwards in an interview, Raphael said of his treatment by the Kubrick Estate and Warner Bros.: "They didn't say I could say what I've said [...] here in the U.K. they have the freedom of speech, so I think with any luck I shall get away with it".[59]

This in part acknowledges that *Eyes Wide Open* is a memoir that purposely exposes Kubrick, regardless of whether the portrait is genial or otherwise. But the extent to which Raphael had access in order to expose Kubrick's private life was limited. Raphael gives Kubrick the nickname Bluebeard, a name taken from the fairy tale character epitomised in Charles Perrault's seventeenth-century version of the story. Bluebeard was a monster of a man with many secrets contained within a room in his house that he prohibited his wife from entering. Entry to the room led to the discovery of bloodied corpses of women to whom he had previously been married.[60] Raphael humorously claims that such a room must have existed in Kubrick's 'castle', where writers before him had died and been "buried in its recesses".[61] Whilst Raphael's comparison is meant in gallows-humour, the insinuation is similar to that of Emma Tennant's memoir of poet Ted Hughes, *Burnt Diaries.* As Middlebrook has argued, "for Tennant, Hughes resembles Bluebeard in being a man who possesses a secret that can ignite [...] overwhelming curiosity".[62] Raphael's decision to refer to Kubrick as Bluebeard reveals just how little he is able to reveal for how little he knows. Kubrick keeps Raphael locked out of his secret room – his private, personal world – and as a result, all Raphael has to go on in understanding the director is speculation and supposition. Raphael is not alone in making leaps of judgment about character based on scant fact and only snippets of understanding. The media, given no access to the 'real' Kubrick, instead created a character of hermetic, paranoid, and obsessive qualities.

4. Conclusion

In many respects, there were two Kubricks; Kubrick the family man and Kubrick the filmmaker, and both personas remained enigmatic and deeply private. Raphael has attempted to justify the ethical righteousness of his work – revealing the humanity he believes sanctioned biographies have robbed Kubrick of – and his freedom to write about whom he chooses, but he knew of Kubrick's desire for privacy and there is no question that it was betrayed. But his ethical reasoning is lost in a work that mixes fiction and non-fiction writing styles so as to leave the reader unsure of whether what is being presented is merely a caricature of a man that even Raphael did not truly know. The mixing of writing styles by Raphael is in line with the tradition of the British memoir and its post-modern irony and satire, but at the same time, the ethical implications, particularly surrounding a figure as private as Kubrick, cannot be ignored. The ultimate effect of these styles is to create distance; distance between the reader and the character of Kubrick, but also revealing a distance that existed between Raphael and Kubrick.

Raphael concludes the memoir by emphasising its post-modern irony, but also the issue of distance. Their 'friendship' – if that is what it can be called – remained amicable, with infrequent contact during the shooting of *Eyes Wide Shut* and with Kubrick extending invitations for Raphael to visit the set.[63] Raphael's final correspondence with Kubrick occurred at Christmas 1998: "Dear Freddie, Looking forward to seeing you. Best Wishes, Stanley".[64] But he never did see Raphael again, since he passed away several months later. The memoir ends with this moment, with Raphael utilising post-modern black humour to suggest that he felt no emotion, instead conflating the news with his hearing that Newcastle United had beaten Everton in the English FA Cup. This news in fact takes priority over Kubrick's death, he notes, with Newcastle's football victory printed above an insert of Kubrick's death on the following day's newspaper.[65] Kubrick has immediately become a printed story in the writer's mind, their relationship at Kubrick's death perhaps as distant as it was when he was alive.

Notes

1 Raphael, Frederic (1999a). Letter to Deborah. Stanley Kubrick Archives (SKA). SK/17/5/13. 10 March 1999, 1.

2 Herr, Michael (2000). *Kubrick*. London: Picador, 11.

3 Raphael (1999a), 1.

4 Gooblar, David (2008). "The Truth Hurts: The Ethics of Philip Roth's 'Autobiographical' Books." *Journal of Modern Literature* 32.1, 36.

5 *Ibid.*, 36-37.

6 Kubrick, Christiane. Home page. Web. 1999. <http://eyeswideshut.warnerbros.com/ck/ckenglish.htm>.

7 *Ibid.*

8 Kubrick, Christiane (2002). *Stanley Kubrick: A Life in Pictures*. London: Little, Brown, 1.

9 Couser, Thomas G (2012). *Memoir: An Introduction*. New York: Oxford University Press, 85.

10 Atlas, James (1996). "Confessing for Voyeurs; The Age of The Literary Memoir Is Now." *The New York Times*, 12 May. Web. <http://www.nytimes.com/1996/05/12/magazine/confessing-for-voyeurs-the-age-of-the-literary-memoir-is-now.html>.

11 *Ibid.*

12 Couser (2012), 15.

13 Hemley, Robin (2011). "Confessions of a Navel Gazer." *Lit From Within: Contemporary Masters on the Art and Craft of Writing*. Eds. Kevin Haworth, Dinty Moore. Athens, OH: Ohio University Press, 13.

14 *Ibid.*

15 *Ibid.*

16 Eakin, Paul John (2004). "Introduction: Mapping the Ethics of Life Writing." *The Ethics of Life Writing*. Ed. Paul John Eakin. London: Cornell University, 2.

17 *Ibid.*

18 Raphael, Frederic (2013). "Stanley Kubrick, Museum Piece." *Commentary*. April. 135.4, 56.

19 Raphael, Frederic (1999b). *Eyes Wide Open*. London: Orion, 53-54.

20 Raphael (2013), 56.

21 *Ibid.*

22 Boyd, William (2012). "In Conversation with Frederic Raphael." *PN Review* 38.5, 27.

23 *Ibid.*

24 McDowell, Frederick (n.d.) "Frederic Raphael - Contemporary Novelists." SKA, SK/1/2/3/6/19.

25 Raphael (1999b), 121.

26 *Ibid.*, 124.

27 *Ibid.*

28 *Ibid.*, 126.

29 *Ibid.*, 36.

30 Miller, Nancy K. (2004). "The Ethics of Betrayal: Diary of a Memoirist." *The Ethics of Life Writing*. Ed. Paul John Eakin. London: Cornell University Press, 151.

31 *Ibid.*

32 Such a low profile meant that a conman, Alan Conway, was able to impersonate the director at celebrity parties throughout the 1990s. See the film *Colour Me Kubrick*. Dir. Brian W. Cook. 2005 for a fictional retelling of Conway's exploits.

33 Raphael (1999a), 1.

34 *Ibid.*

35 For a detailed history of the biopic genre see Custen, George F (1992). *Bio/Pics: How Hollywood Constructed Public History*. New Brunswick: Rutgers University Press. Custen's work traces the evolution of the biopic within the Hollywood studio system and its representation of historical figures.

36 *Ibid.*, 86

37 Lejeune, Philippe (1977). "Autobiography in the Third Person." *New Literary History*, 9.1, 34.

38 *Ibid.*, 35.

39 Kosta, Barbara (1994). *Recasting Autobiography: Women's Counterfictions in Contemporary German Literature and Film*. Ithaca: Cornell University Press, 69.

40 *Ibid.*, 70.

41 Eakin, John Paul (1999). *How Our Lives Become Stories: Making Selves*. Ithaca: Cornell University Press, 159.

42 Eakin (2004), 2.

43 Miller (2004), 149.

44 *Ibid.*

45 *Ibid.*

46 Raphael, Frederic (2006). "The Pumpkinification of Stanley K." *Depth of Field Stanley Kubrick, Film, and the Uses of History*. Eds. Geoffrey Cocks, James Diedrick, Glenn Perusek. Madison, WI: The University of Wisconsin Press, 73.

47 *Ibid.*

48 *Ibid.*

49 *Ibid.*

50 Raphael (1999b), 81.

51 Raphael (2013), 56.

52 *Ibid.*, 58.

53 *Ibid.*, 56

54 Gooblar (2008), 37.

55 *Ibid.*

56 Kubrick, Christiane.

57 *Ibid.*

58 *Ibid.*

59 *One to One with Adam Boulton*. 1999. Sky News. Web. <https://www.youtube.com/watch?v=O5DyCgkql8A>.

60 Middlebrook, Diane (2004). "Misremembering Ted Hughes." *The Ethics of Life Writing*. Ed. Paul John Eakin. London: Cornell University, 43.

61 Raphael (1999b), 37.

62 Middlebrook (2004), 43.

63 Raphael (1999b), 185.

64 *Ibid.*, 186.

65 *Ibid.*

Bibliography

Atlas, James (1996). "Confessing for Voyeurs; The Age of The Literary Memoir Is Now." *The New York Times*, 12 May 1996. Web.

Boyd, William (2012). "In Conversation with Frederic Raphael." *PN Review* 38.5, 25-30.

Churchill, Winston (1930). *My Early Life*. London: T. Butterworth.

Couser, Thomas G (1989). *Altered Egos: Authority in American Autobiography*.

New York: Oxford University Press.
--- (2012). *Memoir: An Introduction*. New York: Oxford University Press.
Cramer, Jeffrey S. (2004). *Walden: A Fully Annotated Edition.* New Haven: Yale University Press.
Crisp, Quentin (1968). *The Naked Civil Servant*. London: Jonathan Cape.
Darling. Dir. John Schlesinger. 1965. DVD. Studiocanal, 2015.
Defoe, Daniel (1992 [1719]). *Robinson Crusoe*. Ware, UK: Wordsworth.
--- (2013 [1720]). *Memoirs of a Cavalier*. Farmington Hills, MI: Gale.
Eakin, Paul John (2004). "Introduction: Mapping the Ethics of Life Writing." *The Ethics of Life Writing*. Ed. Paul John Eakin. Ithaca, NY: Cornell University Press, 1-16.
--- (1999). *How Our Lives Become Stories: Making Selves*. Ithaca, NY: Cornell University Press.
Eyes Wide Shut. Dir. Stanley Kubrick. 1999. DVD. Warner Home Video, 2008.
Franklin, Cynthia G. (2009). *Academic Lives: Memoir, Cultural Theory, and the University Today*. Athens: University of Georgia Press.
Gooblar, David (2008). "The Truth Hurts: The Ethics of Philip Roth's 'Autobiographical' Books." *Journal of Modern Literature* 32.1, 33-53.
Herr, Michael (2000). *Kubrick*. London: Picador.
Hemley, Robin (2011). "Confessions of a Navel Gazer." *Lit From Within: Contemporary Masters on the Art and Craft of Writing*. Eds. Kevin Haworth, Dinty Moore. Athens, OH: Ohio University Press, 8-19.
James, Clive (2015 [1980]). *Unreliable Memoirs*. London: Picador.
Kosta, Barbara (1994). *Recasting Autobiography: Women's Counterfictions in Contemporary German Literature and Film*. Ithaca: Cornell University Press.
Kubrick, Christiane (2002). *Stanley Kubrick: A Life in Pictures*. London: Little, Brown.
Lejeune, Philippe (1989). *On Autobiography*. Minneapolis: University of Minnesota Press.
Middlebrook, Diane (2004). "Misremembering Ted Hughes." *The Ethics of Life Writing*. Ed. Paul John Eakin. Ithaca, NY: Cornell University, 40-50.
Miller, Nancy K. (2004). "The Ethics of Betrayal: Diary of a Memoirist." *The Ethics of Life Writing*. Ed. Paul John Eakin. Ithaca, NY: Cornell University Press, 147-160.
Raphael, Frederic (1995). *A Double Life*. London: Phoenix.
--- (1999). *Eyes Wide Open*. London: Orion.
--- (2006). "The Pumpkinification of Stanley K." *Depth of Field Stanley Kubrick, Film, and the Uses of History*. Eds. Geoffrey Cocks, James Diedrick, Glenn Perusek. Madison, WI: University of Wisconsin Press, 62-73.
--- (2013). "Stanley Kubrick, Museum Piece." *Commentary*. April. 135.4. 55-58.

Sassoon, Siegfried (1974 [1928]). *Memoirs of a Fox-Hunting Man*. London: Faber & Faber.

Schnitzler, Arthur (1999 [1927]). *Traumnovelle/Dream Story*. London: Penguin.

Tennant, Emma (1999). *Burnt Diaries*. Edinburgh: Canongate Books.

Two for the Road. Dir. Stanley Donen. 1967. DVD. Eureka Entertainment, 2015.

Sarah Herbe (Salzburg)

Online Self-Presentation and -Promotion in Jeanette Winterson's Column (2000–2014)

> I love the freedom of the Net. I know we haven't figured out how to use it yet, or even what it's for, but this is the beginning, so much the beginning, and we shouldn't weight the future with too many questions.[1]

1. Introduction

In 2000, the British author Jeanette Winterson launched her website jeanettewinterson.com.[2] One feature of this website was a "column", a rubric to which Winterson would add monthly updates on her personal and professional life. Between 2000 and 2014, Winterson posted 116 column entries of 800 to 1800 words. While there used to be updates almost every month from November 2000 to the end of 2010, the regularity of the updates decreased in 2011, and the final entry was uploaded in February 2014.

When Winterson started her column, websites were still fairly new environments for online self-presentation.[3] Personal home pages had become popular only at the beginning of the 1990s, and "newer autobiographical genres like the Webcam and the blog […] emerged in the later half of the 1990s."[4] Since then, the popularity of online autobiographical self-presentation has climbed to such heights that Anna Poletti and Julie Rak argue that "[n]owhere is the power and diversity of the autobiographical more visible than online, where it is the raison d'être for many of the activities and practices associated with Web 2.0".[5] The emergence of online self-presentation in the 1990s and its constant rise of popularity in various forms and online environments such as MySpace, Facebook or YouTube have generated a valuable corpus of scholarship in the realm of auto/biography studies, only some of which shall be briefly addressed here since they inform my reading of Winterson's column. The key characteristics concerning format and medium, narrative pattern, author and audience as well as the specific content of digital life stories identified by Michael Hardey in 2004 are still helpful starting points for an analysis of online autobiographical writing today. *Identity Technologies: Constructing the Self Online*, edited by Julie Rak and Anna Poletti in 2014, brings together approaches from auto/biography studies and media studies. In one of the contributions, Philippe Lejeune gives an update of autobiographical writing in the twenty-first century by showing how the three genres he has identified as central of autobiographical writing, namely the "retrospective story of a life", the personal diary as well as correspondence are adapted to online environments. In the same collection, Sidonie Smith and Julia Watson suggest fifteen concepts for approaching online self-presentation. For a reading of Winterson's column, the concepts of "temporality" (e.g., "What time or times, whether a specific moment or more general time, does the site set up? [...] Are temporal moments signaled through dates or other chronological distinctions?")[6] and "audiences" (e.g., "What kind of audience does the site call for? Whom does the site explicitly address as its imagined audience? What verbal or visual rhetorics does the site deploy to engage visitors?")[7] are particularly useful.

Two special issues of *Biography* on "Online Lives" (2003 and 2015) do not only provide insights into the variety of forms of online self-expression, and map the rapid changes they have undergone in slightly more than a decade, but offer valuable approaches to analysing these still relatively new forms of expression. According to John B. Killoran, "[a]ny account of autobiographical display in the new medium of the Web must be, in part, an account of genres rooted in older media".[8] Andreas Kitzmann, on the other hand, argues that new technological possibilities will engender new paradigms based on their own material conditions and therefore contends that a "compare and contrast" approach towards online autobiographical presentation misses the point.[9] For a reading of Winterson's column, an awareness of both critical positions is helpful: if we read her column entries in the context of traditional genres of autobiographical writing, their indebtedness to the diary, letters, or travel writing will become visible. A focus on the parameters introduced by an online environment will highlight their impact on both form and content of the column entries as well as their interactive potential, and draws our attention to renegotiations of private and public spaces in an online environment.

While Winterson's website is referred to repeatedly in critical essays on her work,[10] her column has not received much critical attention so far. Winterson's column describes a trajectory of initial enthusiasm about the possibilities offered by the new medium over a phase of disillusionment and eventual abandonment of the column format in favour of a new form of online self-presentation. The column is an example of how online self-presentation evolved over more than a decade, and offers an opportunity to probe into how autobiographical writing can be utilised for public self-presentation and self-promotion.

2. *Questions of Genre*

In her column entries, Winterson deals with choices of life style (the entries betray her growing wish to live environmentally friendly and to eat wholesome, ideally home-grown, food); she comments on developments in national and international politics, and reflects on the functions of art and culture. While she mentions her childhood and youth with her Pentecostal adoptive parents as well as her coming out as a lesbian, autobiographical aspects which are also to be found in some of her fictional work, the column entries focus more on her current concerns and struggles. Some of the entries include photographs of the author, of her house in the country or her shop in Spitalfields; sometimes covers of the books Winterson recommends to her readership are added, and around Christmas, the entries are decorated with festive clip-art ornaments and symbols. There are hyperlinks to other parts of the website, such as to the poem of the month or to pieces of journalism written by Winterson, as well as links to other websites, such as to that of Winterson's favourite astrologer.

The visual make-up of the column entries, the inclusion of hyperlinks and the retrochronological[11] order of the entries (newest entries displayed first) suggest a categorisation of Winterson's column as a 'blog', a "frequently updated web site consisting of personal observations, excerpts from other sources, etc., typically run by a single person, and usually with hyperlinks to other sites; an online journal or diary".[12] When Winterson's column was established, the blog format was still very new: it developed out of online diaries in the late 1990s and experienced its first boom around the turn of the century. While Winterson does not refer to her column as "blog", it can still be regarded as an early example of this emerging form of online self-expression. The heading "column" betrays Winterson's background in print journalism and suggests regular, but not necessarily daily, publication intervals. The heading thus also indicates a bridge between traditions of print publication and newly emerging online forms of expression.

The column entries all start with concrete temporal markers: they are headed by the month and year of composition or upload (the two do not always coincide) and in almost all of them does Winterson comment explicitly on the current month, and what she associates with it. She states repeatedly that "June is a month I really like" (June 2001), while readers learn that she does not like July (July 2010); she believes that August "should be the month of holidays and sunshine and something like happiness" (August 2004) and in January Winterson often tells her readers that "she love[s] a new year" (January 2006). The temporal references are always combined with information about Winterson's current location: her life as presented in her monthly column is characterised by frequent moves and travels not only inside the UK, where she alternately resides in London and in a remote house in the countryside, but between the UK and the US, especially New York, and the UK and continental Europe, particularly France. In about a third of the entries her location is mentioned in the very first paragraph, another third involves extended discussions about her present, past or immediate future destinations or detailed descriptions of where she is at the moment of writing. Her column is in this respect reminiscent of "modern travel writing", much of which "turns on the encounter with material space by way of a mode of transportation – train, plane, or an earlier form of conveyance".[13] The frequent references create an omnipresent sense of place and usually provide the starting points for Winterson's musings about her everyday actions, her concerns about the environment, or current political developments.

While the column is updated only once a month, its dated entries and lack of hindsight (the entries are also not edited once they have been uploaded) are reminiscent of diary entries rather than of retrospective life stories. Since they are always written with an audience in mind, online diaries require, in contrast to personal diaries not meant for imminent publication, "constant care […] to achieve a positive and appealing self-presentation" as well as a "great deal of self-control".[14] The temporal and spatial coordinates provided by Winterson usually at the beginning of the entries presents one such method of self-control. Further, her frequent references to place and time serve to present her as both a cosmopolitan as well as an individual who feels at home in a rural environment, and thus appeals to diverse readerships.

Temporal and spatial anchoring of autobiographical experience, familiar from diaries, letters and travel writing, assumes new importance in online autobiographical writing, where it does not only provide information potentially interesting for a reader following the frequent moves of Winterson, but represents a physical, concrete contrast to the virtual environment of her website. Together with the occasional photograph of Winterson, of her house or her animals this strategy renders the author and her whereabouts palpable for the reader of the column.

Also, Winterson reaches out to her audience and sees the column as a forum for making an impact on their lives. Her column thus partly follows the pattern of "conversion story", identified by Hardey as one of three types of digital life stories (the other two being the family story and the transition or quest story), which he does not limit to stories of religious conversion, but extends to narratives that appeal to readers to follow the author's example.[15] Starting from her own life experience, Winterson advocates a healthy and environmentally friendly life style, encouraging her readership to change their eating, consuming and travelling habits. Her autobiographical writing becomes a "self-help" column in a twofold sense: some passages of the column read as if they were written in an effort of scriptotherapy, "a term proposed by Suzette Henke to signal the ways in which autobiographical writing functions as a mode of self-healing",[16] while others double as self-help literature for her readers, as in the following passage:

> Whatever you can do to cut your carbon emissions, please do it, and lobby local councils and government, wherever you are, to take some responsibility for our planet. We can do a lot as individuals, much more than we think – but we need governments to think globally. If only they would give up their bombs and invest in some carbon-cutting technology instead.
>
> Meanwhile, wash in a bucket, water your plants, and get out the bicycle.

> Oh and listen to the proms and read a few poems. You will be arming your mind instead of arming the world. Me, I am going to do more of everything I love, and do it consciously, not least because time feels short and precious. Or as Mrs Winterson used to say, The Summer is Ended and We Are Not Yet Saved. (August 2006)

However, the sincerity of Winterson's appeals to her audience is occasionally impaired by paratextual interventions of the online environment: while Winterson asks her readers to buy books locally instead of via Amazon.com,[17] a link below at least one of the covers of her books included in the column suggests "Buy now from Amazon".[18]

That the entries were composed as transient news updates rather than as elements of an autobiographical project meant for repeated or cumulative reading becomes apparent when they are read in one go and in the original order in which they were posted: they are repetitive and predictable. The entries posted in August or September invariably deal with Winterson's birthday and address her age, and the Christmas entries, which detail Winterson's routines of gift-making and preparing Christmas meals in places read as if they were copied and pasted from earlier entries. The fact that all the entries are still accessible and archived on her website, however, invites a cumulative reading. Since the entries were not edited once they were uploaded, they present an intriguing form of documentation of fourteen years of the writer's life and work.

3. Structure and (Ir)regularity of Column Entries

In contrast to her memoir *Why Be Happy When You Could Be Normal?* (2011) and the fictionalised version of her life in *Oranges Are not the Only Fruit* (1985), Winterson's column entries follow a rigid structure: she starts with an update on what has happened in her life over the last month, a section that is often linked with a discussion of national or global economic or political developments or current events, such as the economic crisis such or the terror attacks in New York and London. Sections on her work as a writer and recommendations, mostly of literature, cultural events or other books, but also of psychics and astrologers, follow. The entries usually end with a call to action or a piece of advice. This fixed pattern betrays the "pressure towards standardization [of digital storytelling] because of the sheer volume of material online and people's limited tolerance for formats, layouts or sequences whose intent they have difficulty interpreting", identified by Nick Couldry as one of the characteristic features of online narrative forms,[19] but it also supports Winterson's self-presentation as a well-organised person who relies on fixed routines and discipline. The structure of her entries and the regularity with which they have appeared for the first ten years of the column thus support Winterson's claims about the role of discipline in her life:

> The reason that I live as I do – both strictly, in that I am regular in my habits, and simply, in that I avoid pointless activity and pointless clutter, is to keep myself in readiness for work, fit for purpose I suppose, and to keep at bay the enervations of modern life – enervations which are bad for creativity, which is high enough in its own right, without getting strung out by crazy life. (August 2008)

Breaks in the regularity of the entries correlate with phases of mental distress and personal struggle in the life of the writer, as the reader learns on the return of the column: after skipping her first column entry after more than four years of regular uploads, Winterson apologises in July 2006: "Sorry about last month, I just couldn't manage the update, exhausted." In 2007, Winterson cryptically explains the reasons for two months' absence from the column as follows: "Here I am, back on site. It is unusual for me – indeed unknown for me not to update the site each month, but I needed to finish my new book, and there were difficulties elsewhere." (June 2007) After having missed another entry in July 2008, Winterson states:

> All right, I admit it, I have been avoiding the website. Actually I have been avoiding as much as possible that isn't my kids' book because I love writing it, and once again, work has saved me, in the sense of taking me to a better place. (August 2008)

Once this pattern has been identified, the reader of Winterson's column will basically be able to glean hints about Winterson's wellbeing simply from the metadata of the online column by paying attention to the time lag between one entry and the next. In 2010, however, a new facet enters the explanation for missing updates, though it goes hand in hand with struggle and personal distress. Winterson is frustrated with the public reception of the column:

> At last the column is back – many of you have emailed me about this, and I am sorry it has taken so long to make a return. I have to say that […] I just got fed up of this web column being a media bulletin board, where anything I said about my personal life was taken up elsewhere. And in the tone of 'what does she expect??'
> So, I shall have to write as much as I can without really saying too much… which is a bit odd.
> Well, maybe I can say some things. (June 2010)

This passage draws our attention to two central aspects of Winterson's project of online self-presentation: the awareness of her audience and the growing unease about what can be revealed of one's personal life in an online environment.

4. Private Spaces, Public Audiences and Self-Promotion

Winterson started her column in a spirit of enthusiasm about the new and still unknown possibilities the web had to offer. She embraced the freedom of the web, and perceived her online column as a site where, in contrast to interviews or print journalism with a bigger audience, she could communicate openly with her readers. Winterson closes the very first column with the following paragraph:

> I will write again on December 1st - Advent. I hope you'll tell me what you want in these columns, providing it's not too personal, though I have to say that when I was asked recently what had changed my life now that I am 40, the answer had to be THE WONDERBRA. (November 2000)

This first entry does not only indicate Winterson's willingness to communicate directly with her readers, but foreshadows the tension that will become characteristic of the column, namely between revealing and withholding details about her private life. While her comment on the wonderbra is obviously tongue-in-cheek[20] (underlined by the use of capital letters), we find more serious statements about her private life in later column entries. Despite her avowal not to reveal details that are "too personal" in her column, the reader is regularly informed about Winterson's daily routines, her mental and physical health,[21] her dietary regime as well as particulars from her depressing childhood and adolescence, and gets more or less explicit updates on her girlfriends. Her online explicitness about personal life details can be explained by the fact that over the first eight years or so of her column, Winterson perceived the column as a "private space". In 2005 she says:

> Remember this column is personal space. It's not in a newspaper or a magazine. It's talking as I would to you, with all the doubts, hesitations, anger, mistakes, misreadings, but all the moment flooding in. If I start to censor it, we lose a space we share. Remember you can change your mind as time goes on. So can I.
> The problem with being a writer, the problem with public space, is that you say something and it stays put, which is not what happens in conversation. We try things out. We argue with our friends and ourselves. We do that here, in this column. It is not tablets of stone. (May 2005)[22]

In online self-presentation "privacy [...] is an issue of access: to be private is to control or regulate the level of access that the 'outside world' has to one's personal property, body, or thoughts."[23] Access to Winterson's column was never technically restricted by a password, but Winterson controls access to her private life by choosing what to share with her audience. She also makes it very clear that she is in charge of what is being said in her column, even if she allows for interaction with her readers:

> Apparently I am not allowed to use the phrase 'You Guys' – got a long email castigating my failures here. Well, I always get emails doing just that, but in this case, you guys, too bad. This is a letter to friends, not my next book, and it's MY site, so, we'll relax. (December 2002)

Though Winterson does not define "private" or "personal", it becomes clear from entries such as the one of May 2005 quoted above that she uses the concepts in opposition to appearing in print: for her, the online medium is more akin to casual personal conversation or familiar correspondence, and thus limited to a particular audience. An awareness that everything she says in her column will "stay put" as well, and might make its way to an audience beyond that of well-meaning readers of Winterson's books does not surface until 2008:

> It has been a very tough two years – lots of lovely things, yes, but a very tough and testing time. I can't explain why here, because I won't have a private life – because although this is me talking to you, whoever you are, in quite an intimate way, I know that it is also a public place, and I have to be careful not to turn it into Jerry Springer. (August 2008)

Winterson realises at this point that it is beyond her control what readers of the column do with the information about her gained there, and she is evidently frustrated with this situation, and slightly disillusioned by the possibilities of the internet, when she finds out that the revelation about her new girlfriend in September 2009 prompted reporters to seek out her house to catch a glimpse of her new partner. In 2010, she reflects upon how her revelations in her column are linked to the media coverage on her new partner, and admits to her own naivety of having perceived her column as a private space:

> I am still not prepared to talk about it, because I was never interested in doing that – only that in these columns over the last two years, I have written about my personal struggles and deep sadness, and had a huge, and helpful and kind response from readers, and also a lot of messages saying that my willingness to talk about difficult things has been valuable to others. And so I wanted to say that a very good thing had happened unexpectedly and rather beautifully. A gift.
>
> But in our world you cannot be private without being secret…
>
> And I suppose I have been a bit of an idiot, because although I write these columns in what feels to me quite a private way – talking to my readers through my website – it is a public arena.
>
> Part of me never wants to say anything again. But that is not the answer either.
>
> I guess I won't ever resolve these dilemmas. (February 2010)

Before we condemn Winterson for her naivety, we must not forget that when she launched her column in 2000, access to the internet was not as omnipresent and as uncomplicated as it is today: at the end of 2000, only 34 % of British households could access the internet from home, whereas by 2016, this percentage had risen to 89 %.[24] Furthermore, before the rise of social media and before the practice of constant sharing of online content became widespread, the awareness that what one shared online would not be limited to its original environment was not as taken for granted as it is today.

In the passage from February 2000, a further explanation why Winterson perceived her column as a private rather than as a public site is implied: it was based on the assumption that her audience was mainly comprised of the benevolent readers of her novels. Kitzmann argues that for "any Web self-documenter, the audience is not only anticipated, but expected, and thus influences and structures the very manner in which the writer articulates, composes, and distributes the self-document."[25] That Winterson wrote her column entries with the readers of her novels in mind becomes clear from such casual remarks as "[b]ut I am obsessed with time – you've read my books, you know that." (January 2003) The impression that she knew who her audience was will have been furthered by the interaction encouraged by her website. In the early days of Winterson's website, there used to be a message board.[26] Also, there was a contact e-mail address, and while Winterson was always open about the fact that she did not administer the website alone, she referred to many of the messages sent to her in her column entries, and thus established a kind of communication between readers and writer that allowed for some reciprocity, while it was not symmetrical. While interaction with the readership soon became daunting and unmanageable and she tried to divert requests for photographs or interviews to her agent (March 2001), Winterson kept asking her readers for their opinion, for example on new features of the website, but also for advice on life decisions and thus maintained (the impression) of interaction with her audience.

Kitzmann argues that "the online collapse of the public/private divide into a paradoxical mix of intimacy and 'mediatization,' of introversion and self-promotion, can be seen as a sign of the Web's technological 'nature'",[27] and it is indeed the moment of self-promotion that provides a motivation for presenting the column as a private space that allowed Winterson to divulge details about her private life. The following passage illustrates how details of Winterson's private life and the promotion of her novels are linked:

> My girlfriend has her birthday in June and we're going to Capri. Anybody who has read The Powerbook [sic] will know how much I love the

> island, and if you still haven't read The PowerBook, now's your chance, especially with the sexy cover on the front. Some of you don't like the cover, and I respect your views. I do like it, but to answer an email I've had about 100 times - no, I didn't choose it. Random House authors are not allowed to choose their covers. That's marketing. (June 2001)

In a survey of professional websites, many of which include personal information about the person behind the business, Killoran found that, asked about their reasons for including pictures in leisure wear or information about hobbies, professionals would frequently answer that such pieces of information were included to show the prospective client that they were real people, and that this perception helped build and maintain a successful business relationship with their clients. [28] Winterson's motives behind including personal information as well as photographs in her column entries and her website as a whole might be similar.

Since Winterson's column is part of her website, which Jago Morrison has identified as a "marketing tool, a means of promoting new publications, disseminating her views on contemporary culture, and facilitating discussion of both",[29] ultimately everything she chooses to share of her private life there has to be seen in the framework of advertising, and thus self-promotion. This ties in with the fact that Winterson explicitly asks the readers of her column to buy her books – usually at the end of the entries, after the reader has learned new snippets of her life, and thus some kind of contact, even contract, has been established.

The aspect of self-promotion also explains why Winterson chooses to share so many private details with her audience, despite her belief that knowledge of a writer's life should not have an impact on the reception of their work. In 1996 she said,

> the intersection between a writer's life and a writer's work is irrelevant to the reader. [...] The question put to the writer 'How much of this is based on your own experience?' is meaningless. The fiction, the poem, is not a version of the facts, it is an entirely different way of seeing.[30]

This attitude is basically repeated in a reaction to a message by a reader who accuses her of anti-Americanism after she had complained about the omnipresence of TV sets in the US:

> Last month's column pulled in a lot of cross emails from Americans, many of whom seemed to feel that if I had ANY criticisms of America at all, I should give up publishing there, sack, [sic] my agent etc. Others said they were so disappointed with my views that they would never read me again.
> On that basis, we had all better give up reading books now; if the criteria for reading a book is to be in complete harmony with the writer and all their views, world literature has had it.
> Does it also apply to film makers, musicians, painters? Should we stuff as much personal information as possible in the front of our books, just in case someone has a good time under false pretences? (October 2002)

The autobiographical details provided in her column are thus evidently not intended to affect how readers approach her books, but to guarantee that they buy them in the first place, and that the audience does not lose interest in the writer in the gap between the publications of books. Divulging selected autobiographical details in her column also represents an act of taking control of her public image.

5. The End of the Column

The number of column entries decreased after 2008, when Winterson first expressed frustration at its public nature. While there are still eight entries in 2009, there are only five in 2010 and 2011 each; there is a slight rise to seven entries in 2012 before the two final ones are uploaded in 2013 and 2014. Many of the final entries deal with the publication of Winterson's *Why Be Happy When You Could Be Normal?* (2011), which she refers to as "[p]art memoir, part manifesto" (November 2011), but never as "autobiography". While readers are not informed about what led to the composition of this book (they will only find out when they read the book that Winterson has made contact with her biological mother), they learn how Winterson tries to "sell the memoir" to the publisher and are informed about the details of the publication process. After its publication, Winterson keeps readers updated on the success of the book. The column thus becomes a running commentary on another autobiographical project.

The petering out of her column does not only coincide with the publication of her memoir, but with Winterson's move to Twitter. At the beginning of 2011, Winterson is still sceptical about Twitter:

> A lot of people have asked me why I don't TWITTER.
> I would never remember to do it – that's number one. Number two is the horrible communality of it – the bogus sharing. I would feel ridiculous and exposed. Number three – what would I twitter about? Feeding the birds? Fighting my way to London on a Great Western Train? The awful answer is yes – for that appears to be the nature of Tweets.
> BUT – if I am able to do something useful – like get into schools and excite the kids towards reading, towards language, towards higher education, then maybe I WILL get tweeting. But first I have to persuade our Education Secretary, Michael Gove, to let me go forth and multiply the numbers of poorer kids wanting more than a job in Carphone Warehouse.
> I'll write him a letter. I'll let you know how it goes.... (January 2011)

Here, Winterson's preference for more traditional forms of communication, such as the letter, is still expressed. Later that year, however, she tells her readers that she might join Twitter after all: having contributed to a project in which writers were asked to rewrite books in the form of tweets, she found out that she "enjoyed it so much that [she was] wondering if Twitter might have something in for [her] after all" (September 2011). She joins the next month, and asks the readers of her column to follow her on https://twitter.com/Wintersonworld (October 2011). Meanwhile, it is clear that the format of the column has become out-dated: Winterson asks her readers if she should "change this column thing for a weekly BLOG" or even a video blog in 2012, but the fact that she ends this request with the invitation, "[l]et me know and follow me on Twitter@Wintersonworld" (January 2012) already indicates her preferred future online environment.

The column project is thus now completed. Contrary to many other online life-writing projects that were launched in the early twenty-first century,[31] it is still available online today (2017). Its status has changed from a prominently placed feature on the writer's website to a feature that is filed under "Archive", with the added description "Click here to access an archive written for the site over the years".[32] The heading "column" has disappeared. Instead, Winterson's Twitter feed is now displayed at the bottom of her website. The style and content of her tweets is reminiscent of her column entries: Winterson expresses outrage about political developments such as the Brexit vote, advertises her public appearances and latest publications, and shares private photographs, for example of her wedding in 2015. The compressed form is made up for by the higher frequency of tweets.

A thorough analysis of Winterson's self-presentation on Twitter would be the subject of another paper: critical approaches to reading Twitter feeds as presentation and performance of the self already exist.[33] As a conclusion to the present essay suffice it to say that reflections on how to live her life well and how to straddle her public and private personae are largely absent from Winterson's tweets. In the column entries, such autobiographical contemplations often went hand in hand with reflections on the medium through which Winterson presented herself to the public: this form of thinking about the self and how it is expressed to an audience is no longer there either. This altered approach towards online self-presentation expresses tacit acceptance of its publicness and of the fact that the controlled distribution of details about an author's private life – a picture here, a line about the wife's greatness there – can serve to keep one's readership interested. With the help of the Twitter medium, Winterson's followers are kept up to date about the author's work and life in a more immediate fashion than was the case with the column entries. The focus of the tweets on announcing Winterson's public appearances, her publications and journalism, as well as the re-tweeting of messages and links that praise Jeanette Winterson serve to highlight the self-promotional drive that was ultimately the motivation of the column entries as well. Winterson's self-presentation as 'author' is paramount.

Notes

1 Winterson, Jeanette. "August 2001." Web. 27 July 2016. <http://www.jeanettewinterson.com/archive/august-2001/> All column entries are available here: <http://www.jeanettewinterson.com/column-year/2000/>. For better readability, references will be made in brackets by references to month and year of their upload.

2 For a detailed account of the lawsuit that led to the launch of this website, see Mota, Miguel (2004). "What's in a Name? The Case of Jeanettewinterson.com." *Twentieth Century Literature* 50.2, 192-206.

3 In this essay, I shall use "online autobiographical writing" and "online self-presentation" interchangeably.

4 Killoran, John B. (2003). "The Gnome in the Front Yard and Other Public Figurations: Genres of Self-Presentation on Personal Home Pages." *Biography* 26.1, 80.

5 Poletti, Anna, and Julie Rak (2014). "Introduction: Digital Dialogues." *Identity Technologies: Constructing the Self Online*. Eds. Anna Poletti and Julie Rak. Wisconsin Studies in Autobiography Madison, US: University of Wisconsin Press, 3.

6 Smith, Sidonie, and Julia Watson (2014). "Virtually Me: A Toolbox About Online Self-Presentation." *Identity Technologies: Constructing the Self Online*. Eds. Anna Poletti and Julie Rak. Wisconsin Studies in Autobiography. Madison, US: University of Wisconsin Press, 90.

7 *Ibid.*, 74.

8 Killoran (2003), 79.

9 See Kitzmann, Andreas (2003). "That Different Place: Documenting the Self within Online Environments." *Biography* 26.1, 48-65.

10 For example in the following articles: Morrison, Jago (2006). "Who Cares About Gender at a Time Like This? Love, Sex and the Problem of Jeanette Winterson." *Journal of Gender Studies* 15.2, 169-80; Mota (2004), or van der Wiel, Reina (2009). "Trauma as Site of Identity: The Case of Jeanette Winterson and Frida Kahlo." *Women: A Cultural Review* 20.2, 135-56.

11 Philippe Lejuene discusses retrochronology as a feature of online diaries, calling it "the new way in which they process time spatially". He says that the "past of the text is not behind it but in front of it, or rather under it, floating to the surface only to be pushed down in turn by the next entry." Lejeune, Philippe (2014). "Autobiography and New Communication Tools." Trans. Katherine Durnin. *Identity Technologies: Constructing the Self Online*. Eds. Anna Poletti and Julie Rak. Wisconsin Studies in Autobiography. Madison, US: University of Wisconsin Press, 252.

12 "weblog, n." *OED Online*. Oxford University Press, 2016. Web. 25 July 2016.

13 Smith, Sidonie, and Julia Watson (2010). *Reading Autobiography: A Guide for Interpreting Life Narratives*. 2nd ed. Minneapolis and London: Minnesota Press, 43.

14 Lejeune (2014), 252.

15 Hardey, Michael (2003). "Digital Life Stories: Auto/Biography in the Information Age." *Auto/Biography* 12.3, 193.

16 Smith and Watson (2010), 279.

17 See for example the January 2011 entry.

18 See <http://www.jeanettewinterson.com/archive/september-2011/≥. On the interaction between online text and paratext, see Smith and Watson (2014), 85-87.

19 Couldry, Nick (2008). "Mediatization or Mediation? Alternative Understandings of the Emergent Space of Digital Storytelling." *New Media & Society* 10.3, 382.

20 The occasion of this statement at a reading in Toronto has been reported by Leah Darke in "A Thief in the Vaults of Literature." *The Globe and Mail* 25 Nov. 2000: n. pag. Web. 3 February 2017.

21 See for example the May 2002 entry: "First Ruth Rendell, then Martin Amis, and now me. What is it with writer's [sic] and dental work? I decided that at the ripe old age of 42, it was time to get a new crown fitted and finally extract a baby tooth that has been sitting in there since I was, well, a baby. The tooth is now in an envelope waiting for the Tooth Fairy to do something with it."

22 See also June 2005 or October 2006.

23 Kitzmann (2003), 55.

24 See Cooper-Green, Emma-Jane. "Internet Access: Households and Individuals." Office for National Statistics, 2002. Web 26 July 2016. <https://www.ons.gov.uk/> and Prescott, Cecil. "Internet Access - Households and Individuals 2016." Office for National Statistics. Web. 30 September 2016. <https://www.ons.gov.uk/> respectively.

25 Kitzmann (2003), 56.

26 See Mota for further observations on the interactive features: "Furthermore, Winterson's website, while clearly an attempt on one level to control the production and circulation of the author's name, nevertheless encourages the kind of interactive participation by its readers that ensures play around the name and identity of the author. That Winterson provides her fans with a voice on the site by encouraging email exchanges not only with her but also among themselves has the effect of enacting and positioning "Jeanette Winterson" in a variety of ways. Some correspondents, for example, may use the e-mail list as a forum for discussing issues having little or nothing to do with Jeanette Winterson, relegating the name of the author to the margins of her own domain. And of course others can readily build links to jeanettewinterson.com from their own websites, thereby incorporating into potentially very different performative spaces whatever constructions of author and authority may exist within Winterson's own site." (Mota [2004], 200).

27 Kitzmann (2003), 58.

28 See Killoran (2003).

29 Morrison (2006), 171.

[30] Winterson, Jeanette (1996). *Art Objects: Essays on Ecstasy and Effrontery*. New York: Vintage, 27.

[31] See for example Lejeune's remarks on the disappearance of early online diaries (252).

[32] <http://www.jeanettewinterson.com/column-year/2000/>.

[33] Zizi Papacharissi applies content and discourse analysis "to examine performative strategies" of the self in tweets; see Papacharissi, Zizi (2012). "Without You I'm Nothing: Performances of the Self on Twitter." *International Journal of Communication* 6, 1989. In a media studies contribution, Marwick and boyd find that on Twitter, "[s]ome techniques of audience management resemble the practices of 'micro-celebrity' and personal branding, both strategic self-commodification." (Marwick, Alice E., and danah boyd [2011]. "I tweet honestly, I tweet passionately: Twitter users, context collapse, and the imagined audience." *New Media & Society* 13.1, 114).

Bibliography

"blog, n." *OED Online*. Oxford University Press, 2016. Web. 25 July 2016.

"weblog, n." *OED Online*. Oxford University Press, 2016. Web. 25 July 2016.

Cooper-Green, Emma-Jane. "Internet Access: Households and Individuals." Office for National Statistics, 2002. Web 26 July 2016. <https://www.ons.gov.uk/>.

Couldry, Nick (2008). "Mediatization or Mediation? Alternative Understandings of the Emergent Space of Digital Storytelling." *New Media & Society* 10.3, 373-91.

Darke, Leah (2000). "A Thief in the Vaults of Literature." *The Globe and Mail* 25 Nov. 2000: n. pag. Web. 3 February 2017.

Hardey, Michael (2003). "Digital Life Stories: Auto/Biography in the Information Age." *Auto/Biography* 12.3, 183-200.

Killoran, John B. (2003). "The Gnome in the Front Yard and Other Public Figurations: Genres of Self-Presentation on Personal Home Pages." *Biography* 26.1, 66-83.

Kitzmann, Andreas (2003). "That Different Place: Documenting the Self within Online Environments." *Biography* 26.1, 48-65.

Lejeune, Philippe (2014). "Autobiography and New Communication Tools." Trans. Durnin, Katherine. *Identity Technologies: Constructing the Self Online*. Eds. Anna Poletti and Julie Rak. Wisconsin Studies in Autobiography. Madison, US: University of Wisconsin Press, 247-58.

Marwick, Alice E., and danah boyd [2011]. "I tweet honestly, I tweet passionately: Twitter users, context collapse, and the imagined audience." *New Media & Society* 13.1, 114-133.

McNeill, Laurie, and John David Zuern (2015). "Online Lives 2.0: Introduction." *Biography* 38.2, v-xlvi.

Morrison, Jago (2006). "Who Cares About Gender at a Time Like This? Love, Sex and the Problem of Jeanette Winterson." *Journal of Gender Studies* 15.2, 169-80.

Mota, Miguel (2004). "What's in a Name? The Case of Jeanettewinterson.Com." *Twentieth Century Literature* 50.2, 192-206.

Papacharissi, Zizi (2012). "Without You I'm Nothing: Performances of the Self on Twitter." *International Journal of Communication* 6, 1989-2006.

Poletti, Anna, and Julie Rak (2014). "Introduction: Digital Dialogues." *Identity Technologies: Constructing the Self Online*. Eds. Anna Poletti and Julie Rak. Wisconsin Studies in Autobiography Madison, US: University of Wisconsin Press, 3-22.

Prescott, Cecil. "Internet Access - Households and Individuals 2016." Office for National Statistics. Web. 30 September 2016. <https://www.ons.gov.uk/>.

Smith, Sidonie, and Julia Watson (2010). *Reading Autobiography: A Guide for Interpreting Life Narratives*. 2nd ed. Minneapolis and London: Minnesota Press.

--- (2014). "Virtually Me: A Toolbox About Online Self-Presentation." *Identity Technologies: Constructing the Self Online*. Eds. Anna Poletti and Julie Rak. Wisconsin Studies in Autobiography. Madison, US: University of Wisconsin Press, 70-95.

van der Wiel, Reina (2009). "Trauma as Site of Identity: The Case of Jeanette Winterson and Frida Kahlo." *Women: A Cultural Review* 20.2, 135-56.

Winterson, Jeanette (1996). *Art Objects: Essays on Ecstasy and Effrontery*. New York: Vintage.

--- (2001). *Oranges Are Not the Only Fruit*. London: Vintage.

--- (2012). *Why Be Happy When You Could Be Normal?* London: Vintage, 2012.

--- (2000-2014). *Column*. Web. 27 July 2016. <http://www.jeanettewinterson.com/column-year/2000/>.

Simone Herrmann

Graphic Isolation? Imagining Contemporary Britain in Graphic Memoirs

Britain is currently suffering from an identity crisis: The 2016 EU referendum, which has instigated Britain's withdrawal from the EU, the so-called 'Brexit', not only puts to the test a more than forty-year-old connectedness with the EU,[1] but also summons a ghost supposedly long-dead: Britain's *splendid isolation*. In these insecure times, with threats lurking not only outside national borders but also within, the question arises where the UK and its citizens position themselves. Where do they belong? Who are their associates? What does being British mean? Despite the majority having voted 'leave', the narrow results of the referendum reflect a deep split among Britain's population.[2] Although many a European would exclusively like to remember Churchill's call for a 'United States of Europe',[3] Britain has usually perceived itself on a global rather than a European scale,[4] and a feeling of *Euroscepticism*[5] has been growing now since the 1990s.[6] It has become apparent that a majority of the British people are unable to identify themselves as part of the community the EU and its member states have striven to be ever since the EU's official formation in 1993. In the light of Britain's looming withdrawal from the EU, predictions of what will become of Euro-British relations are near to impossible.

However, some of today's atmosphere might be captured in contemporary British literature, and particularly so in autobiography since it is supposed to "present the truth of the individual self, how the self relates *to the world, to society*, to family, to spouse or a lover, to friends and rivals, *to the system and values that govern life*".[7] Authors thus represent dialectical negotiations of the private self and the world surrounding him or her.[8] Graphic autobiographies,[9] or graphic memoirs, are a special case in this respect. In addition to thinking carefully about the visual aesthetics of individual characters, such as clothes and hairstyles that might contextualise a scene within a particular timeframe, authors of graphic memoirs have developed further visual strategies to position their narratives socio-politically. Such content might often not be discussed prominently as the main theme of a narrative, but it might well be expressed in a picture hanging on the wall or the TV running in the background of individual panels, for example.

In contextualising Britain and Euro-British relations in recent graphic memoirs, two strategies stand out in particular: On the one hand, authors focus on the representation of domestic British society by embedding their narratives in *historical* contexts, constituting a sense of British national identity as well as crossing national borders in search of common European identity markers. On the other hand, Britishness is by no means a fixed and exclusive construction but has to be negotiated in both a *contemporary* European and global context, by delimitation against or association with different cultural settings.

Four graphic memoirs have exemplarily been chosen to demonstrate how these two distinct structures and strategies are employed by contemporary British authors. The first part of this paper, which reflects on historical aspects of Great Britain during parts of the twentieth century, will discuss Raymond Briggs' *Ethel & Ernest – A True Story* (1998) and Mary M. and Bryan Talbot's *Dotter of her Father's Eyes* (2012). While the former outlines the life of Briggs' parents as a couple like a chronicle between 1928 and 1971, structured around episodes of social importance for Great Britain and featuring the author/illustrator/narrator only as a minor character, the latter is framed by the relationship of only one of the authors, Mary M. Talbot, with her father. Her life-story is, in contrast to Briggs', not narrated strictly chronologically, but is composed at various time levels and even includes as meta-narrative a biography of Lucia Joyce, James Joyce's daughter. Noticeably, however, both narratives negotiate the protagonists' pasts as parts of their parents' lives whilst they simultaneously reverberate distinct concepts and momentums in British social history.

In contrast, the second part of this paper will focus on works by two representatives of a younger generation of artists who share more recent episodes of their lives with the readers that specifically, though not necessarily intentionally, challenge their own understanding of Britishness by contact with other cultures. Marc Ellerby's *Ellerbisms* (2012) is the story of the author's love to a Swedish girl, following the couple not only through the changing phases of their relationship, but also on their varying stops around the world. While Ellerby's story traces the lovers' relationship from their first meeting until their separation after roughly four years, *A Long Day of Mr. James-Teacher* (2011) by James Harvey focuses on the emotions and experiences of the protagonist during only a minor part, a single day, of his time as language teacher in South Korea. While the Talbots and Briggs give the reader an insight into the events that *have formed* their identity, Ellerby's and Harvey's protagonists, and in extension they themselves, reflect on the question what *forms* their notion of British identity. The ensuing paper will try to shed light on the specific techniques these authors use in their graphic memoirs.

1. Drawing History – Forming Identity

In autobiography, an author is the producer of not only life-history,[10] but, particularly in visual life-narratives, also of national history. Even though many authors agree that their representation of a life-story is at best "approximate truth",[11] their accounts of socio-political events and developments usually adhere to historical facts. This functions as a means to authenticate a narrative and classify it as autobiography rather than fiction. Autobiographical texts thus become valid sources for interdisciplinary scholars like historians and sociologists,[12] and many of them agree that comics in general might well provide and support awareness of historical culture.[13] However, the question is *which* events and circumstances authors choose to represent. For, with their life-accounts and memories, authors also reflect upon personal perceptions of national identity and, consequently, history. As Renan argues:

> Two things […] constitute [the nation]. One lies in the past, one in the present. One is the possession in common of a rich legacy of memories; the other is present-day consent […], the will to perpetuate the […] heritage that one has received in an undivided form. […] The nation […] is the culmination of a long past of endeavours, sacrifice, and devotion. Of all cults, that of the ancestors is the most legitimate. For the ancestors have made us what we are.[14]

If these "endeavours, sacrifice[s], and devotion[s]" have now shaped a certain nation, Great Britain in this paper's context, they have also shaped the nation's citizens, and the potential for identification with their nation. In this sense, the memory of historical events is vital for personal and national identity as well as in the process of imagining Britain, since identity and history are inseparable.

Raymond Briggs (1998) and Mary M. and Bryan Talbot (2012) dispute the meaning of personal and national history for the individual's perception of identity in their graphic memoirs. Using their parents' stories, the authors determine the significance of one aspect inherent in British society: class-consciousness.

2. *"What's the Poverty Line?"*[15] *– Imagining Class*

It is particularly through his mother that Briggs expresses notions of British class-consciousness in his memoir. The narrative begins in 1928, when Briggs' parents, Ethel and Ernest, meet. At that time, Ethel is employed as a housemaid,[16] but although she is a mere servant, she identifies with her wealthy employers by euphemistically defining her position as being an honourable "lady's maid". Ernest, as the child of a working-class family, has a more negative opinion of her employers, insulting them rudely as 'plutocrats' to whom Ethel was a mere "skivvy".[17] While Ethel and Ernest have a similar working-class background, the reader observes a couple that takes a completely different stance towards the upper classes and eventually also to social mobility. Although Ethel does theoretically not mind her husband's, and ultimately her own, background, reality regularly gets the better of her in practical matters. Accordingly, Ethel's worst nightmare is Ernest's stepmother, who, for her, is the personification of negative working-class attributes. Not only is she dirty, smelly and uneducated,[18] but she also displays the same lower-class accent Ethel so utterly abhors in Ernest.[19] Hence, Ethel emphasises where possible that "We're NOT working-class!"[20] Equally, Ethel's striving for social mobility results in her distancing herself from anything 'common',[21] beginning with praise for their outstandingly luxurious newlyweds' house.[22] Nonetheless, their son, Raymond, as the auto-/biographer, feels the effects of his mother's ambitions the most since she insists on grammar-school education as a means to his social ascent.[23] At least as a child, Briggs depicts himself as being rather indifferent towards the topic, wishing, for example, for a pair of boots of the kind his friends, common boys, wear.[24]

Domestic social changes form another focus for Briggs in imagining his version of Britain. Positive as well as negative developments are for the most part mediated[25] through Ernest Briggs when he is reading the daily newspaper. During one of these instances, Ernest, and through him Ethel and the reader, is informed of the introduction of the welfare state in Britain towards the end of the Second World War.[26] For the working-class man Ernest, this happy news is an important issue since "It's what the workers have always fought for. WE'VE WON!" Ernest's positive sensations are visually intensified through the situation in which the action of reading the newspaper is embedded: the merry Christmas preparations, including decorating the house, become the expression of his joy. The page ends in a panel paralleling Ernest's hopeful views of the economic future with the blissful angel that is supposed to crown their Christmas tree. As the angel exceeds the frame of the panel, the focus is completely laid on this tiny figure's symbolism: the hope that is nurtured in Ernest's hands. This is a contrast to the preceding page, where the atmosphere is dominated by dark colours, crying faces and the theme of death.[27]

In her memoir *Dotter of her Father's Eyes*, Mary M. Talbot reflects on similar class experiences, particularly with her father. In comparison to Briggs, though, it is not her parents' anxiety to distance themselves from their social background and thus to create an appearance of superiority that characterises their expression of class-consciousness, but her parents' attempts to strengthen their educated middle-class status as teachers in an industrial working-class area of the 1950s. By representing her mother in casual business dresses in contrast to the housewives next door, who usually wear aprons, Talbot expresses a keen awareness of her family's higher social status. Only twice is her mother represented with an apron doing housework – for practical reasons, it appears.[28] However, by including a footnote at the bottom of the page stating that Talbot's "mother wouldn't have been seen dead in a frilly apron,"[29] the authors emphasise that the domestic connotation of the apron contradicted her self-image as a professional. In *Ethel & Ernest*, on the other hand, Briggs' mother Ethel *never* manages to cast off her apron despite her ambitions to manifest her family's position as (lower) middle-class.

Thus, both Briggs and Talbot agree on the apron as a symbol of the drudgery of domestic work.

The class difference between these two hard-working women, Ethel Briggs and Mrs Atherton (Mary M. Talbot's mother), also becomes obvious in their educational background and resulting independence.[30] For example, Briggs' depictions of his working-class mother display his criticism of the class-based gender biases of that era against housewives. His mother is found reading only children's letters[31] or birthday cards.[32] It is Briggs' deliberate choice of reading material that transfers his criticism to the reader. Simple readings are fine, it appears, and this stresses the traditional picture of the dependent as well as unintelligent woman. Likewise, the newspaper as medium of political information is only summarised to her by her husband Ernest. Ethel's reflections on politics are not taken seriously by her husband, who claims "Oh Et! You just don't understand politics!"[33]

In contrast, Talbot sees her educated family background as the "wrong cultural and linguistic capital for the playground" at school, because she is insulted as 'posh' by her classmates.[34] Although Talbot equates a northern accent with working-class status as her parents did, she succeeds in sensitively representing her 'native' Lancashire accent while at the same time revealing that her parents' urge to speak accent-free is an expression of actual class-insecurity. Her experiences in school, however, differed very much from family life. Attending a typical Lancashire 1950s/60s Catholic school, she is faced with religious conservatism in the classroom. Here, Talbot is forced to comply with conservative paradigms of gender distinction.[35] In this environment, her liberal family background often causes frictions concerning the religious assumptions at school.[36] Even though the Anglican Church predominates in Britain, Catholicism is still very present in British society. Talbot's story is in this sense exemplary of a heterogeneous British national identity that constantly had to rely on these inward discourses and negotiations.

3. Shared Suffering: Remembering the Great Wars

Although Briggs is able to draw a neat picture of Britain's social structure as well as of those issues most worrying to the average citizen until

1970, it is Briggs' engagement with his and his parents' experiences of the Second World War which are shared by many British people and form a major basis of British national identity. As Renan states, "suffering in common unifies more than joy does. Where national memories are concerned, griefs are of more value than triumphs, for they impose duties, and require a common effort".[37]

Whereas Briggs also portrays his parents' private aftermath of the First World War, indicating that every family had suffered losses,[38] it is the inter-generational memory of their routine at home during the Second World War which he specifically emphasises. His own memories of that period seem to be characterised by carefree childhood activities. Accordingly, we observe the author as a boy converting his parents' shelter preparations into a playground and learn that he associates gasmasks not with the horror of poisonous gas, but with the advertising song of the Air Raid Precautions (A.R.P.).[39] Similarly, Briggs spends moments of decidedly historical importance, like King George V's famous radio speech on the declaration of war on Germany, doing activities that children are often found doing subconsciously: singing or whining.[40] Like so many children during that time, Briggs was also evacuated to the countryside,[41] which appeared to be a safe haven in contrast to the constant bomb alerts troubling the larger English cities and Greater London.[42]

Nonetheless, Briggs experienced the war-time restrictions and dismay through his parents' stories. The biography of his parents, then, is a mediation of the stories they shared with him during their lives, ranging from their memories of self-made bomb-shelters in private houses[43] to their efforts in the war,[44] including the psychological strains of his father dealing with the horrible sight of dead people.[45] In its composition, then, *Ethel & Ernest* is the author's interpretation of his parents' life-story. Although Briggs claims his narrative to be "a true story" in its subtitle, the events are condensed for narratological purposes – presenting 43 years in not even a hundred pages requires an intensification of all the emotions displayed. Although Briggs attempts to present his graphic memoir as an objective, distanced narration by choosing an omniscient narrator, he achieves the opposite by combining biographical and autobiographical features. Depicting positive as well as negative scenes of his childhood and adult years results in a multi-facetted nostalgic picture of Ethel and Ernest as good parents and persons, no matter how disheartening and dangerous times might have been.

The narrative frame of *Dotter of Her Father's Eyes* is formed by a present-day scene that triggers Mary M. Talbot as narrator to tell the reader about her childhood memories.[46] With a first-person narrator, the unfolding memoir can be regarded as being more personal than Briggs' narrative in the way Talbot represents her point of view; at the same time, though, it is highly reflective of her relationship with her father and analytical concerning her father's character. Being born in 1954,[47] "the year rationing ended",[48] Mary M. Talbot herself can neither relate to the Second World War, nor does she recall her parents' involvement and experiences during that time. Yet, since *Dotter of Her Father's Eyes* is also the biography of Lucia Joyce, James Joyce's daughter, it is in the biographical part of the narrative that Mary M. and Bryan Talbot relate to both World Wars. These are, however, merely marginal notes to contextualise Lucia Joyce's development and travels through Europe in 1914[49] and 1935.[50] By dealing with two of the most unsettling experiences of the twentieth century in this short form, it might appear now that the authors simply disregard the significance of these events for British and ultimately a whole continent's cultural identity.[51] Still, weaving only minor scraps of history into the narrative is a technique the Talbots use to juxtapose Mary's and Lucia's story with international history, of which the two World Wars are only one part, and consequently to identify their interests as well as influences outside of Britain. Mary M. and Brian Talbot therefore argue in their graphic memoir for a notion of history as vital to a British identity that is not limited to the Second World War but acknowledges the relevance of events on a global scope, beyond domestic interests. This inclination can already be observed in the variety of books Talbot engages with as a child, reading not only British classics[52] like Lewis Carroll's *Alice's Adventures in Wonderland* or J.R.R. Tolkien's *The Hobbit*,[53] but also books of international renown, such as *Emil and the Detectives* by Erich Kästner.[54] Furthermore, though certainly compelled by her father, Talbot is trained in the languages most widespread in Europe: Spanish,[55] German and French.[56]

Figure 1: Mary M. Talbot and Bryan Talbot, Dotter of her Father's Eyes (2012). © Mary M. Talbot and Bryan Talbot. Used by permission of Mary M. Talbot. All rights reserved.

In contrast to Lucia Joyce's biographical narrative thread, which in fact 'Europeanises' the entire narrative through setting and atmosphere, the plot-line of Mary M. Talbot's younger self is fixed in a British setting geographically, but regularly points towards a larger global context in cultural terms.[57] Although Great Britain was only marginally involved in the Vietnam War, she remembers this conflict[58] as one of the great international crises of her childhood years and eventually expresses the delicate nature of such events for a witnessing as well as worrying world public.[59]

For the Talbots, this and similar events provide the basis of a shared identity, an identity that is not limited by national borders but inspired by the richness of Western cultures. As Figure 1 shows, their marriage is based on shared experiences and interests but also worries such as humanity's expansion into space, American Western movies, and ultimately, the atomic threat during the 1970s.[60] Through such references, *Dotter of her Father's Eyes* becomes an example of a trans- and intercultural text by presenting the "interconnectedness of cultures, their common history and values".[61]

Briggs does not entirely isolate Britain from these events in *Ethel & Ernest*, but projects them, unlike the Talbots, onto Britain and its interior affairs. As Briggs' mother Ethel is nervous about Nazi Germany's advance towards Britain, he remembers her not expressing concern about the nation or the people, but reacting to such a threat at a personal level: "Adolf Hitler in Wimbledon Park!"[62] The repetition of the same large-scale single-panel depiction of the Briggs' terraced house turns into a motif that expresses the concentration on the home at both the literal and metaphorical level. Consequently, the reader is given a possibility to experience the emotions of the protagonists through a familiar motif: the pride in buying a new house,[63] the despair after its destruction in the war,[64] the hope arising with its reconstruction[65] and the sadness of Raymond Briggs when he inherits his childhood home after his parents' death.[66] Even if only the latter picture can be assumed to express the immediate emotion of the author, as it is the only version of the house Briggs is able to personally remember, the repetition of this motif highlights the graphic novel's focus on the domestic, both in terms of the family and of the home country. In addition, Ethel enunciates a notion of

Britons being superior and different from *them*, in which *them* covers nearly every other ethnic, national or religious group around the globe. While considering various conflicts in the world, between Irish Catholics and Protestants, Arabs and Jews, Serbs and Croats as well as Hindus and Moslems, Ethel is convinced that the British way is the best and only way: "Why can't they all just be like us and live in peace?"[67] Such an uncritical understanding reflects the general belief in a powerful, though waning British Empire in the first half of the twentieth century.[68]

Whereas Briggs reflects on his parents' definition of the British people as constituted by the grandeur of the British nation, the Talbots draw a picture of British culture which is, through shared experiences in history, equally informed by European as well as global connections. As younger British graphic authors do not have the same historical experiences as Briggs and the Talbots, they have to rely on other sources of identification. Therefore, they emphasise the individual protagonists' recent experiences through which they subconsciously negotiate between *flexible* Euro-British and global British cultural affiliations.

5. "... a Trip abroad Might Do Me Some Good":[69] Britain in a Mobile World

A more recent graphic memoir is Marc Ellerby's *Ellerbisms* (2012), in which the author illustrates his relationship with the Swede Anna and, through his choice of setting, reflects on his British identity[70] in both a contemporary European and global context. The opening sequence at Gatwick airport already introduces one of the main motifs of Ellerby's graphic memoir: mobility.[71] Not only do he and his friends travel through Britain and Europe without any restrictions, but his circle of friends is additionally enriched by people from varying European nations.[72] Though Ellerby does not derive any direct benefits from the Schengen agreement as a UK citizen, his experiences nevertheless mirror the enthusiastic and unrestricted travelling of millions of young Europeans today, who have profited from the reduction of border controls ever since the establishment of the Schengen area in 1995. The reader is at this point already presented with references that place the protagonist's ties outside of Britain. Particularly his girlfriend Anna and her home country of Sweden have left a profound impression on him and become the centre of his personal negotiations of Britain, and ultimately himself, as part of Europe. Here, Ellerby focuses not on the nation but on a general notion of communities as "products of affective bonds"[73] to locate his affiliations.

Since British and Swedish cultures are, in Ellerby's representation, different in their manifestations, his depictions of positive surprises and peculiarities during his travels through Sweden are rather detailed. The reader accompanies him through fascinating experiences, such as the Swedish Christmas tradition of *julebord*.[74] His attitude towards the impressions these trips have left on him is conveyed through the size of the panels: In a double page with exactly same-sized panels, Ellerby demonstrates how equally important every single memory is for him as author. The positive picture he has of Sweden and its people makes every experience appear as memorable as his first tasting of reindeer meat.[75]

Naturally, a foreign experience includes contact with foreign languages. The protagonist exhaustively celebrates the learning of only a single Swedish word: *tack* or thanks.[76] Nevertheless, Ellerby as protagonist appears unappreciative of Anna's everyday attempts to master English, while he reveals a keen empathy for her situation as author. His and Anna's diverse experiences mirror the many facets of the European experience of (younger) people today. Despite these cultural and national differences Ellerby still does not dissociate from Anna, but, on the contrary, starts to appreciate her even more. His love seems to be based on an exoticised picture of her. After their holiday in Sweden, the author-protagonist expresses the beneficial influence of this holiday on his emotions for Anna.[77] The question arises whether Ellerby does so because of their wonderful shared experiences or because of his fascination with the culture his "Swedish beauty" was born into.[78]

Figure 2: Marc Ellerby, *Ellerbisms* (2012). © Marc Ellerby. Used by permission of Marc Ellerby. All rights reserved.

6. "... This Stupid Island"?[79] *– Identification outside the National Context*

Ellerby's longing for new affiliations is repeated on a global scope in his travels to Canada and the USA. Particularly the prospect of going to Canada fills the author and his girlfriend with excitement.[80] Just like in his representation of his positive memories of Sweden, Ellerby uses same-scale panels for standard travelling scenes such as the flight to Canada and queuing for customs to express how equally important the impressions during the journey were for him. By choosing to draw his and Anna's faces in a completely different way from the rest of the memoir, with eyes as vertical lines and fixed smiles, Ellerby highlights the predominance of their euphoria during this time. Canada has, at least as represented in his graphic memoir, the potential to become a place of comfort and, after all, escape for him.[81]

The flipside to the author's positive views on other nations is an overly negative picture of the UK, as presented in Figure 2. For the panels, Ellerby employs similar settings as for the journey to Canada but turns them into unpleasant experiences. While before a crying baby on the plane could not disturb their happiness, it now interferes with their nap. Their sadness about leaving Canada develops into a physical sickness when coming back to England. After his trips abroad, Ellerby is now confronted with the shortcomings of his life in Britain in comparison with Sweden,[82] Canada[83] or the USA.[84] "Fucking England. Ugh!"[85] and "I can't wait to get off this stupid island"[86] become mantras to express unhappiness with his daily routines in Britain.[87]

Ellerby's graphic memoir shows that identity is manifest in the little differences of life, as Seyla Benhabib argues: "no identity can be constituted without difference; the other is never merely an other but always in – and for – itself".[88] In this sense, Ellerby discusses essential distinctions between his British and Anna's Scandinavian character: Whereas cold climates and snow create a feeling of joy and ultimately home for Anna, his British reaction is neutral and reserved.[89] Furthermore, while Ellerby's friends come from all over continental Europe, he still distinguishes between himself as British and them as "Bloody Europeans!"[90] Although this might only be a joke, it nevertheless reflects a subtle yet persistent distinction between people from the continent and the United Kingdom. Hence, Ellerby's self-perception occurs both in a British and a European context, as social identity may be shaped by the values and emotions of multiple groups.[91] Despite his differentiation between European and his own British behavioural patterns, he draws a picture of a modern Britain that opens up to the world and is by no means Eurosceptic. Since his identity is influenced by his international and European peers and vice versa,[92] these aspects point to a nearly trans-national development.[93]

7. Buying a Rubber Horse Head: Reflecting on British Identity Abroad

In the short account of his time as a foreign language teacher in South Korea, *A Long Day of Mr James-Teacher* (2011), James Harvey approaches the topic of cultural encounters in a different way, that is, by locating his narrative entirely in a foreign setting. In contrast to Ellerby, who constantly expresses his wish to leave the UK, the opening panels in Harvey's memoir create a feeling of home for a British readership through the well-known sight of rain.[94] Though the setting is still neutral at this point, a melancholic atmosphere is created. However, the use of the South Korean currency symbol (*won*) on the subsequent page and its repetition on various occasions throughout the narrative functions as a constant reminder of the different culture.[95] Despite this non-British setting, the readership addressed in Harvey's memoir is definitely British: He uses British reference points, for instance the comparison of South Korean products with popular British equivalents, giving details in footnotes.[96] The foreign setting is reinforced by the varying forms of respectful address: Harvey himself is not addressed as 'Mr Harvey' by the school children, as he would be in Britain, but he is referred to as 'James-teacher'[97] in the same manner as Harvey's supervisor is 'Kang-teacher'.[98]

The key issue for Harvey in South Korea is a feeling of estrangement at various levels, which remains strong even after four months abroad.[99] Not only is the language cryptic for him (represented in the graphic memoir as blurred lines),[100] it is first and foremost the culture's different sense of duty and respect that causes problems for him. Hence, frictions arise particularly with the local 'Kang-teacher' with regard to the evaluation of his work ethic. Harvey represents his supervisor as demanding, strict and ever-shouting. In Figure 3, the author embodies this emotional problem by depicting Kang-teacher in an erect posture ready for duty while Harvey appears smaller in a hunched posture.[101] As a consequence of this persistent alienation, Harvey does not socialise with the people surrounding him, neither with his colleagues during lunchtime at school,[102] nor with his fellow foreign language teachers.[103]

An additional crux in his conflicts with Kang-teacher is Harvey's lack of motivation to finish his tasks, which is at the same time an early indication that being a teacher is not his vocation. Although he is supposed "to teach the kids about Western culture",[104] he is rather clueless about the essence of *his* own culture. One of the two aspects coming to his mind is the British sense of humour. He remembers that he once bought a rubber horse head, and his idea of how to deal with it in the classroom, including the interpretation of a popular song with the title 'Pony', attests to a British sense of humour in the tradition of Monty Python. The only other aspect he supposedly knows about Western culture is "animation".[105] Harvey's problem then is that *Western culture* seems to be too broad a term for him to grasp and to ultimately teach others. The things he knows come from his knowledge about himself as an individual and his British cultural roots. Although it becomes only evident in marginal details, Harvey implicitly distinguishes between British culture and Western culture. In this sense, he is a counter-example to the Talbots: While Mary's life is mostly set in Britain, she is able to value the achievements of Western culture. In contrast, Harvey's time outside Britain does not lead him to recognise any shared European or Western heritage, which leaves him without teaching material.

Thus, the representation of his conflict with Kang-teacher is an expression of the author's insight that he has failed as teacher. The realisation that "I have no idea what I'm doing" is painful but necessary in the process of character formation.[106] In the final panels of the memoir, Harvey again seizes on the motif of rain that frames the narrative from the first to the very last panel, hence emphasising his resignation.[107]

Figure 3: James Harvey, *A Long Day of Mr. James-Teacher* (2011). © James Harvey. Used by permission of James Harvey.

Ellerby and Harvey are only two representatives of a young generation of British graphic authors who try to cope with the processes of globalisation in the twenty-first century. While Briggs and the Talbots can rely on clear notions of their national identity *despite* and *because of* their age and the experiences they have gathered of both common sufferings and successes in the past century, younger authors do not have this repertoire of historical experiences to draw upon in their memoirs.[108] Their narratives are defined by the lives they have lived. Yet, these younger authors/illustrators do not have to rely on national history in their versions of constructing British identity to the same extent as Briggs and the Talbots. Their 'liberty' is the post-modern individual's self-reflexivity.[109] In presenting his protagonist as moving freely between the American continent and various European states and, eventually, establishing affiliations, Ellerby provides a prime example that to *acknowledge* national identities does not mean to be *bound* to them. Furthermore, whilst Harvey emphasises his alienation in South Korea and highlights cultural differences, Ellerby focuses on the shared features and values in a trans-cultural Europe. Nevertheless, a dissolution of clear national identification can already be observed in the Talbots' memoir, which shows a high awareness of Britain's past and future place in a larger European as well as global project.

In the light of these recent British graphic memoirs and their European as well as international orientation, it can be hoped that despite the government's plans to withdraw from the EU, a large part of the British population will still want to remain culturally involved with Europe and the world. If we assume that the worldviews of the authors discussed above are representative, then Britain is by no means on its way back into splendid isolation, but will maintain a liberal stance and open-mindedness towards international cultural influences.

Notes

1 It was, however, not a feeling of pure solidarity which "created the momentum for the 'turn to Europe'" (Gifford, Chris [2014]. *The Making of Eurosceptic Britain*. Farnham: Ashgate, 12), but Britain's post-imperial phase together with the post-war financial hardships that brought forth the rapprochement between the EU and the UK.

2 Whereas the Remain campaign succeeded in Ireland, Scotland and the City of London, most voters in Wales and the rest of England were convinced by the Leave campaign. Likewise, younger voters tended to favour remaining in the EU, while a majority of voters aged 45+ were persuaded by the Leave campaign (BBC News. "EU referendum: The results in maps and charts." *BBC* 24 June 2016. Web. 1 August 2016. <http://www.bbc.com/news/uk-politics-36616028>).

3 Churchill, Winston. "Speech delivered at the University of Zurich, 19 September 1946." *Council of Europe – Documents and Archives*. Web. 29 October 2015 <http://www.coe.int/t/dgal/dit/ilcd/Archives/selection/Churchill/ZurichSpeech_en.asp>.

4 Despite his pro-European plea, Churchill was always aware of a British context outside of the EU: "'We are with Europe, but not of it. We are linked, but not comprised. We are interested and associated, but not absorbed'" (Crowson, N.J. [2011]. *Britain and Europe – A Political History since 1918*. Abingdon: Routledge, 12).

5 Euroscepticism "not only means a persistent opposition to the idea of an integrated European political and economic order but a deeper and more fundamental reproduction of Britain and Britishness in opposition to the integrationist project" (Gifford [2014], 171).

6 *Ibid*., 5.

7 Hetata, Sherif (2003). "The Self and Autobiography." *PMLA* 118.1, 123-125, 124 (emphasis added).

8 Marcus, Laura (1994). *Auto/biographical Discourses: Theory, Criticism, Practice*. Manchester: Manchester University Press, 4.

9 Another possible term for this paper's purpose would be 'autography', which shifts the focus of (graphic) autobiography from the written form to the visual. For an extended discussion of the different terms, see Kukkonen, Karin (2013). *Studying Comics and Graphic Novels*. Chichester: Wiley Blackwell. However, since memoir supposedly is more intimate and confessional than auto(bio)graphy, I will use the term memoir throughout (Ludwig, Christian [2015]. "Narrating the 'Truth': Using Autographics in the EFL Classroom." *Learning with Literature in the EFL Classroom*. Eds. Werner

Delanoy, Maria Eisenmann and Frauke Matz. Frankfurt am Main: Peter Lang, 300).

10 Marcus (1994), 4.

11 Versaci, Rocco (2007). *This Book Contains Graphic Language – Comics as Literature*. New York: Continuum, 58.

12 Marcus (1994), 8/9.

13 Gundermann, Christine (2014). "Geschichtskultur in Sprechblasen: Comics in der politisch-historischen Bildung." *Aus Politik und Zeitgeschichte* 64.33-34, 27.

14 Renan, Ernest (1990). "What Is a Nation?" *Nation and Narration*. Ed. Homi K. Bhabha. London: Routledge, 19.

15 Briggs, Raymond (1998). *Ethel & Ernest – A True Story*. London: Jonathan Cape, 27.

16 Briggs (1998), 3ff.

17 *Ibid.*, 7/8.

18 *Ibid.*, 25.

19 *Ibid.*, 16.

20 *Ibid.*, 24 (original emphasis).

21 *Ibid.*, 17.

22 *Ibid.*, 11ff.

23 *Ibid.*, 58ff.

24 *Ibid.*, 45.

25 Other media gain in importance, too, during the course of the narrative, mirroring the technological progress Briggs' parents had to deal with. Although television is mentioned as well, for example when Ernest watches the first moon landing at the end of the 1960s (*Ibid.*, 88), Briggs stresses especially the historical importance of the radio (as well as the newspaper) during the Second World War (*Ibid.*, 34).

26 *Ibid.*, 50.

27 *Ibid.*, 49.

28 Talbot, Mary M. and Bryan Talbot (2012). *Dotter of her Father's Eyes*. Milwaukee: DarkHorse Books, 13; 56.

29 Talbot and Talbot (2012), 13.

30 Although Mary M. Talbot's mother is educated and employed as a teacher, which leaves an impression of a rather progressive family, Mrs Atherton is still married to a choleric patriarch whom the Talbots characterise for instance through a quote from James Joyce as "'feary father'" (*ibid.* 28/29).

31 Briggs (1998), 35.

32 *Ibid.*, 21.

33 *Ibid.*, 37.

34 Talbot and Talbot (2012), 31.

35 *Ibid.*, 17ff.

[36] *Ibid.*, 57.

[37] Renan (1990), 19.

[38] Briggs (1998), 6.

[39] *Ibid.*, 32.

[40] *Ibid.*, 33/34.

[41] *Ibid.*, 34.

[42] *Ibid.*, 44/45.

[43] *Ibid.*, 36ff.

[44] *Ibid.*, 40/41.

[45] *Ibid.*, 49.

[46] Talbot and Talbot (2012), 4.

[47] Before the narrative even starts, the binding of the book includes a ration book dated 1952-53 in a collage, reminding the reader of a noticeboard. This creates a very personal access to history, as the reader can imagine sitting in front of a desk and collecting all those treasured memories of the past. Also, since the ration book is not drawn but photocopied, this inter-medial approach creates on the one hand a highly sensory experience for the reader, and on the other hand adds to the credibility and realism of the narrative as an authentic memoir.

[48] Talbot and Talbot (2012), 5.

[49] *Ibid.*, 38.

[50] *Ibid.*, 84.

[51] Cf. Leggewie, Claus (2011). *Der Kampf um die europäische Erinnerung*. München: C.H. Beck.

[52] Mary M. Talbot's choice of childhood books subconsciously functions as an example of the disengagement of culture-specific productions in children's literature. For an elaborate study on the topic, cf. O'Sullivan, Emer (2005). *Comparative Children's Literature*. Oxon: Routledge.

[53] Talbot and Talbot (2012), 24.

[54] *Ibid.*, 14.

[55] *Ibid.*, 61.

[56] *Ibid.*, 56.

[57] For a further discussion of the narrative structure of this text, see Markus Oppolzer's contribution in this volume.

[58] *Ibid.*, 31/32.

[59] In her assumption that the 'witnessed' events had an impact on various cultures through the media, Talbot, for example, opposes philosopher Jean Baudrillard, who would deny the cultural significance of televised events since television is a mere construction of reality. Cf. Baudrillard, Jean (1994). *Simulacra and Simulation*. Ann Arbor: The University of Michigan Press.

[60] Talbot and Talbot (2012), 61.

61 Ludwig (2015), 308.
62 Briggs (1998), 32.
63 *Ibid.*, 10.
64 *Ibid.*, 43.
65 *Ibid.*, 55.
66 *Ibid.*, 102.
67 *Ibid.*, 33.
68 *Ibid.*, 42.
69 Ellerby, Marc (2012). *Ellerbisms*. Manchester: Great Beast Comics, 18.
70 For Ellerby, 'British' identity is not homogeneous. He, for instance, reflects on differences between northern and southern English mentality (Ellerby [2012], 156). Yet, these differences are minor, being at most manifest in the types of products available in shops.
71 *Ibid.*, 13.
72 *Ibid.*, 48.
73 Benedict Anderson quoted in: Bowers, Terrence N. (2010). "Nationhood in the Age of Enlightenment." *Reading the Nation in English Literature – A Critical Reader*. Eds. Elizabeth Sauer and Julia M. Wright. London and New York: Routledge, 158.
74 Ellerby (2012), 120.
75 *Ibid.*, 88/89.
76 *Ibid.*, 87.
77 *Ibid.*, 88.
78 *Ibid.*, 62.
79 *Ibid.*, 30.
80 *Ibid.*, 167.
81 *Ibid.*, 172.
82 *Ibid.*, 90.
83 *Ibid.*, 173.
84 *Ibid.*, 30.
85 *Ibid.*, 173.
86 *Ibid.*, 30.
87 A certain sadness and negativity stems to some degree from his self-perception as an 'emo' (*Ibid.*, 13).
88 Benhabib, Seyla (2007). *Situating the Self – Gender, Community and Post-modernism in Contemporary Ethics*. Cambridge: Polity Press, 197.
89 Ellerby (2012), 134.
90 *Ibid.*, 48.
91 Schlenker-Fischer, Andrea (2009). *Demokratische Gemeinschaft trotz ethnischer Differenz. Theorien, Institutionen und soziale Dynamiken*. Wiesbaden: VS Verlag für Sozialwissenschaften, 28.

92 Appiah, Kwame Anthony (2007). *The Ethics of Identity*. Princeton, NJ: Princeton University Press, 20.

93 Müller, Anja and Clare Wallace (2011). "Neutral Spaces and Transnational Encounters." *Cosmotopia – Transnational Identities in David Greig's Theatre*. Eds. Anja Müller and Clare Wallace. Prague: Litteraria Pragensia, 5.

94 Harvey, James (2011). *A Long Day of Mr James-Teacher*. ChalkMarks, 1.

95 *Ibid*., 2.

96 *Ibid*., 14.

97 *Ibid*., 12.

98 *Ibid*., 2.

99 *Ibid*., 5.

100 *Ibid*., 18.

101 *Ibid*., 17.

102 *Ibid*., 12.

103 *Ibid*., 2ff.

104 *Ibid*., 5.

105 The exact meaning of "animation" remains unclear: Considering the author in his role as illustrator, animation might refer to his drawing skills. However, in the context of his teaching career, animation might equally refer to entertaining children rather than professionally teaching them (*ibid*. 9/10).

106 *Ibid*., 18.

107 *Ibid*., 24.

108 This is not to argue that Ellerby and Harvey lack any sense of historical awareness. In their texts, British society is alive with commemorative holidays and events, about which schools are only one institution to actively teach those who were not fortunate or unfortunate enough to be witnesses. However, their memoirs are free from any conscious contextualisations with historical events.

109 Marcus (1994), 4.

Bibliography

Appiah, Kwame Anthony (2007). *The Ethics of Identity*. Princeton, NJ: Princeton University Press.

Baudrillard, Jean (1994). *Simulacra and Simulation*. Ann Arbor: The University of Michigan Press.

BBC News. "EU referendum: The results in maps and charts." *BBC* 24 June 2016. Web. 1 August 2016. <http://www.bbc.com/news/uk-politics-36616028>.

Benhabib, Seyla (2007). *Situating the Self – Gender, Community and Post-modernism in Contemporary Ethics*. Cambridge: Polity Press.

Bowers, Terrence N. (2010). "Nationhood in the Age of Enlightenment." *Reading the Nation in English Literature – A Critical Reader*. Eds. Elizabeth Sauer and Julia M. Wright. London and New York: Routledge. 155-163.

Briggs, Raymond (1998). *Ethel & Ernest – A True Story*. London: Jonathan Cape.

Churchill, Winston. "Speech delivered at the University of Zurich, 19 September 1946." *Council of Europe – Documents and Archives*. Web. 29. October 2015 <http://www.coe.int/t/dgal/dit/ilcd/Archives/selection/Churchill/ZurichSpeech_en.asp>.

Crowson, N.J. (2011). *Britain and Europe – A Political History Since 1918*. Abingdon: Routledge.

Dahlgreen, Will (2015). "EU referendum: Brexit ahead by 2." *YouGov* 28 September 2015. Web. 30 October 2015. <https://yougov.co.uk/news/2015/09/28/eu-referendum-brexit-leads-2/>

Ellerby, Marc (2012). *Ellerbisms*. Manchester: Great Beast Comics.

Gifford, Chris (2014). *The Making of Eurosceptic Britain*. Farnham: Ashgate.

Gundermann, Christine (2014). "Geschichtskultur in Sprechblasen: Comics in der politisch-historischen Bildung." *Aus Politik und Zeitgeschichte* 64.33-34, 24-29.

Hall, Stuart (1997). "The Spectacle of the 'Other'." *Representation: Cultural Representations and Signifying Practices*. Ed. Stuart Hall. London: Sage, 223-290.

---, and Paul du Gay (1996). *Questions of Cultural Identity*. London: Sage.

Harvey, James (2011). *A Long Day of Mr. James-Teacher*. ChalkMarks.

Hetata, Sherif (2003). "The Self and Autobiography." *PMLA* 118.1, 123-125.

Kellner, Peter (2016). "Analysis: the big dividing lines on the EU are age, education and newspaper readership." *YouGov* 6 January 2016. Web. 10 January 2016. <https://yougov.co.uk/news/2016/01/06/big-dividing-lines-eu-age-education-and-newspaper-/>.

Kukkonen, Karin (2013). *Studying Comics and Graphic Novels*. Chichester: Wiley Blackwell.

Leggewie, Claus (2011). *Der Kampf um die europäische Erinnerung*. München: C.H. Beck.

Ludwig, Christian (2015). "Narrating the 'Truth': Using Autographics in the EFL Classroom." *Learning with Literature in the EFL Classroom*. Eds. Werner Delanoy, Maria Eisenmann and Frauke Matz. Frankfurt am Main: Peter Lang, 299-320.

Marcus, Laura (1994). *Auto/biographical Discourses: Theory, Criticism, Practice*. Manchester: Manchester University Press.

Müller, Anja, and Clare Wallace (2011). "Neutral Spaces and Transnational Encounters." *Cosmotopia – Transnational Identities in David Greig's Theatre*. Eds. Anja Müller and Clare Wallace. Prague: Litteraria Pragensia, 1-13.

O'Sullivan, Emer (2005). *Comparative Children's Literature*. Oxon: Routledge.

Renan, Ernest (1990). "What Is a Nation?" *Nation and Narration*. Ed. Homi K. Bhabha. London: Routledge, 8-22.

Schlenker-Fischer, Andrea (2009). *Demokratische Gemeinschaft trotz ethnischer Differenz. Theorien, Institutionen und soziale Dynamiken*. Wiesbaden: VS Verlag für Sozialwissenschaften.

Talbot, Mary M., and Bryan Talbot (2012). *Dotter of her Father's Eyes*. Milwaukee: DarkHorse Books.

Versaci, Rocco (2007). *This Book Contains Graphic Language – Comics as Literature*. New York: Continuum.

Markus Oppolzer (Salzburg)

Teaching (British) Autobiographical Comics

1. Introduction

Within the past ten years there has been a renewed interest in (autobiographical) comics and their use in the EFL classroom. This can be ascribed to a number of factors,[1] but most importantly to a redefinition of the role of literature in the classroom and the competences that can and should be trained through narrative texts.[2] Since autographics represents a crucial genre outside mainstream (superhero) comics,[3] both for its popularity and critical acclaim,[4] it was only a matter of time until life writing in the comics medium would find its way into classrooms. There is still little theoretical engagement with the teaching of autobiographical comics as a distinct genre in the EFL context. The few articles that do exist either treat them as one type of literature (e.g. to teach intercultural communicative competence, aspects of language, or gender) or as comics (e.g. to train visual literacy), but not as a text type with very specific characteristics that students should be aware of. With the exception of Wolfgang Hallet's recent introductory essay to *Autobiographies: Presenting the Self* (2015), there have not been many attempts to link the engagement with autobiographical writing in the classroom back to the leading theories in literary studies. In this article I first clarify the terminology, then I discuss the existing publications and the rationalisations they offer why and how to teach (autobiographical) comics and, finally, I introduce three key concepts that teachers and students should keep in mind when dealing with life narratives in the comics medium. Since this is a volume on British autobiographies, I shall pick my examples accordingly, though the basic observations apply in equal measure to every other narrative belonging to the genre.

2. *Terms*

In "Narrating the 'Truth': Using Autographics in the EFL Classroom", Christian Ludwig "supports the view that comics are a medium in their own right", but deplores the lack of a "uniform terminology in comics studies" as much as "a clear distinction between comics and graphic novels".[5] Michael A. Chaney is wary of the latter term and sees it "commercially rather than aesthetically imposed, not to mention misleading. Nearly all of the graphic novels studied in this volume, for instance, make referential claims to the author's lived reality and therefore are not technically novels at all".[6]

Though I cannot provide a clarification of terms that pleases everyone, I find Danny Fingeroth's classification in *The Rough Guide to Graphic Novels* (2008) very helpful. He understands 'comics' as a narrative medium that uses specific modes or types of signs to tell a story, in the case of comics a combination of images and words juxtaposed in a sequence: "Just like prose or film, the comics medium encompasses a variety of different formats, all of which share the same basic language, but deploy it in a different form".[7] In this sense a 'graphic novel' is a longer, self-contained and maybe more complex variety of comics publication that is sold in book form and often marketed to an older, more sophisticated audience. The other two widespread formats are comic strips and comic books. All three represent viable publication formats for autobiographical narratives.[8]

The terminology in autobiography studies is no less confusing. Sidonie Smith and Julia Watson propose 'life writing' as an umbrella term for all content that "takes a life, one's own or another's, as its subject. Such writing can be biographical, novelistic, historical, or explicitly self-referential and therefore autobiographical".[9] However, the noun 'autobiography' as a genre label has become "vigorously challenged",[10] as Smith and Watson put it, for its specific cultural connotations.[11] Randy Duncan, Matthew J. Smith and Paul Levitz suggest 'memoir' as an alternative term, especially in the context of comics, as it allows for greater subjectivity, they argue, a less formal approach and a focus on shorter spans of time.[12] This is more in line with contemporary autobiographical acts that refuse to present a whole life as a "master narrative"[13] that comes with a rigid, teleological pattern into which the heterogeneous and contradictory mass (mess?) of one's experiences are supposed to fit. Smith and Watson prefer the more inclusive concept of 'life narrative', "a general term for acts of self-presentation of all kinds and in diverse media that take the producer's life as their subject, whether written, performative, visual, filmic, or digital".[14] Gillian Whitlock suggests 'autographics' as a replacement for 'graphic memoir' which avoids the association of 'graphic' with 'violent' or 'explicit', stresses the centrality of visual self-representation and foregrounds the negotiation of identity and subject positions in the process of artistic endeavour.[15] Since the adjective 'autobiographical' seems less contentious, I shall refer to 'life narratives in the comics medium' as 'autobiographical comics' or 'autographics' as an alternative.

3. Comics in the Classroom

Ansgar Nünning and Carola Surkamp include comics in their list of appropriate types of literature for the classroom,[16] but do not treat it as a narrative medium in its own right. Still, by implication, their extensive list of advantages that literary texts can have for language teaching applies to comics in equal measure.[17] I present just a few important points here: a genuine purpose for communication, developing empathy and critical thinking skills, questioning one's own attitudes and beliefs, insights into other cultures, adopting other perspectives, literary literacy, as well as an active, creative and affective engagement with texts.

Many ideas of how to adopt standards of literary teaching to the narrative medium of comics have been suggested, such as to "translate a panel or a short sequence into prose"[18] or to re-enact a sequence,[19] to write a diary entry or role biography,[20] to add speech balloons or new panels to (wordless) sequences,[21] to put panels in the right order and explain the choice,[22] or to verbalise the missing information in the gaps between storyboard images.[23] Ansgar Nünning and Carola Surkamp's pre-, while- and post-reading activities are equally relevant here,[24] as is Daniela Caspari's extensive list of creative activities for the foreign language classroom.[25]

In an edited publication on the use of graphic novels in schools Wolfgang Hallet declares that the general aim is to explore their specific narrative strategies,[26] which requires an expansion of reading competences to include visual literacy, film literacy and multiliteracies.[27] After this general introduction Roswitha Henseler offers some practical ideas on how to teach P. Craig Russell's adaptation of Neil Gaiman's *Coraline*, proposing an interesting combination of teaching aesthetic reading, narratology and visual literacy at the same time.[28]

Hallet's own "AutobioGraphic Novels" returns to the concept of narrative competence across media.[29] After providing a brief history of American autobiographical comics by focusing on Will Eisner, Art Spiegelman and Chester Brown, he stresses their potential for the EFL classroom as templates for the visual self-representation of teenagers who do have some experience of performing autobiographical acts in social media. This is a more genuine use of autographics in the classroom than activities that can be equally well done with any narrative medium. Hallet also emphasises the importance of getting students engaged in creative work, for which he points out several websites that help to create comics. Contrary to these fascinating ideas that would have warranted a more extensive presentation, his main activity seems too formalist in nature. Using Freytag's pyramid, an established pattern of representing the structure of plays, students analyse a sequence of eight pre-selected panels from Chester Brown's *I Never Liked You* by identifying their specific narrative functions in the sequence. For the worksheet the panels have been taken out of their original context and resized. Students should then remember a "conflict situation"[30] they experienced and plot it in such a way that it fits the prescribed pattern. Though this activity provides scaffolding for fledgling comics artists and highlights universal patterns of storytelling that could serve as a basic orientation, this may be somewhat limiting as a creative response to a literary text and especially in view of a medium that takes more liberties and is known for its experimentation. More importantly, there is little information on what autobiographical writing involves on a conceptual level.

This task also raises a number of general questions concerning the use of self-created comics in the language classroom: How many panels are necessary to tell a whole sequence the way that comics usually narrate? What do students need to know about the language of comics and its narrative strategies to be able to do that? Since eight panels may not suffice, should page design be taught as a constitutive element of comics narration? Should students work out these sequences at home, as time is always an issue? How, when and where could these texts then be presented and discussed? Since storyboarding and the creation of comics sequences can easily be confused, how should they be kept apart? Satisfying answers to all of these questions would take up too much space, but Monika Schäfers offers an interesting activity that highlights the difference between storyboarding and narrating and another one for the presentation of the results in the form of a gallery walk.[31] I shall return to creative activities in the context of diary comics later in the article.

4. The Language of Comics

Two interlinked and almost ubiquitous claims about comics are that they "provide struggling readers with mental imagery" and that "most students have a very positive attitude toward comics and enjoy dealing with them in class".[32] Both of these statements have to be qualified. The first can become problematic when teachers expect comics to be complex literary texts *and* more easily accessible at the same time. If the intricacies of the narrative are not to be found in the language, they are likely to be (hidden) in the visuals. Hallet is right in claiming that traditional reading is facilitated by complementary pictures,[33] but such graphic novels are usually designed for educational purposes.[34] He stresses that a developed visual literacy is a prerequisite for a successful engagement with complex images. Most writers acknowledge this fact sooner or later. Carola Hecke states that "comics require a higher degree of reader involvement than other types of narrative because they contain images that can be abstract or symbolic, often bear multiple connotations, and frequently go beyond the depicted subject matter".[35] In a similar fashion, Charles Hatfield argues that comics are "challenging (and highly teachable) because they offer a form of reading that resists coherence, a form at once seductively visual and radically fragmented. Comic art is a mixed form, and reading comics a tension-filled experience".[36] He goes on to say that the "very discontinuity of the page urges readers to do the work of inference, to negotiate over and over the passage from submissive reading to active interpreting".[37] It is, of course, true that this mainly applies to complex graphic novels, such as Mary M. and Bryan Talbot's *Dotter of her Father's Eyes* (2012), but Tim Stafford points out that we should not underestimate the complexity of comics for younger learners:

> We may assume that children have knowledge and prior experience of reading comics but this is not necessarily true and, even if they have, it is still vital that we take the time to ensure that they fully understand the technical aspects of comic book narratives.[38]

That students are fascinated and motivated by comics is a possibility,[39] but not more likely than with any other text that has been carefully chosen for the EFL classroom. Even if we were to assume that students are eager to embrace comics, the decisive bottleneck is the teachers' willingness to learn a new 'language': "In fact, many teachers can't read the pictures, or better said, don't take the time to read the pictures".[40] Another argument that is frequently put forward in this context is that boys are weak readers and "seem to prefer plurimedial comics to (purely written) monomedial texts".[41] The reversal of this statement would suggest that female students and pre-service teachers are more critical of comics than their male counterparts, which Hecke confirms based on personal experience.[42] Though I cannot prove the opposite with a study, this does not conform to my own observations. There may be reservations at the beginning and preferences in terms of genres, artists and individual books throughout a course, but I am reluctant to generalise. I would rather see a chance to reach different learner types and foster students' active engagement with different genres and media.

Although the language of comics makes use of an intricate combination of two modes – the visual and the verbal –, it is possible to look at them individually for educational purposes. This usually involves a focus on dialogue or on visual literacy. Contrary to prose fiction but similar to film, the dialogues in comics include more paratextual information: "The panels show verbal communication in relation to its non-verbal, visual context, and they do not isolate utterances from their natural visual context".[43] In short, comics have a potential to train pragmatic and sociolinguistic competences as the context of language use is always depicted. Some critics also stress that the language is authentic or natural,[44] but this depends on the genres, the artists or even the specific situations and thus applies equally to all literary texts: while diary comics rely on short, everyday exchanges, maybe even transcripts of remembered dialogues, the verbal narrator in Mary M. and Bryan Talbot's *Dotter of her Father's Eyes* is very articulate and does not shy away from Latinate words. In fact, it is quite impossible to remember even the most important conversations of one's life in any detail, so the dialogues in autobiographical comics are more or less convincing reconstructions. In films, intonation, modulation and sentence stress are directly audible, but comics employ typography, especially bold print, italics and font size, to visualise such features of speech.[45] An advantage in contrast to film may be that students read at their own speed and have more time to study the details of conversations.[46]

Depending on one's understanding of 'visual literacy' and its applicability to comics or the alternative concept of 'multiliteracies',[47] the necessary reading skills for an engagement with comics may or may not be adequately covered. Hallet adds three literacies to the usual assortment of reading competences – visual literacy, film literacy and multiliteracies – to cover different aspects of the meaning-making process: the reading of individual images, the influence of film language on many contemporary comics and the combination of verbal and visual signs.[48] Alternatively, Hecke suggests "comics literacy" – in analogy to film literacy – to capture all forms of meaning-making that the medium requires.[49] This highlights the fact that there are aspects of reading comics that cannot be subsumed under general reading skills. It is impossible to treat these questions now, but I shall return to the question of visual literacy in the context of embodiment.

5. The Cultural Context

As inexperienced readers are tempted to confuse life writing with truth-telling, it is indispensable to approach these texts with some critical distance. The development of inter- and transcultural competences is one of the central concerns of teaching literature in the classroom that naturally influences or – for some – even preconditions the use of (autobiographical) comics. Frank Erik Pointner and Dirk Vanderbeke address the important issue of stereotypes, which is especially relevant in the context of comics.[50] According to McCloud, cartooning is based on "amplification through simplification",[51] which means that the complexity of images is stripped down to specific details that capture 'the essence' of cultures, people and situations. Naturally, this has often led to the adoption of widely available cultural stereotypes as a visual shorthand. Pointner bases his discussion of identities and identity construction in comics on McCloud's concept and offers a number of relevant case studies.[52] These may be taken from purely fictional texts, but the same principle applies to all comics. Vanderbeke discusses a wide spectrum of comics, including autobiographical texts, briefly sketches their potential use for cultural studies and roughly determines for which level they may be suitable. In this context he acknowledges the importance of Raymond Briggs' *Ethel & Ernest* as an entry point for a discussion of the British class system, especially its diachronic dimension.[53] He references the article by Sabine and Wolfgang Hochbruck, who foreground the centrality of this aspect in the comic and base their activities on the inherent tensions between Ethel's ambitions to move up the social ladder and Ernest's proud acceptance of his working-class background.[54] Vanderbeke touches upon Art Spiegelman's *Maus* and *In the Shadow of No Towers* which he classifies as "a very complex and artistically demanding comic on 9/11".[55] He ends his survey of autobiographical comics and their relevance for cultural studies with Marjane Satrapi's *Persepolis*: "Of course, the context here is not British or American but Iranian; however, for intercultural studies these graphic novels are undoubtedly suitable as an introduction to a foreign culture".[56] This is perfectly fine as long as the comic serves as a starting point and is complemented by further cultural explorations.

When Carola Hecke reports on a school project that involved Jessica Abel's semi-autobiographical *La Perdida* and Satrapi's *Persepolis*, she observes in a footnote that "graphic novels, like all other types of literature and cultural representations, never simply show a real world, but always a more or less fictionalised as well as complexly mediated version of this world".[57] Accordingly, additional sources were used to contextualise the books. However, within the same article she suggests that "students should put themselves, to the greatest extent possible, in a given character's place",[58] which Hecke proposes in the context of creative activities, to "allow a closer look seemingly from within".[59] This highlights the difficulties of teaching literature, cultural studies and autobiographical writing at the same time. While this change of perspective and a strong identification with characters are necessary to gain access to the text and understand it 'from within', the "analytical approach", as Hecke calls it,[60] is equally necessary, but requires the exact opposite – a critical distance to characters and a certain suspicion towards their beliefs and attitudes. It would be a mistake to confuse Marjane Satrapi with 'the typical Iranian woman', her depiction of Iran with the country or the use of her younger self as a character with the actual experiences, though the events depicted may be based on them. As stated above, the only solution may be a gradual process that takes students from close identification to a more critical stance with the help of additional texts.

6. The Centrality of Genre

It is no coincidence that Tim Stafford chooses "Reading Visuals", "Picture Books", "Comic Books", "Film", "Genre" and "Adaptation" as the six main chapters of *Teaching Visual Literacy in the Primary Classroom.*[61] After introducing the four (narrative) media that he finds particularly suited for primary school, he acknowledges the central importance of genre to make sense of any given text and finishes with adaptations to demonstrate how stories change when they are realised in different media. Stafford is highly aware of the fact that almost all (literary) texts are produced, marketed, sold and reviewed with specific genre labels in mind, no matter if they conform to expectations or not: "The concept of genre is a key part of literacy teaching and an understanding of it enables children to develop not only their own writing, but also their critical and analytical reading skills".[62] He goes on to argue that it is "inextricably bound up with audience expectation – the two are indivisible".[63] To activate students' schemata and provide an initial framework of analysis, to raise, clarify and discuss their expectations, and "to consolidate genre knowledge"[64] is especially important in the context of autobiographical comics.

Students have to realise that even the sub-genres of autographics – such as travel writing, reporting (journalism),[65] autofiction (postmodern autobiographies),[66] illness narratives, coming-of-age, slice-of-life, diary comics – have their own traditions and rely on different forms and narrative strategies. To illustrate that fact I would like to pick diary comics as an example. Isaac Cates explains that they were "originally a reaction against the fashioned closure of the memoir, the narrative structural devices that such writing borrows from fiction" and, in their present form, often modelled on James Kochalka's *American Elf*, "hardly conform to generic expectations about memoir or autobiography".[67] They are "often concerned with describing brief sensory impressions or preserving the emotional charge of a single moment" and do this in the form of "a four-panel strip".[68] Usually, "the first three panels set up a fourth-panel punch line or a revelation; alternatively, the punch line comes in panel three, followed by a panel of reaction".[69] Of course, this imposes "constraints on the diary cartoonist in how much experience he or she can represent", so that "a handful of brief moments, one sustained reflection, or a single event or anecdote" is all the cartoonist can get across within the confines of a four-panel strip.[70] Cates even compares some diary comics to sonnets or haikus,[71] which seems appropriate considering the lyrical quality these strips can achieve.

Adam Cadwell's *The Everyday* (2012), a collected edition of his webcomics, is a good example of these qualities. Here is his distillation of a whole day into one brief moment of exceptional importance:

Figure 1: An intimate moment as visual poetry; © 2012 Adam Cadwell.

One should keep in mind, though, that despite its length, or rather because of its brevity, the diary comic can be fairly complex, as "Incomplete Mouse" by Adam Cadwell demonstrates:

Figure 2: A flashback within a four-panel strip; © 2012 Adam Cadwell.

There are several reasons why a focus on diary comics can be a great asset for the EFL classroom: first of all, many webcomics are diary comics (e.g. http://www.joedecie.com/), which means that they are available online and for free.[72] Since many up-and-coming British comics artists depend on short narratives published online, in anthologies or with small presses, the comic strip or the slice-of-life (short) story are the more widespread forms. Diary comics are short and can be easily dealt with during one lesson. They showcase a whole range of sophistication – both thematically and artistically – from the everyday and mundane to the lyrical and philosophical, which means they are suitable for different age groups and levels. As the following strip by Cadwell illustrates (see Figure 3) even very odd or whimsical moments have their place.

Figure 3: A weird coincidence worth recording; © 2012 Adam Cadwell.

Figure 4: What is Adam thinking? © 2012 Adam Cadwell.

As Figure 4 illustrates. some of them use very little language and may offer interesting starting points for creative writing activities, from introductory texts that set up the scene via the addition of speech and thought balloons to continuations and diary entries. They may also serve as an early model for autobiographical writing by students: diary comics in the strip format are only four panels long, which means that teachers do not have to adapt the task in terms of length or complexity.

7. The Autobiographical I

All autobiographical writing is built on a central paradox that becomes more obvious with comics: we tend to indulge the "assumption that there is a homology among the author, narrator, and protagonist",[73] that they are, in fact, the same person, but "the multiplicity of selves", fragmented across the verbal and the visual channels, is "plainly visible in graphic memoir".[74] While a prose autobiography has a fairly consistent first-person narrator who also functions as the narrative's focaliser,[75] an autobiographical comic often combines several levels of narration and focalisation. This is one of Rocco Versaci's major arguments: "[…] comics are capable of demonstrating a broader and more flexible range of first-person narration than is possible in prose".[76] For "the variety of first-person perspectives"[77] in comics he names direct address, thought balloon, text box and "alter ego"[78] – an avatar of the narrator in the comic.

Since autobiographical narratives *are* based on the lives of real people, the ethical dimension of life writing becomes clear. Students have to learn that there are limits to the extent to which they can use photos or biographical details in their own life writing. It is an important thought experiment to find out for oneself which biographical details and photos one is willing to share with other people and for what purpose. A recent issue of *Der fremdsprachliche Unterricht Englisch* (136; 2015) entitled *Autobiographies: Presenting the Self* contains a number of fascinating activities for the classroom that all raise the central question of what students are willing to share of their personal lives. The frequent violation of their private spaces by peers and adults, combined with an almost exhibitionist desire to be seen and recognised, is a central tension in the lives of many teenagers that has to be addressed in the classroom.

Both the narrator as the older self and various incarnations of the younger selves have to be seen as personae in the original Latin sense of the word, as characters in a play through which the (implied) author is speaking. This complicates the seeming simplicity or transparency of life writing.[79] For students, it is essential to keep different manifestations of the autobiographical 'I' apart. An important activity in this context is to copy several pages (A4) of an autobiographical comic onto A3 sheets and let students identify the different elements by using colours and commenting in the margins what they have identified and how they would interpret the different points of view – visually/literally and metaphorically. Every group of three to four students receives one page and they can focus on different aspects: the narrator's voice-over in captions, the dialogue, the thought balloons, body postures and facial expressions that reveal the characters' attitudes and reactions etc.[80] Bernd Rüschoff promotes the idea of "shared or cooperative reading", which Stephen Cary calls a "buddy read".[81] This form of reception is easier with comics and encourages an immediate negotiation of meaning in pairs or groups. To showcase what can be found on just one page of an autobiographical comic, I use page 13 of *Dotter of her Father's Eyes* (see Figure 5).

Here we find young Mary, the daughter of two teachers, encountering a new world. While her mother is out working, she has to stay with neighbours for an hour. Though they live just "across the backs", they are working class and engage in a very different life-style: smoking, eating chips and watching television. Mary Talbot, the writer, is indirectly present in the form of the voice-over narrator, who comments on this encounter. She also wrote the speech balloons for her younger self, the baby-sitter and her own mother. Then there is Bryan Talbot's visual interpretation of characters and their interaction through overall style and a choice of body postures, facial expressions and specific shots, such as a high-angle establishing shot in panel one or an eye-level half-subjective visual point of view that brings us close to young Mary watching TV for the first time. This split between scriptwriting and visual interpretation led to a few misunderstandings. This becomes apparent when Mary Talbot corrects her husband ("NB: My mother wouldn't have been seen dead in a frilly apron.") in a caption in the bottom left corner of the page, which offers an interesting insight into the creative process. We do not know how detailed Mary Talbot's script was for this scene, but there is always room for interpretation.[82] Finally, the neighbour's 'point of view' (her attitude) in the form of direct speech should not be forgotten.

Figure 5: An illustration of the intricacies of the comics page; © 2012 Mary M. and Bryan Talbot.

The first three panels characterise Mrs. Corless brilliantly through three images and four sentences, but this is, of course, not what happened, but how Mary Talbot, about 50 years after the event, remembered her when she was writing the script and how her husband visualised the scene in a second creative step. To be able to do that within three panels, he had to resort to stereotyping.

I do not suggest that this is the kind of analysis one should be doing with students in school, but they should be aware of the fact that Mary Talbot selected memories from her childhood and re-created scenes for a specific purpose fifty years after they had taken place. When "private memories are shaped into a narrative for public consumption",[83] the process "requires creating connections between incidents that did not exist in real life".[84]

As a feminist critic, Mary Talbot is clearly interested in the social roles of men and women across history. Using the account of Lucia Joyce's life as a point of comparison, she explores the situation of women at three points in time – the early twentieth century, the 1950s and '60s of her childhood and, finally, the early twenty-first century – and draws readers' attention to similarities and differences.

A far more widespread and even more unusual feature of autographics is the complete or partial absence of a verbal narrator. Using Jeffrey Brown's *Clumsy* as his example, David Herman analyses the effect of such an absence:

> [...] rather than using an older narrating self to provide explicit assessments of the meaning or impact of events encountered by the younger experiencing self, and thereby distancing the world of the telling from the world of the told, Brown's texts can be viewed as a tentative, provisional, still-unfinished attempt to come to terms with the events they portray.[85]

Such a strategy has a marked influence on the reader:

> [...] the absence of commentary by an overt narrating I requires readers to draw their own conclusions about exactly how the teller's current understanding (and evaluation) of his earlier experiences may have shaped his presentation of events in the storyworld.[86]

This is a double-edged sword for a teaching context: on the one hand, students are more likely to speculate and develop different theories about the narrative; on the other hand, they may miss the guiding voice of the narrator and find it hard to judge the meaning or importance of certain scenes in relation to the larger concerns and themes of the text.

8. Embodiment

"The ability to recover memories, in fact, depends on the material body. There must be a somatic body that perceives and internalises the images, sensations, and experiences of the external world".[87] While the autobiographical self may only have fragmented memories left – an image here, an ominous feeling there – he or she has to recreate situations over and over again in which the younger selves are making these experiences – maybe for the first time – as something completely new, exciting or devastating, but powerfully present all the same. "In both cartoons and comics we recognise an immediacy, a process of visual distillation that endeavors to capture the essence of moments, of circumstances, of people".[88] Life writing in the comics medium is a writing of, on and through the bodies of one's younger selves. This makes 'embodiment' such a vital issue in all autobiographical writing,[89] but especially in autographics,[90] where "the relationship between bodily identity and subjectivity" is even more intense due to "the requirement to produce multiple drawn versions of one's self".[91] Charles Hatfield comments that we get to see "how the cartoonist envisions him- or herself; [how] the inward vision takes an outward form",[92] but this is only half the truth: "embodiment is an active, cultural process of rendering the body meaningful".[93] Thus, culturally available body images play an important role in how artists understand and depict themselves in comics. A second important point has to do with the internalisation that Smith and Watson talk about and the externalisation that Hatfield addresses. Here is Hatfield again:

> The cartoon self-image, then, seems to offer a unique way for the artist to recognize and externalize his or her subjectivity. [...] Thus the cartoonist projects and objectifies his or her inward sense of self, achieving at once a sense of intimacy and a critical distance. It is the graphic exploitation of this duality that distinguishes autobiography in comics

> from most autobiography in prose. Unlike first-person narration, which works from the inside out, describing events as experienced by the teller, cartooning ostensibly works *from the outside in*, presenting events from an (imagined) position of objectivity, or at least distance.[94]

In other words: the default setting of focalisation in prose autobiographies is internal, which means that we have to reconstruct the storyworld 'from the inside out', whereas the comics medium requires the artist to translate inner states into readable signs: facial expressions, body postures, 'lighting', composition, choice of colours etc. To get to the feelings of characters the readers have to work 'from the outside in', as Hatfield puts it.

Writing thought balloons for characters in specific situations is a great way to check whether students are able to identify with them and how they understand the inner lives of characters, but it also makes sense to tie these findings back to a more analytical approach and ask them to mark and/or describe those signs on which their interpretations are based. The reading of bodies and their signals is an essential skill that we need countless times every day; yet, because this process is automatic and subconscious, students need to be made aware of it. Contrary to real life, where the signs and signals are fleeting and have to be analysed in split seconds, comics offer an opportunity to study them in detail. Due to the principle of 'amplification through simplification' and the artistic orchestration of scenes to achieve specific effects, the visual signs are more likely to be noticed and can be discussed in pairs and groups to check one's reading against that of others. Hatfield argues that autographics are ideal for such a reading: "Whereas first-person prose invites complicity, cartooning invites scrutiny".[95]

Embodiment, bodily identity and visual self-representation play a central role in present youth culture, so comics may be a medium of choice to address such issues. However, to complete my overview, I would rather draw attention to two sub-genres of autographics that intensify the engagement with one's own body and these are illness and disability narratives. Next to the diary comic, these twin genres seem to be favourites among British comics artists. Al Davison's *The Spiral Cage* is a classic of this type, focusing on the impact of spina bifida on Davison's life, but there are more examples.[96] Katie Green's *Lighter Than My Shadow* (2013) is a detailed history of suffering from anorexia throughout her teenage years. Due to its length of over 500 pages and an almost exclusive focus on the eating disorder, teachers are probably reluctant to confront students so intensely with the topic, but it is a fascinating case study of embodiment and of a metamorphic and metaphoric body that – throughout the comic – keeps transforming back and forth between Katie's emaciated physical self and her self-image as a bloated and disgusting person, between a healthy and a sick body, and between a solid presence and a ghostlike, fragmented, even uncanny self.

9. Autobiographical Truth

One of the most quoted comments on autographics in Charles Hatfield's *Alternative Comics* is that "the genre isn't about literal but rather about emotional truths".[97] Every critic in the field stresses the fact that "it is impossible to draw strict boundaries between factual and fictional accounts of someone's life, since memory is always incomplete and the act of telling one's life story necessarily involves selection and artful construction".[98] Yet, this does not keep the public from buying and perusing autobiographies, hoping for true insights, only to be bitterly disappointed when it turns out that parts of these narratives have been invented.[99] Talking about autographics, Hatfield feigns surprise how anyone can confuse drawn images in little boxes, separated by white space, with reality:

> […] autobiography has become a distinct, indeed crucial, genre in today's comic books – despite the troublesome fact that comics, with their hybrid, visual-verbal nature, pose an immediate and obvious challenge to the ideal of 'non-fiction'. They can hardly be said to be 'true' in any straightforward sense.[100]

Most importantly, the question whether a book is truthful or not is beside the point. We should rather ask when and why readers are willing to accept something as the truth: "the question of whether any given narrative belongs to fiction or autobiography is ultimately one that readers must negotiate".[101] When artists want to "create a sense of authenticity",[102] they have to rely on specific markers they can employ to convince readers of the narrative's truth. Elisabeth El Refaie dedicates a whole chapter of her study *Autobiographical Comics* to "Performing

Authenticity".[103] Here is a brief overview of the key strategies that she lists: claims in the peritexts (e.g. direct genre classification in the blurb); truth claims in the narrative itself; the artist sharing the same name with the protagonist and resembling him/her visually; being painfully honest or ironic about one's life; meta-narrative comments to explain 'what really happened'; details that signal familiarity with what is depicted; either photorealism or a "consciously assumed amateurish style"[104] that rings true due to its handmade quality; or documentary evidence.[105] Concerning the last point, Christian Ludwig comments that "inserting 'real' images and photographs into the text is another strategy used to cement the claim to accuracy and, in a way, truth".[106]

This also means that there are not "instances of objective truth" in an autobiographical comic, as Ludwig suggests in relation to Mary M. and Bryan Talbot's *Dotter of her Father's Eyes* (2012), but only signs and signifiers that suggest to the readership that the narrative is more or less based on real events. The very first page of *Dotter* offers such a playful approach to authenticity, as it features the following 'poem' framed by pressed flowers: "Once upon a time / And long ago / A King and a Queen / Had a Daughter. // Her Name was / Marushka / Or Lucia / Or Lucy Maria / or Mary".[107] Not only does this beginning undermine the truth claims of the narrative from the get-go by borrowing the most significant genre marker of fairy tales, but it also highlights the constructedness of the whole text: deliberately confusing the two names and treating Lucia Joyce as if she were Mary Talbot's soul mate or twin is a highly subjective, wish-fulfilling fantasy of Talbot's that she strategically and deliberately worked into the book.

We have to return to the critics for a moment to get this into perspective: "Most comics memoirists are not obsessed with detailing the verifiable facts of the past, but rather with communicating how they feel about the past".[108] An autobiographical comic is always "a performance of identity",[109] based on culturally available "practices of self-representation".[110] Memory becomes "a continuous process of re-interpreting, or re-membering, the events of a life in the light of current interests and concerns".[111] Accordingly, "'experience' is already an interpretation of the past and of our place in a culturally and historically specific present".[112] This may seem rather theoretical, but there is no other way to understand how Mary M. Talbot is making sense of her own and Lucia Joyce's lives in light of feminist criticism. Her experiences become meaningful by inscribing them into a larger narrative of the twentieth century that is concerned with shifting gender roles and the rights of women. In the meantime, she has published a biography, *Sally Heathcote: Suffragette* (2014), with Kate Charlesworth and her husband, which has recently been followed by *The Red Virgin and the Vision of Utopia* (2016), a biography of Louise Michel, the French anarchist, feminist and teacher. This is clearly not a coincidence.

Without a doubt, this is more the territory of university courses, but if autobiographical comics are to become a part of the school canon, the question of truth is unavoidable, especially as students are eager to know. There are several ways to explore the grey areas between fact and fiction with students.[113] The most obvious one is to follow Werner Delanoy's recommendation and avoid the "single-text approach",[114] studying related texts, especially intertexts and paratexts, ranging from YouTube interviews with the creators via their websites to blurbs of the actual books and reviews. These may comment on or present the same information from a different angle and thus help to put the subjective view presented in the autobiographical text in perspective. Students could also look for El Refaie's markers of authenticity that I listed above to understand the writers' strategies and judge their effectiveness. Discussing impressions and findings in pairs and groups provides students with a second or third opinion that may challenge their own reading. And, finally, creating their own (short) autobiographical comics is probably the best way to understand how the process of selecting and arranging personal details imbues elusive memories with meaning or even shapes them into a consistent narrative. In this context, Adam Cadwell's *The Everyday* (2012) or other diary comics could serve as models. The strip is a genuine form(at) of publishing diary comics, allows for a wide range of content and only requires aspiring artists to create four interrelated panels.

10. Conclusion

In this article I have retraced a renewed interest in the educational possibilities of comics that has been noticeable for about ten years. The rise of the graphic novel, which introduced comics to bookstores and made them culturally more viable, has done its share to draw new readers to the medium and let educators explore the use of comics as a special type of literature, but also to study the medium in its own right. As multimodal texts that employ familiar narrative strategies from prose and film, but also utilise a unique language, they can serve to develop various literacies.

A quick survey has shown that autobiographical comics are already very popular in the increasing number of publications dealing with comics in the classroom, but there are two noticeable limitations that I have tried to address. In terms of formats, comic strips and serialised narratives published as comic books are equally relevant, as are travel writing, reporting (journalism), autofiction (postmodern autobiographies), illness narratives, coming-of-age, slice-of-life, and diary comics in terms of genre. My major point, however, was an argument in favour of greater genre competence among students. I focused on three essential characteristics of autobiographical comics – the different incarnations of the autobiographical I, the central role of embodiment and the pitfalls of believing too naively in autobiographical truth – which I find essential for any discussion of autographics with older students.

Notes

1 I list a few publications and releases between 2005 and 2007 that suggest such a turning point: *Teaching Comics* (*Der fremdsprachliche Unterricht Englisch* 73) was edited by the late Martin Schüwer and offered an excellent introduction to comics in the classroom. It also contained one article on (auto)biographical comics that is particularly relevant in the context of this volume: Sabine and Wolfgang Hochbruck's "Britische Alltagsgeschichten im Comic-Roman: Raymond Briggs' *Ethel and Ernest*". In the same year Charles Hatfield published one of the foundational texts of comics and autographics studies. Though only a third of *Alternative Comics: An Emerging Literature* is dedicated to autobiographical comics, chapter 4 (on the problem of authenticity in this genre) is still an essential read for anyone interested in the subject. 2006 saw the publication of Alison Bechdel's *Fun Home*, whose literary and cultural impact in general has been enormous. To provide one example, in 2015 the Broadway musical adaptation of the comic won five Tony Awards for best musical, best book, best score, best per-

formance by an actor in a leading role and best direction (http://www.tonyawards.com/en_US/nominees/shows/20141202141755731 4329.html). Also in 2006 Hillary Chute and Marianne DeKoven edited a special issue of *Modern Fiction Studies* (52:4; Winter 2006), entitled "Graphic Narrative", which contained a number of excellent articles on 'autographics' – a term that Gillian Whitlock introduced in this volume to denote autobiographical texts in the comics medium. A year later Marjane Satrapi's successful animated adaptation of *Persepolis* drew a lot of attention and made even more people aware of her autobiographical comic. Though Rocco Versaci's *This Book Contains Graphic Language: Comics as Literature* (2007) is clearly indebted to Hatfield's *Alternative Comics*, chapter 2, "Creating a 'special reality': Comic Book vs. Memoir", is an indispensable starting point for anyone interested in this type of literature.

2 In *Englische Literatur unterrichten 1: Grundlagen und Methoden* (Seelze: Kallmeyer/Klett, 2010), Ansgar Nünning and Carola Surkamp provide a summary of relevant competences (22-38) and argue in another chapter, ("Kanonfrage und Textauswahl", 39-50), in favour of a wider variety of genres and media (49), such as comics, radio plays, feature films and TV shows. A redefinition of literacy, mostly in the wake of the New London Group's plea for a pedagogy of multiliteracies, plays an equally important role in the rediscovery of comics for the EFL classroom, usually in the context of media literacy and/or visual literacy (see 23-24).

3 See Hatfield, Charles (2005). *Alternative Comics: An Emerging Literature*. Jackson: University Press of Mississippi, 112.

4 See Duncan, Randy, Matthew J. Smith and Paul Levitz (2015). "Comic Book Genres: The Memoir." *The Power of Comics: History, Form, and Culture*. 2nd ed. London and New York: Bloomsbury, 229.

5 Ludwig, Christian (2015). "Narrating the 'Truth': Using Autographics in the EFL Classroom." *Learning with Literature in the EFL Classroom*. Eds. Werner Delanoy, Maria Eisenmann and Frauke Matz. Frankfurt am Main: Peter Lang, 299; see also 301.

6 Chaney, Michael A. (2011). "Introduction". *Graphic Subjects: Critical Essays on Autobiography and Graphic Novels*. Ed. Michael A. Chaney. Madison, WI: The University of Wisconsin Press, 5.

7 Fingeroth, Danny (2008). *The Rough Guide to Graphic Novels*. London: Rough Guides, 4. For the widely established critical consent that comics are a medium and the 'graphic novel' a form(at) of publication, see also McCloud, Scott (1994). *Understanding Comics: The Invisible Art*. New York: HarperPerennial, 6; Chute, Hillary L. (2010). *Graphic Women: Life Narrative and Contemporary Comics*. New York: Columbia University Press, 3; Schüwer, Martin (2005). "Teaching Comics: Die unentdeckten Potenziale der grafischen Literatur." *Der fremdsprachliche Unterricht*

Englisch 73, 3; El Refaie, Elisabeth (2012). *Autobiographical Comics: Life Writing in Pictures*. Jackson, MI: University Press of Mississippi, 19-20; Hatfield (2005), 5-6; Hochbruck & Hochbruck (2005), 26.

8 The failure to see comic strips, comic books and graphic novels as interconnected and sharing the same language leads to a confusion about their historical development and ties. Frank Erik Pointner, for example, claims that "the idiosyncratic language comics have developed" can be traced back to the time when "they first came into existence in the late 1930s" (Pointner, Frank Erik [2013]. "Teaching Comics as Comics." *Teaching Comics in the Foreign Language Classroom*. Eds. Christian Ludwig and Frank Erik Pointner. WVT-Handbücher zur Literatur- und Kulturdidaktik: Band 4. Trier: WVT, 27). However, the language of comics had developed for over half a century in newspaper comic strips and even before that if we acknowledge Rodolphe Töpffer (1799-1847) as the inventor of the medium's 'language'.

9 Smith, Sidonie, and Julia Watson (2010). *Reading Autobiography: A Guide for Interpreting Life Narratives*. 2nd ed. Minneapolis, MN, and London: University of Minnesota Press, 4.

10 *Ibid.*, 3.

11 See *Ibid.*, 2-3.

12 Duncan et al. (2015), 230-231.

13 Smith & Watson (2010), 3.

14 *Ibid.*, 4.

15 Whitlock, Gillian (2006). "Autographics: The Seeing 'I' of the Comics." *Modern Fiction Studies* 52.4, 966.

16 See Nünning & Surkamp (2010), 49.

17 See *Ibid.*, 17.

18 Pointner (2013), 58.

19 See Hecke, Carola (2011). "Graphic Novels as a Teaching Tool in High School and University English as a Foreign Language (EFL) Classrooms." *Amerikastudien / American Studies* 56.4, 664-665.

20 See *Ibid.*

21 See *Ibid.*, 664; Schüwer (2005), 6; Schäfers, Monika (2012). "This Is Not A Diary: Narrative Strategien von grafischer Literatur erschließen." *Der fremdsprachliche Unterricht Englisch* 117, 24.

22 See Schäfers (2012), 24; Hecke (2011), 664.

23 See Schäfers (2012), 24.

24 See Nünning & Surkamp (2010), 71-82.

25 See Caspari, Daniela (1994). *Kreativität im Umgang mit literarischen Texten im Fremdsprachenunterricht: Theoretische Studien und unterrichtspraktische Erfahrungen*. Frankfurt am Main: Peter Lang, 157-225.

[26] See Hallet, Wolfgang (2012). "Graphic Novels: Literarisches und multiliterales Lernen mit Comic-Romanen." *Der fremdsprachliche Unterricht Englisch* 117, 8.

[27] See *Ibid.*, 5.

[28] See Henseler, Roswitha (2012). "Story-orientierte Aufgaben zu einer graphic novel stellen". *Der fremdsprachliche Unterricht Englisch* 117, 10-13.

[29] See Hallet, Wolfgang (2012). "AutobioGraphic Novels." *Der fremdsprachliche Unterricht Englisch* 117, 34-38.

[30] *Ibid.*, 37.

[31] See Schäfers (2012), 24, 26.

[32] Hecke (2011), 654. See also Schüwer (2005), 5; Vanderbeke (2006), 369; Kimes-Link, Ann, and Ivo Steininger (2012). "American Born Chinese." *Der fremdsprachliche Unterricht Englisch* 117, 28.

[33] See Hallet (2012), 3. See also Rumlich, Dominik (2013). "The Benefits of Comics for Language Learning at the Lower Secondary Level: A Practical Approach." *Teaching Comics in the Foreign Language Classroom.* Eds. Christian Ludwig and Frank Erik Pointner. WVT-Handbücher zur Literatur- und Kulturdidaktik: Band 4. Trier: WVT, 99.

[34] See Oppolzer, Markus (2012). "Teaching *Frankenstein* through Comics: A Critical Look at Classics Illustrated." *Transfer in English Studies.* Eds. Sabine Coelsch-Foisner, Manfred Markus and Herbert Schendl. ASE 100. Wien: Braumüller.

[35] Hecke (2011), 657; see also 661.

[36] Hatfield (2005), xiii.

[37] *Ibid.*, xiv.

[38] Stafford, Tim (2011): *Teaching Visual Literacy in the Primary Classroom.* London and New York: Routledge, 56.

[39] See Schüwer (2005), 4-5, Hallet (2012), 2, and Ludwig (2015), 302, for this claim.

[40] Cary, Stephen (2004). *Going Graphic: Comics at Work in the Multilingual Classroom.* Portsmouth, NH: Heinemann, 58. See also Hochbruck & Hochbruck (2005), 27.

[41] Hecke (2011), 654. See also Schüwer (2005), 5.

[42] See Hecke (2011), 665.

[43] *Ibid.*, 654.

[44] See Rumlich (2013), 108. See also Cary (2004), 24, 33, 101-2.

[45] Sec Rumlich (2013), 103, 108-109. See also Ludwig (2015), 304.

[46] See Schüwer (2005), 5.

[47] For the concept of 'visual literacy' see Hecke (2011), 657, Schäfers (2012), 22, and Rumlich (2013), 99-100; for multiliteracies see Cary (2004), 32, Ludwig (2015), 315-6, and Rüschoff, Bernd (2013). "Comics in Language

Learning: The Pedagogical, Didactic, and Methodological Framework." *Teaching Comics in the Foreign Language Classroom.* Eds. Christian Ludwig and Frank Erik Pointner. WVT-Handbücher zur Literatur- und Kulturdidaktik: Band 4. Trier: WVT, 11.

48 Hallet (2012), 5.

49 Hecke (2011), 659; see also 660.

50 See Pointner (2013), 65-7, and Vanderbeke (2006), 370. In "Introduction: Towards a Methodology for Teaching Cultural Studies" (Linke, Gabriele [ed.] [2011]. *Teaching Cultural Studies: Methods – Matters – Models* Heidelberg: Winter, 8, 12-13) Gabriele Linke raises exactly the same point concerning cultural studies in general.

51 See McCloud (1994), 30.

52 See Pointner (2013), 52-8, 65-7.

53 See Vanderbeke (2006), 371.

54 See Hochbruck & Hochbruck (2005), 27, 30, 32.

55 Vanderbeke (2006), 372.

56 *Ibid.*, 374.

57 Hecke (2011), 663.

58 *Ibid.*, 665.

59 *Ibid.*

60 *Ibid.*

61 Stafford (2011), vii.

62 *Ibid.*, 113.

63 *Ibid.*, 115.

64 *Ibid.*

65 See Versaci (2007), 109-38, for an introduction.

66 See Duncan, Smith & Levitz (2015), 231.

67 Cates, Isaac (2011). "The Diary Comic." *Graphic Subjects: Critical Essays on Autobiography and Graphic Novels.* Ed. Michael A. Chaney. Madison, WI: The University of Wisconsin Press, 211, 209.

68 *Ibid.*, 220, 209.

69 *Ibid.*, 217.

70 *Ibid.*

71 *Ibid.*, 218.

72 Two other prominent British examples – Adam Cadwell's *The Everyday* and Marc Ellerby's *Ellerbisms* – were printed as books and therefore removed from their websites – a frequent fate of successful webcomics (http://www.marcellerby.com/ellerbisms/).

73 Herman, David (2011). "Narrative Worldmaking in Graphic Life Writing." *Graphic Subjects: Critical Essays on Autobiography and Graphic Novels.* Ed. Michael A. Chaney. Madison, WI: The University of Wisconsin Press, 232.

74 D'Amore, Jonathan (2012). "Serial Self-Portraits: Framing Student Conversations About Graphic Memoir." *Teaching Comics and Graphic Narratives*. Ed. Lan Dong. Jefferson, NC: McFarland, 212.

75 Smith and Watson claim the same for all autobiographical texts: "The multifacetedness inherent in autobiographical writing produces a polyphonic site of indeterminacy rather than a single, stable truth" (2010, 16; see also 74). This is, of course, true as autobiographical texts always include other voices, visual material or different "layers of the self" (Duncan et al. [2015], 238), but the comics page is inherently fragmented and the gaps are much more visible.

76 Versaci (2007), 36.

77 *Ibid.*, 38.

78 *Ibid.*, 41.

79 See Smith & Watson (2010), 63.

80 This idea is based on Evelyn Arizpe and her team's "annotations of images" in *Visual Journeys through Wordless Narratives* (2014), 79-80, and Michael Benton's use of jottings to have students explore a poem in *Secondary Worlds* (1992), 80, 87-88, 118.

81 Rüschoff (2013), 21. See also Cary (2004), 32, 69.

82 See Versaci (2007), 53.

83 El Refaie (2012), 8.

84 Duncan et al. (2015), 244.

85 Herman (2011), 240.

86 *Ibid.*

87 Smith & Watson (2010), 49.

88 Chute (2010), 12.

89 See Smith & Watson (2010), 49-54, 239-240.

90 See El Refaie (2012), 49-92, and Duncan et al. (2015), 240-243, 250.

91 El Refaie (2012), 51, 4.

92 Hatfield (2005), 114.

93 El Refaie (2012), 52.

94 Hatfield (2005), 115.

95 *Ibid.*, 117.

96 For a discussion of the book see Versaci (2007), 54-57; Oppolzer, Markus (2011). "Beyond *The Spiral Cage*: Al Davison's Counterstories of Self-Empowerment." *From the Cradle to the Grave*: *Life-Course Models in Literary Genres*. Eds. Sabine Coelsch-Foisner and Sarah Herbe. Heidelberg: Winter, 69-83; and the two essays on masculinities by Paul McIlvenny. See the list of British autobiographical comics for further examples, especially John Stuart Clark, Darryl Cunningham and Nicola Streeten.

97 Hatfield (2005), 113.

[98] El Refaie (2012), 12. See also Smith & Watson (2010), 15-18; Herman (2011), 232; Chaney (2011), 3; Duncan et al. (2015), 243; Versaci (2007), 36, 58.

[99] See Versaci (2007), 34-36, for a discussion of the James Frey case (*A Million Little Pieces*).

[100] Hatfield (2005), 112. See also Chaney (2011), 7; Versaci (2007), 36.

[101] Chaney (2011), 4.

[102] El Refaie (2012), 7.

[103] *Ibid.*, 135-178.

[104] *Ibid.*, 155.

[105] *Ibid.*, 158-165.

[106] Ludwig (2015), 303.

[107] Talbot, Mary M. and Bryan Talbot (2012). *Dotter of her Father's Eyes*. Milwaukie, OR: Dark Horse, 1. This may even represent an intertextual reference to James Joyce's *Portrait of the Artist as a Young Man* – not too far-fetched considering that Talbot's father was a Joyce scholar.

[108] Duncan et al. (2015), 246.

[109] *Ibid.*, 251. See also Smith & Watson (2010), 61; El Refaie (2012), 135-139; Hatfield (2005), 125-126.

[110] Chaney (2011), 6.

[111] El Refaie (2012), 16.

[112] Smith & Watson (2010), 31.

[113] Smith & Watson's "Group and Classroom Projects" (287-293) are targeted at a college audience, but some of the activities can also be adapted for the EFL classroom.

[114] See Delanoy, Werner (2015): "Literature Teaching and Learning: Theory and Practice." *Learning with Literature in the EFL Classroom*. Eds. Werner Delanoy, Maria Eisenmann and Frauke Matz. Frankfurt am Main: Peter Lang, 24.

A Selection of British Autobiographical Comics:

Cadwell, Adam (2012). *The Everyday*. Manchester: Great Beast Comics.

Campbell, Eddie (2009). *Alec: The Years Have Pants*. Marietta, GA: Top Shelf.

Clark, John Stuart (2010). *Depresso*; or: *How I Learned To Stop Worrying And Embrace Being Bonkers!* London: Knockabout.

Cunningham, Darryl (2010). *Psychiatric Tales*. London: Blank Slate.

Dakin, Glenn (2001). *Abe: Wrong for all the Right Reasons*. Marietta, GA: Top Shelf.

Davison, Al (2003). *The Spiral Cage*. Los Angeles, CA: Active Images.

Decie, Joe (2011). *The Accidental Salad*. London: Blank Slate.
--- (2013). *The Listening Agent*. London: Blank Slate.
East, Oliver (2008). *Trains are ... Mint*. Blank Slate.
Ellerby, Marc (2012). *Ellerbisms: A Sporadic Diary Comic*. Manchester: Great Beast Comics.
Green, Katie (2013). *Lighter Than My Shadow*. London: Jonathan Cape.
Hatcher, Gill (2014). *The Beginner's Guide to Being Outside*. London: Avery Hill.
Hughes, David (2009). *Walking the Dog*. London: Jonathan Cape.
Mackintosh, Ross (2011). *Seeds*. London: Com.x.
Moreton, Simon (2014). *Days: Comics 2011-2012*. London: Avery Hill.
Richards, Barnaby (2014). *Beetroot: An Unreliable Memoir*. London: Blank Slate.
Streeten, Nicola (2011). *Billy, Me & You: A Memoir of Grief and Recovery*. Brighton: Myriad Editions.
Syder, Ed (2011). *My Skateboard Life*. London: Blank Slate.
Talbot, Mary M. and Bryan Talbot (2012). *Dotter of her Father's Eyes*. Milwaukie, OR: Dark Horse.

Bibliography

Arizpe, Evelyn, Teresa Colomer and Carmen Martínez-Roldán (2014). *Visual Journeys through Wordless Narratives: An International Inquiry with Immigrant Children and* The Arrival. London: Bloomsbury.
Bechdel, Alison (2006). *Fun Home: A Family Tragicomic*. New York: Houghton Mifflin.
Benton, Michael (1992). *Secondary Worlds: Literature Teaching and the Visual Arts*. Buckingham: Open University.
Cary, Stephen (2004). *Going Graphic: Comics at Work in the Multilingual Classroom*. Portsmouth, NH: Heinemann.
Caspari, Daniela (1994). *Kreativität im Umgang mit literarischen Texten im Fremdsprachenunterricht: Theoretische Studien und unterrichtspraktische Erfahrungen*. Frankfurt am Main: Peter Lang.
Cates, Isaac (2011). "The Diary Comic." *Graphic Subjects: Critical Essays on Autobiography and Graphic Novels*. Ed. Michael A. Chaney. Madison, WI: The University of Wisconsin Press, 2011, 209-226.
Cazden, Courtney et al. [The New London Group] (1996). "A Pedagogy of Multiliteracies: Designing Social Futures." *Harvard Educational Review* 66.1, 60-92.

Chaney, Michael A. (ed.) (2011). *Graphic Subjects: Critical Essays on Autobiography and Graphic Novels*. Madison, WI: The University of Wisconsin Press.

--- (2011). "Introduction." *Graphic Subjects: Critical Essays on Autobiography and Graphic Novels*. Ed. Michael A. Chaney. Madison, WI: The University of Wisconsin Press, 3-9.

Chute, Hillary L. (2010). *Graphic Women: Life Narrative and Contemporary Comics*. New York: Columbia University Press.

D'Amore, Jonathan (2012). "Serial Self-Portraits: Framing Student Conversations About Graphic Memoir." *Teaching Comics and Graphic Narratives*. Ed. Lan Dong. Jefferson, NC: McFarland, 210-219.

Delanoy, Werner (2015). "Literature Teaching and Learning: Theory and Practice." *Learning with Literature in the EFL Classroom*. Eds. Werner Delanoy, Maria Eisenmann and Frauke Matz. Frankfurt am Main: Peter Lang, 19-47.

Dong, Lang (ed.) (2012). *Teaching Comics and Graphic Narratives*. Jefferson, NC: McFarland.

Duncan, Randy, Matthew J. Smith and Paul Levitz (2015). "Comic Book Genres: The Memoir." *The Power of Comics: History, Form, and Culture*. 2nd ed. London and New York: Bloomsbury, 229-262.

El Refaie, Elisabeth (2012). *Autobiographical Comics: Life Writing in Pictures*. Jackson, MI: University Press of Mississippi.

Fingeroth, Danny (2008). *The Rough Guide to Graphic Novels*. London: Rough Guides.

Hallet, Wolfgang (2012). "AutobioGraphic Novels." *Der fremdsprachliche Unterricht Englisch* 117, 34-38.

--- (2015). "Autobiographies: Selbst-Erzählung und Selbst-Darstellung in der Fremdsprache." *Der fremdsprachliche Unterricht Englisch* 136, 2-7.

--- (2012). "Graphic Novels: Literarisches und multiliterales Lernen mit Comic-Romanen." *Der fremdsprachliche Unterricht Englisch* 117, 2-9.

Hatfield, Charles (2005). *Alternative Comics: An Emerging Literature*. Jackson: University Press of Mississippi.

Hecke, Carola (2011). "Graphic Novels as a Teaching Tool in High School and University English as a Foreign Language (EFL) Classrooms." *Amerikastudien / American Studies* 56.4, 653-668.

Henseler, Roswitha (2012). "Story-orientierte Aufgaben zu einer graphic novel stellen." *Der fremdsprachliche Unterricht Englisch* 117, 10-13.

Herman, David (2011). "Narrative Worldmaking in Graphic Life Writing." *Graphic Subjects: Critical Essays on Autobiography and Graphic Novels*. Ed. Michael A. Chaney. Madison, WI: The University of Wisconsin Press, 231-243.

Hochbruck, Sabine, and Wolfgang Hochbruck (2005). "Britische Alltagsgeschichte im Comic-Roman: Raymond Briggs' *Ethel & Ernest*." *Der fremdsprachliche Unterricht Englisch* 73, 25-32.

Kimes-Link, Ann, and Ivo Steininger (2012). "American Born Chinese." *Der fremdsprachliche Unterricht Englisch* 117, 28-33, 49.

Linke, Gabriele (2011). "Introduction: Towards a Methodology for Teaching Cultural Studies." *Teaching Cultural Studies: Methods – Matters – Models*. Ed. Gabriele Linke. Heidelberg: Winter, 2011, 7-14.

Ludwig, Christian (2015). "Narrating the 'Truth': Using Autographics in the EFL Classroom." *Learning with Literature in the EFL Classroom*. Eds. Werner Delanoy, Maria Eisenmann and Frauke Matz. Frankfurt am Main: Peter Lang, 299-320.

Ludwig, Christian, and Frank Erik Pointner (eds.) (2013). *Teaching Comics in the Foreign Language Classroom*. WVT-Handbücher zur Literatur- und Kulturdidaktik: Band 4. Trier: WVT.

McCloud, Scott (1994). *Understanding Comics: The Invisible Art*. New York: HarperPerennial.

McIlvenny, Paul (2003). "Disabling Men: Masculinity and Disability in Al Davison's Graphic Autobiography *The Spiral Cage*." *Bending Bodies*. Eds. Søren Ervø and Thomas Johansson. Aldershot: Ashgate, 238-258.

--- (2002). "Graphic Fictions of Masculinity and the Body in the Autobiographical Comic *The Spiral Cage*." *Revealing Male Bodies*. Eds. Nancy Tuana et al. Bloomington and Indianapolis, IN: Indiana University Press, 100-124.

Oppolzer, Markus (2011). "Beyond *The Spiral Cage*: Al Davison's Counterstories of Self-Empowerment." *From the Cradle to the Grave: Life-Course Models in Literary Genres*. Eds. Sabine Coelsch-Foisner and Sarah Herbe. Heidelberg: Winter, 69-83.

--- (2012). "Teaching *Frankenstein* through Comics: A Critical Look at Classics Illustrated." *Transfer in English Studies*. Eds. Sabine Coelsch-Foisner, Manfred Markus and Herbert Schendl. ASE 100. Wien: Braumüller, 159-181.

Nünning, Ansgar, and Carola Surkamp (2010). *Englische Literatur unterrichten 1: Grundlagen und Methoden*. 3rd ed. Seelze: Kallmeyer/Klett.

Pointner, Frank Erik (2013). "Teaching Comics as Comics." *Teaching Comics in the Foreign Language Classroom*. Eds. Christian Ludwig and Frank Erik Pointner. WVT-Handbücher zur Literatur- und Kulturdidaktik: Band 4. Trier: WVT, 27-68.

Rumlich, Dominik (2013). "The Benefits of Comics for Language Learning at the Lower Secondary Level: A Practical Approach." Eds. Christian Ludwig and Frank Erik Pointner. WVT-Handbücher zur Literatur- und Kulturdidaktik: Band 4. Trier: WVT, 95-124.

Rüschoff, Bernd (2013). "Comics in Language Learning: The Pedagogical, Didactic, and Methodological Framework." Eds. Christian Ludwig and Frank Erik Pointner. WVT-Handbücher zur Literatur- und Kulturdidaktik: Band 4. Trier: WVT, 5-25.

Satrapi, Marjane (2007). *The Complete Persepolis*. New York: Pantheon.

Schäfers, Monika (2012). "This Is Not A Diary: Narrative Strategien von grafischer Literatur erschließen." *Der fremdsprachliche Unterricht Englisch* 117, 22-27.

Schüwer, Martin (2005). "Teaching Comics: Die unentdeckten Potenziale der grafischen Literatur." *Der fremdsprachliche Unterricht Englisch* 73, 2-8.

Smith, Sidonie, and Julia Watson (2010). *Reading Autobiography: A Guide for Interpreting Life Narratives*. 2nd ed. Minneapolis, MN, and London: University of Minnesota Press.

Stafford, Tim (2011). *Teaching Visual Literacy in the Primary Classroom*. London and New York: Routledge.

Vanderbeke, Dirk (2006). "Comics and Graphic Novels in the Classroom." *Cultural Studies in the EFL Classroom*. Eds. Werner Delanoy und Laurenz Volkmann. Heidelberg: Winter, 365-379.

Versaci, Rocco (2007). *This Book Contains Graphic Language: Comics as Literature*. New York and London: Continuum.

Whitlock, Gillian, and Anna Poletti (eds.) (2008). *Autographics*. *Biography* 31.1.

Whitlock, Gillian (2006). "Autographics: The Seeing 'I' of the Comics." *Modern Fiction Studies* 52.4, 965-979.

Katrin Röder (Potsdam)

Acknowledging Anger, Problematising Shame: Affirming New Identities in British Women's Disability Autobiographies

1. Introduction

Autobiographical writing holds an important place among the cultural practices that represent disability. G. Thomas Couser has argued that disability has become "one of the pervasive topics in contemporary life writing".[1] According to Couser, the surge of autosomatography (an umbrella term that covers autobiographical accounts of illness and disability) must be understood in the context of the civil rights movements in the second half of the twentieth century,[2] its fundamental endeavour being to "destigmatize various anomalous body conditions".[3] Disability autobiography (a term used for autobiographical texts whose authors mostly identify as disabled) is

> a response – indeed a retort – to the traditional misrepresentation of disability in Western culture generally. [...] written from inside the experience in question, it involves self-representation by definition and thus offers an opportunity for personal revaluation of that condition.[4]

Relying on Paul John Eakin's concept of narrative identity[5] as well as on Couser's approach to disability autobiography as a cultural practice of empowerment, this article discusses texts by disabled British and Irish women, a corpus that has largely been neglected by scholarship. It demonstrates that the autobiographical narratives included in Lois Keith's anthology *Mustn't Grumble. Writing by Disabled Women* (1994) affirm embodied difference by challenging the stereotypes of passivity and helplessness associated with disabled women.[6]

G. Thomas Couser has argued that most disability and illness memoirs are characterised by a "comic masterplot" which focuses on the individual's physical, intellectual or spiritual transcendence of impediment, at times also on recovery.[7] He has shown that comic plot models represent disability in purely negative terms of personal tragedy, as a defect of the individual body which must be overcome by medication and surgery. In the following, I will investigate the ways in which the contributors to Keith's anthology respond to the narrative tradition of the comic masterplot as well as to the tragic model of disability which prevails in sociology and the media.[8] My analysis seeks to demonstrate that the autobiographical texts in Keith's anthology generate new plot models and novel, counter-normative forms of identities through narrative oscillations and feed-back processes between positive and negative affects,[9] representing disabled bodies as sites of resistance against dominant discourse.

Although physical or cognitive impairment can preclude the (unassisted) composition as well as publication of autobiography,[10] the popularity of disability memoirs (produced by a single author or in collaboration) is unbroken.[11] I will use the term "disability" in accordance with the broad definition given in the British Equality Act of 2010: "A person has a disability for the purposes of the Act if he or she has a physical or mental impairment and if the impairment has a substantial and long-term adverse effect on his or her ability to carry out normal day-to-day activities".[12] As many forms of mental illness (depression, schizophrenia, bipolar disorder) have a substantial and long-term negative effect on people's ability to carry out normal day-to-day activities, they meet the criteria for disability defined in the Equality Act and are mentioned in the guidance accompanying the Act.[13]

Autobiographical accounts of experiences of chronic illness and disability are available in print but are also part of TV documentaries, personal videos and blogs.[14] In the new media, they often take the forms of shorter self-portraits or diaries and are accompanied by photographs, illustrations, poems, videos and readers'/viewers' responses.[15] Thus, disability autobiography is available in different forms (diachronic, episodic)[16] and genres (for example book-length narratives, short personal vignettes, diaries, letters, poems, collages, soliloquies). Whereas a great amount of critical literature on contemporary American disability memoirs has been produced in the last decades,[17] contemporary British disability autobiography has received much less critical attention.[18] For this reason, this article focuses on a significant but largely overlooked corpus of British and Irish disabled women's autobiographies and discusses their specific models of plot and identity construction.

2. Disability Autobiography, Gender and Identity Formation

Michelle Fine and Adrienne Asch have emphasised that cultural responses to disability are severely gendered. From an ableist perspective, disability is seen as synonymous with being dependent, helpless, and childlike; thereby contradicting stereotypical notions of masculinity such as physical strength, autonomy, virility and independence.[19] The stereotypes associated with disability replicate all that is embodied in the caricature of the "ideal female": "emotionality, passivity, dependence".[20] Therefore, the connection between femininity and dependence is often regarded as a "redundant intersection".[21] As Mary Jo Deegan, Nancy Brooks, Rosemarie Garland-Thomson and Barbara Faye Waxman Fiduccia have shown, the cultural perception of a redundant intersection of femininity and dependence has very harmful consequences for disabled girls and women who carry a double social handicap and face a "double dose of discrimination and stereotyping and multiple barriers to achieving their life goals".[22] They are even more subject to gender-based violence than non-disabled women, but are less likely to seek help. Furthermore, "women of color, low income women and lesbians incorporate additional layers of identity but also receive an extra dose of bias and discrimination".[23] These observations are confirmed by female disabled authors with ethnic minority backgrounds as well as by lesbian disabled authors who contributed autobiographical texts to Lois Keith's collection.[24] For all these reasons, many female autobiographers criticise the negative images attached to disability and illness (passivity, helplessness, dependence) as well as articulate specifically feminist, queer, religious, or national identities in their narratives.[25]

As expressions of "the subjectivity of self-representational agency",[26] autobiographies by disabled women tell alternative truths that can be vital contributions to social change. Whereas Jenny Morris and Carol Thomas argued in the 1990s that non-disabled feminists "failed to address the concerns of disabled women, sometimes actively excluding them from participation in feminist events,"[27] Susan Wendell and Rosemarie Garland-Thomson have successfully integrated feminist theory and disability studies.[28] In *Unruly Bodies*, Susannah B. Mintz connects disability theory and contemporary American feminist autobiography, showing that the texts by Nancy Mairs, Lucy Grealy, Georgina Kleege, Eli Clare, Connie Panzarino and May Sarton challenge "the troping of disability [...] as deviance, helplessness, insufficiency and loss" and "speak openly about a form of embodiment often excluded from the conversation in both disability and feminist discourse".[29]

As Mintz has demonstrated, the identities constructed in autobiographical writing by disabled women are often "fundamentally both relational and discontinuous", as well as / or "unfixed, restless". They are characterised by multiplicity, demystifying the isolated "I" as an ideologically motivated fiction.[30] Many female autobiographers whose identities comprise multiple layers of embodied difference (ethnicity, sexual orientation, class, religion, age) situate their selves within networks of others with shared experiences without reducing the meaning of gendered selfhood to a stable or consistent characterisation.[31] Furthermore, Mintz has shown that the stories told in women's autobiographies neither rely on absolute characteristics nor "abide by the standards of sworn truth"; they resist traditional patterns of men's life writing which tend to focus on cognitive capacities and achievements

> by returning to the body, explicitly representing the self in terms of such body markers as race, sexuality, class, motherhood, instances of physical trauma [...]. Such texts 'talk back' to dominant cultural paradigms and work to validate unrecognized categories of identity and experience.[32]

In the following, I seek to show that Lois Keith's anthology *Mustn't Grumble* contains autobiographical accounts of disabled women which do not represent the connection between femininity and dependence as merely a redundant intersection. Many contributors were/are feminist activists who had fought/fight hard against an image of women which reduces them to passive, helpless objects. They are fully aware that their grasp of independence is fragile,[33] fearing as well as fighting against the loss of autonomy experienced by many disabled women whose lives are determined by adverse social conditions and insufficient medical treatment. Although the texts show that their authors strive to assert their right to lead full, self-determined lives, they neither deny the reality of the physical and emotional pain and suffering that their impairment causes them, nor the fact that disabled people need social and medical support.[34] Furthermore, many texts in Keith's collection show that the common attitude towards disability not only replicates the notion of the passive female but reinforces the notions of dependence and helplessness that turn disabled women and girls into passive, mute objects of physical, sexual and emotional abuse as well as victims of oppression.[35] The texts in Keith's anthology are closely related to feminist disability activism. They disclose and criticise the stigmatisation and oppression that disabled girls and women with multiple layers of identity have to face. As such, they contain strategies of empowerment and share many of the characteristics that Mintz has identified in her analysis of feminist American autosomatographies: the construction of relational/communal, fluid, multi-layered forms of identity, the challenging of dominant cultural paradigms and of hegemonic, absolute notions of truth, the focus on impairment, illness, trauma, race, sexuality, class and motherhood as body markers and the affirmation of unrecognised categories of identity and experience.[36] In my analysis, I will concentrate on the ways in which the autobiographical texts in Keith's collection focus on affect[37] as an important aspect of embodiment, narrative identity formation and political activism that was heretofore overlooked in critical discussions of disability autobiographies.[38]

3. Lois Keith's 'Mustn't Grumble'

Lois Keith's anthology of writings (memoirs, poems, stories, essays) by mostly British women with disabilities is a significant part of early feminist disability activism in Great Britain.[39] Published one year before the passing of the British Disability Discrimination Act, it comprises texts by female authors with different disabilities: Nasa Begum, for example, suffered from a neurological condition that caused muscle degeneration, Ellie O'Sullivan had arthritis, Gohar Kordi is blind and Pam Mason suffers from an anxiety disorder. The authors in Keith's collection come from and belong to different social classes: Celeste Dandeker, for example, is a choreographer, Kate Bromfield is a teacher, Kaite O'Reilly and Janice Pink have emphasised their working-class backgrounds. Furthermore, Keith's anthology is characterised by cultural and sexual diversity as, for example, Gohar Kordi was born in Iran and Nasa Begum is of Pakistani origin. Maria Jastrzębska (born in Warsaw), Suna Polio, Elsa Beckett, Janice Pink and Aspen identify as lesbian. As yet, the significance of Keith's collection has not been fully acknowledged: G. Thomas Couser,[40] Tom Shakespeare[41] and Susannah Mintz[42] only mention it in passing.[43] Janet Price and Margrit Shildrick have disapproved of Keith's anthology, arguing that it suggests that the only significant view on disability comes from disabled people. Furthermore, they have professed that it reproduces a limited understanding of the social model of disability, that it represents the disabled person as "distinctly other in her corporeal specificity, whilst at the same time striving to attain standards of normativity" and that it leaves the body as a site of resistance to dominant discourse out of consideration.[44] I seek to show that Price and Shildrick have failed to acknowledge that many texts in Keith's anthology subvert normative, essentialist notions of disability and normality and value the disabled body as a site of resistance.

Keith's collection generates a flexible community of female authors who cherish their multiple layers of identity instead of repressing them.[45] Keith (a paraplegic since she was hit by a motorist) states in her introduction that she collected the texts among her own friends and acquaintances and among the women who answered her announcements in newspapers, magazines and on flyers.[46] In her introduction, Keith argues that her selection of texts is not based on a homogeneous notion of what the lives of disabled women are supposed to look like or how contributors are supposed to position themselves towards their disabilities. It is a collection of very heterogeneous texts, containing the voices of women from different classes, ethnic backgrounds and with different disabilities that speak in polyphony and sound in consonance or dissonance.[47] Although Keith and the editor from The Women's Press prefer texts that inscribe disabled women as active rather than passive, and angry rather than compliant, the excerpts of Keith's correspondence with some of the contributors included in the appendix show that she values and publishes texts containing viewpoints that differ from her own:

> I haven't felt the need to 'agree' with all the contributors. As well as women who are political about being disabled, there is also writing by women who reject the pressures they feel imposed on them to make some sort of 'correct' view.[48]

Nonetheless, most contributors affirm their identities as disabled women[49] and challenge or even defy the tragic view of disability without denying or transcending the reactions of hostile social environments, the experiences of pain and suffering or the changes of their view points and senses of identity which are related to their impairments.[50] The title of the first edition of Keith's anthology is ironic because the texts included in it acknowledge anger instead of suppressing it:

> "Mustn't grumble" is what women say to each other when what they really want to do is have a good moan about the things which make them feel fed up. [...] We tell each other stories about the ridiculous things strangers in the supermarket say, we moan about doctors, employers, inaccessible buildings, our illness or impairments, and what society and the world in general does to us. [...] This book contains a lot of wonderful, poetic, powerful and funny grumbling.[51]

In Keith's collection, anger is a "survival strategy" and a very productive affect because it gives writers the chance to criticise the social and political conditions that cause oppression and suffering.[52] In addition, many texts contain narrative reparative responses to anger that call for the removal of the problems created by disabling societies.[53] Roz Rushworth's short autobiographical text "Mustn't Grumble", whose title is taken from the name of a drama group,[54] focuses on anger and on her response to this affect: "'Mustn't grumble'", readers learn, is Rushworth's retort to intrusive questions asked by strangers, it is "what I say to people when I really mean 'stop asking me stupid questions' but I'm too polite to say it!"[55] In her text, Rushworth (disabled because of arthritis) recounts how her life changed dramatically when she became a wheelchair user and her friends began to forsake her: "My life had no purpose, no one needed me, I couldn't get a job, I was useless".[56] Her son, however, reminds her of her desire to write: "'You have all the time in the world now and no kids to disturb you. [...] Go back to your writing.'" Following her son's advice, the narrator describes how she decided to write about her anger:

> If I could put my hurt and frustrated feelings down on paper it might help to bring them into the open. I found it hard to begin with but, once the pen started, the ink began to flow and I couldn't stop. [...] I noticed within days [...] the change in me. I was beginning to come to terms with my disability, the frustration was slowly subsiding. Where there had been anger and tears, there was laughter [...]. [...] I joined VALID, a group for disabled writers. We put out our own quarterly magazine. [...] What a joy to be among those who accept me for myself. I am able to talk freely about my disability. [...] I made new friends and a new life, and once again enjoyed life to the full.[57]

At this point, I would like to state that I do not follow Smith and Watson in their focus on the distinction between the "narrator" as the agent of discourse and the "narrated 'I'" as the subject of history on the one hand

and the "historical 'I'" (the flesh-and-blood author) on the other hand.[58] Relying on Paul John Eakin's concept of narrative identity, I consider identities to be provisional discursive narrative constructs generated in autobiographical writing.[59] Although Eakin stresses the normalising dimensions of autobiographical writing, arguing that autobiography is a genre that creates conformity by establishing authors as "normal individuals in the minds of others", his performative approach can be productive for the analysis of disability autobiographies and coming-out texts if it is modified in a way that enables us to investigate them as narrative spaces in which provisional counter-normative forms of identity are created:[60] by expressing herself in writing, the narrator in Rushworth's text explains, she is able to affirm her identity as a disabled woman as well as to develop a reparative response to her anger that envisions social change:

> I know there are still problems for me to face, obstacles to climb over, but I have accepted myself for who I am, a person with a disability. Being able to express this in my writing has helped me so much to come to terms with it all. All that is left now is to change the attitudes of society. To let them see that we understand our own needs. With our guidance they could get things right. We do need their support and help. I am sure if we keep on pressing this point home we will all be able to live richer and fuller lives, if only we can be given the chance to prove this.[61]

Rushworth's text has an optimistic, hopeful ending that addresses disabled as well as non-disabled readers. In it, she affirms her way of life as a disabled author and argues that she prefers it to that of non-disabled people: "I am grateful for my disability, because without it I wouldn't have this [i. e. her new life as a writer] to look forward to, I would still be trying to keep up with the rat race".[62] Similar to Rushworth, many contributors to Keith's anthology are determined to lead lives that are worth living according to their own standards, comprising mobility, access to facilities, work, creative self-expression (in writing, visual, or performative arts), political activism and, last but not least, friendships, love and sexual relationships. Therefore, many texts in Keith's collection can be described as "quality-of-life writing", a term which Couser has used for autosomatography in general.[63] In fact, the autobiographical texts in Keith's collection have a eudaimonic dimension because they focus on aspects that make a life worth living. In this way, they challenge common assumptions according to which the lives of disabled people are necessarily unhappy and tragic as well as dominant legal and medical definitions of valuable lives and life quality.[64] In addition, they demonstrate that the possibility of living a full life does not depend on the disabled individual alone but on the qualities of the social support and medical care this person receives, a position that is in accordance with the social (British) model of disability which asserts that it is not the individual's impairment which causes disability but that disability "is the outcome of social arrangements which work to restrict the activities of people with impairments by placing social barriers in their way".[65] Although the autobiographical texts in Keith's collection represent the lives of disabled women as gratifying forms of existence, they reject the patterns of narratives of triumph in which heroic individuals transcend the negative experiences that are connected with their disabilities.[66] By contrast, they acknowledge these experiences alongside the negative affects activated by them (anger, distress, shame). In addition, they formulate reparative responses that are informed by positive affects and emotional attitudes (joy, interest, love/self-love, pride, hope), calling for the removal of the social causes of suffering and oppression. As a result, the texts are characterised by narrative oscillations between negative and positive affects and emotional attitudes which create novel plot models as well as novel, counter-normative forms of identity.

Pam Mason's autobiographical text on her life with mental illness, entitled "Agoraphobia: Letting Go", is characterised by complex narrative feed-back processes between fear, hope and joy, especially in the passages which describe how the narrator passed through her fear and was able to enjoy her visits to distant places like Liverpool.[67] Mason's text reveals the severely gendered cultural repression of female anger as the origin of Mason's mental illness, defying earlier associations of her mental illness (which she calls "That Feeling") with demonic possession[68] or with medical scare-words like "mad, schizophrenic, 'in the head', neurotic".[69] Through the help of her female psychologist Jacqui, the narrator discovers that her illness was caused by family problems and the "years of pressure" connected with them.[70] "Agoraphobia: Letting Go" has a happy ending and inspires hope, but it does not follow the traditional comic plot model of autosomatography: it neither transcends the reality of suffering and oppression connected with mental illness nor celebrates a heroic individual's triumph over adversity. The narrator defies the pressure of normalization which informs conventional happy endings and states that she still has eating disorders, gets agoraphobic at times of stress and suffers from depression.

As she recognises that the improvement of her mental condition depends on the acknowledgement of her anger, she begins to challenge the severely gendered stereotypes of proper behaviour: "Like most women, I had learned to eat my own anger, not let it show. [...] That Feeling was a bundle of 'wrong' emotions: anger, fear, need, love." Instead of fighting against "That Feeling", she regards it as a "vital message": "[...] I now know what I want, and need, my life to be".[71] Here, the disabled body is a valued and affirmed site of resistance against dominant medical and social discourses, offering an alternative approach to what counts as a valid, meaningful response to the social environment. The self- and body images created in this text are neither essentialist nor homogeneous but relational, complex, contingent, provisional and fluid.[72] They change perpetually and comprise parts that cannot be fully controlled, that subvert the norms of appropriate female behaviour. Thus, the self- and body images generated in Mason's text are based on a revaluation of the narrator's emotional responses to her social environment that involves self-esteem and self-love. Instead of telling the story of an heroic individual's triumph over impairment and adversity, the narrator emphasises that she was very lucky because the improvement of her condition was contingent upon good medical treatment and a supportive social environment in the early 1980s, comprising a good therapist, home visits, student grants, dole and housing benefits and the intense attention of the NHS.[73] At the end, she expresses her anger about the social situation of people with mental illnesses in the early 1990s: "It makes me furious that the escape routes I took have been closed off by government cuts".[74]

In addition to anger, shame is a complex affect that informs many texts in Keith's collection. It is strongly connected with personal, social and cultural processes of identity formation and communication.[75] Shame is inseparably linked to positive affects/emotional attitudes: "one must have expected good things to have come from the other person before the other's contempt produces shame".[76] In her autobiographical vignette "The Visit", Ellie O'Sullivan, a British film maker who died in 1999,[77] recounts her experiences of fear and shame during the visit of a female Social Service worker who grades her with regard to the help she needs at home because of her arthritis. The narrator expects to be regarded as a fraud and a burden and is worried about how the disclosure of her physical weakness will affect her daughter who is present during the interview.[78] In order to remain mobile, she must admit her weakness (the cause of her shame) and tell the Social Service worker that she needs a bath chair to get out of the bathtub by herself. This concession is at odds with her self-image as an active, resourceful and independent woman. The narrator expresses this sense of inner division when she describes her strange feelings about the fact that she is labelled an impaired person in the medical records.[79] In the sheltered space of female communication, the moment in which the narrator admits her weakness and need of support becomes a moment of strength, which leads to an improvement of her situation:

> I finish and see the woman before me soft with sympathy. "Don't worry," she says kindly, "we'll get the chair installed as quickly as possible." I don't look at Charlotte. I want to ask her forgiveness. I want to tell her how ashamed I am, that she needn't worry, that I'm okay. But she is already moving towards me, her arms encircling my legs, reassuring me, protecting me.[80]

In this communicative setting, the other person's contempt which normally activates shame is never actualised but exists as an apprehension in the narrator's mind, revealing how much she depends on good responses from others, that is, on their acknowledgement of her strength and abilities. Contrary to her expectations, the narrator receives "good things" (love, support) from others precisely because she has disclosed and shared the cause that made her feel ashamed. Despite this positive turn of events, the text does not end on a triumphant note. The final scene focuses on her swollen hands and painful movement.

Although many texts in Keith's collection describe their authors' confrontations with the contempt of their social environment, some of them even question the social norms that provoke shame: Nasa Begum's short autobiographical text "Snow White" includes scenes in which she describes how she met with discrimination as a black disabled girl. Begum suffered from a neurological condition that resulted in spine curvature and muscle degeneration. She was a British writer and disability activist of Pakistani origin who died in 2011.[81] In "Snow White", the narrator acknowledges her childhood dreams of being an actress, of becoming the friend of the only disabled Asian girl at her school as well as of being accepted by her white schoolmates.[82] Her childhood desires met with derision and were destroyed by complications connected with her illness and unfortunate incidents. Her hope of "becoming the first Pakistani Snow White" was crushed because she had to go into hospital for an operation, the orange dress she wanted to buy in the shop owned by the Asian girl's parents was sold to somebody else and she and the Asian girl were viewed as outsiders at their special school for disabled children.[83] Despite the fact that her story is constructed along the lines of disasters and disappointments, it does not affirm but challenge and demystify the tragic model of disability, exposing the rampant racism and ableism of her social environment, the lack of a multicultural approach in teaching as well as the inadequate education disabled children received in hospitals and schools by the help of her sarcastic humour:[84]

> It took me a long time to understand why people who did not know me in my neighbourhood called me "spastic", "bandy legs" or "Ironside" and why people with disabilities called me "paki" or "nigger". Eventually I learned that wherever I went I would probably stand out as being different from the majority and I had to be prepared to accept being called either paki or bandy legs, and sometimes both.[85]

At the end of the text, the narrator finds it hard to believe that she "was denied the right to have the same education as my sisters".[86] She is proud of her multi-layered identity as a black disabled woman, rejecting the dominant concept of normality:

> [...] I've come a long way since the days of Snow White and orange dresses. I've reclaimed my identity by refusing to accept a concept of 'normality' which tells me I must walk, have fair skin and try to blend in by wearing Western clothes.[87]

Again, the self-image created here is neither essentialist nor homogeneous but relational and complex, based on a critical revaluation of the negative images of herself produced by her environment which she in part internalised.

Mary Duffy's autobiographical poem is characterised by the acknowledgement of experiences of stigmatisation and oppression as well as by an attitude that questions shame-inducing norms of embodiment. Duffy is an Irish photographer, writer, performer, painter and disability activist; she was born without arms because of the impact of thalidomide. From the very beginning of her poem onwards, Duffy uses a specific graphic realisation of the first person pronoun singular ("i" instead of "I") that can be seen as an expression of her rejection of the concept of the ableist, sovereign subject of traditional autobiography. As such, it might point to embodied difference, resembling an upper body without arms. The poem is written in free verse, it consists of eight sections which are arranged in a chronological order. They focus on Duffy's birth, childhood and life as a woman, describing her relationship to her parents, her grandmother, her sisters, friends, her lover and herself. In section one ("somebody's daughter / CHILD"), the speaker recounts her parents' ambivalent attitude towards her, promising to "love me so much / it wouldn't make any difference" but attempting to normalise her body at the same time. They discouraged her from "using my feet", trying to "make my body conform" by the help of artificial arms and bionic limbs which were to help her "develop a body image that included arms".[88] After dropping their attempts to make her body conform, her parents continued to send ambivalent messages. They regarded her as "the perfect offspring who never leaves the nest", taught her "to be independent, / to be strong, / to have my own opinions, / to earn my own living" and ignored her sexuality.[89] In section six (entitled "HOLE"), the speaker affirms her sexuality, describing how she prepared for making a video about her birth at art college which "involves being naked".[90] She expresses her worst fears of "being unlovable" and of being confronted with her friends' grotesque reactions to her body, gathering round and trying to help her insert a tampon.[91] This scene is very complex, combining elements of nightmare, violence and mockery ("they poke and push and prod / but they can't find the hole".[92] In it, the speaker confronts her readers with their own grotesque reactions when faced with descriptions of female disabled bodies. In section seven, the speaker recounts a conversation with her disabled lover who regards disability as an impassable protection shield from "a hostile world", "a guarantee against rejection", wishing, however, she were "more whole, complete, and beautiful".[93] At the beginning of the final section ("making choices / DIGNITY"), she responds to her lover's wish, affirming that "i am all these things ... / whole, complete and beautiful," arguing that "our disabilities do not guarantee freedom from fear of rejection".[94] Her expression of self-love and pride involves the creation of counter-normative concepts of embodied identity and beauty which do not transcend experiences of the fear of rejection. She states that she leaves her partner because "i accept myself as i am" and does not regard a love relationship "as security / against hurt, pain and anger".[95] In the final part of the text, Duffy appropriates lines from another poem ("After a While"), re-inscribing their expression of self-love through an affirmation of embodied difference.[96] Similar to the video in which Duffy performs as Venus de Milo, the final part of "Making Choices" is an expression of self-love through which she affirms her identity as a disabled woman.[97] As such, Duffy's video as well as her poem create a relational, non-essentialist, complex self- and body image through reparative oscillations between negative (rejection, hurt, pain, anger) and positive (dignity, self-acceptance, self-love, strength, endurance, pride, joy, pleasure, beauty) affects, emotional attitudes and experiences.[98] In contrast to her soliloquy which accompanies the video in which she performed as Venus de Milo,[99] Duffy's affirmation of embodied difference in "Making Choices" includes descriptions of experiences of "rejection", "hurt, pain and anger", but not of shame.[100] Instead, Duffy's autobiographical poem confronts readers with their shamefaced responses to disabled women's bodies (section six), affirming embodied difference and wholeness by challenging the social norms that endorse shame. Although Duffy's focus is on the individual self at the end of "Making Choices" as well as in her video, neither of these expressions should be mistaken as a representation of an essentialist, homogeneous, isolated, sovereign self. In both cases, Duffy's body becomes a site of resistance, re-inscribing the self- and body images as well as concepts of beauty that dominate societies and cultures.

4. Conclusion

I hope to have demonstrated that the autobiographical texts included in Lois Keith's anthology resist both the narrative tradition of the comic masterplot as well as the tragic model of disability. Instead of transcending pain, suffering and oppression, the texts acknowledge these experiences together with the negative affects activated by them. They expose and criticise the social causes of suffering and call for their removal. Opposing the rigid dominant concepts of normality and beauty, they generate new plot models that cannot be classified as either tragic or comic. Furthermore, the short autobiographical texts in Keith's collection produce relational, non-essentialist, counter-normative, provisional forms of identity through complex narrative oscillations between negative (anger, fear, shame, distress) and positive affects and emotional attitudes (enjoyment, interest, love, pride, hope). The majority of autobiographical texts in Keith's anthology describe the lives of women with disabilities as forms of existence which can be affirmed under favourable social conditions. Many texts (especially those by Rushworth, Begum, Mason, Duffy, Kordi and Pink) emphasise cultural difference, that is, they affirm counter-normative, multi-layered forms of identity (all authors are female and disabled, some of them are also non-white, lesbian and working-class) as well as ways of life that differ from those of non-disabled people.[101] For these reasons, they anticipate the new British social model which establishes disability as an "affirmative identity and a distinct collective movement" and which emphasises a politics of difference as well as the necessity of social change.[102] According to Alice Hall, the British model differs from the American rights-based model which focuses on the qualities of personhood disabled people share with the non-disabled part of the population. However, the autobiographical texts in Keith's anthology do not construct disability as a monolithic, exclusivist category of identity. Instead, they affirm the multiple layers of cultural difference of which disabled women's identities are composed and which connect them with other communities.

Notes

1 Couser, G. Thomas (2009). *Signifying Bodies. Disability in Contemporary Life Writing*. Ann Arbour: The University of Michigan Press, 4.

2 On the beginnings of the disability rights movement in Britain in the 1970s as well as on the foundation of the social model of disability in Britain see Thomas, Carol (1999). *Female Forms: experiencing and understanding disability*. Buckingham: Open University Press, 14. The social model asserts that it is not the individual's impairment which causes disability but that disability "is the outcome of social arrangements which work to restrict the activities of people with impairments by placing social barriers in their way" (*Ibid.*, 14). It has been criticised for its failure to acknowledge the significance of impairment, see Price, Janet, and Margrit Shildrick (2002). "Bodies Together: Touch, Ethics, and Disability." *Disability/Postmodernity: Embodying Disability Theory*. Eds. Mairian Corker and Tom Shakespeare. London, New York: Continuum, 62-63.

3 Couser (2009), 4, 6.

4 *Ibid.*, 7.

5 According to Eakin, identities are created in and through autobiographical narratives, see Eakin, Paul John (2008). *Living Autobiographically. How We Create Identity in Narrative*. Ithaca/London: Cornell University Press, x, 2.

6 On these stereotypes see Asch, Adrienne, and Michelle Fine (1988). "Introduction: Beyond Pedestals." *Women with Disabilities. Essays in Psychology, Culture, and Politics*. Eds. Michelle Fine and Adrienne Asch. Philadelphia: Temple University Press, 3.

7 Couser, G. Thomas (1997). *Recovering Bodies. Illness, Disability, and Life Writing*. Madison: University of Wisconsin Press, 183-185.

8 The tragic model of disability is criticised by Sally French and John Swain, see French, Sally, and John Swain (2008). "There but for Fortune." *Disability on Equal Terms*. Eds. John Swain and Sally French. Los Angeles, London, et al.: Sage, 7-20.

9 My classification of positive and negative affects as well as my description of the feed-back processes between them are based on Silvan Tomkins's cybernetic theory of affects, see Tomkins, Silvan (1995). "What Are Affects?" *Shame and Its Sisters. A Silvan Tomkins Reader*. Eds. Eve Kosofsky Sedgwick and Adam Frank. Durham/London: Duke University Press, 74.

10 Couser (1997), 182.

11 Christy Brown's *My Left Foot* (1954), Christopher Nolan's *Under the Eye of the Clock* (1987), John Hawkridge's *Uphill All The Way* (1991), Kamran Nazeer's *Send in the Idiots* (2006) and Daniel Tammet's *Born on a Blue Day* (2006) are examples of book-length autosomatographies written by Irish and British men. Richard Hammond wrote his autobiography in cooperation with his wife: Richard and Mindy Hammond: *On the Edge* (2007). Gohar Kordi's *An Iranian Odyssey* (1991) is a disability autobiography written by a British woman with a migrant background. For a critical discussion of the text see Mintz, Susannah B. (2005). "Dear (Embodied) Reader: Life Writing and Disability." *Women's Life Writing and Imagined Communities*. Ed. Cynthia Huff. New York: Routledge, 143-149. Joan Ross's *I Can't Walk But I Can Crawl* (2005), Leanne Grose's *Just a Step* (2008), Meg Kingston's *The Monster and the Rainbow* (2010) and Amanda Green's *My Alien Self* (2012) are examples of recent book-length autosomatographies written by British women.

12 Office for Disability Issues (2011). *Equality Act 2010. Guidance*. London: Office for Disability Issues, 4.

13 *Ibid.*, 8-9.

14 A recent TV documentary that covers autobiographical accounts of people with mental illnesses in Britain is BBC 3's "Don't Call Me Crazy", see "Don't Call Me Crazy." BBC 3 broadcast 28 June – 12 July 2013. Web. <https://www.youtube.com/watch?v=NHms2hTDuL4>. A growing number

of people share their day-to-day experiences of living with a chronic illness and disability with their audience on YouTube, see Helloim nikita (2016). "My Mental Health Story." 14 April 2016. Web. <https://www.youtube.com /watch?v=hKnI7n22Nx0>.

15 A great number of blogs cover autobiographical accounts of lives with physical and mental impairments, for example on the website "Time to Change", see Time to Change (2016). Web. <https://www.time-to-change.org.uk/personal-stories>. Some disability blogs (for example Jan Sutton's blog) use the format of diaries, see Jan Sutton: "Life after the ILF: We are all valuable enough to have a reasonable quality of life." 12 July 2015. Jan Sutton's blog. Web. <http://jansutton.blogspot.de/>.

16 On diachronic and episodic forms of autobiography see Eakin (2008), 11.

17 See Mintz, Susannah B. (2007). *Unruly Bodies. Life Writing by Women with Disabilities*. Chapel Hill: University of North Carolina Press, Couser (1997) and Couser (2009). Alice Hall's chapter on disability autobiographies focuses on US-American, South African and Japanese examples, see Hall, Alice (2014). *Literature and Disability*. London/New York: Routledge, 129-149. Campling, Jo (1981). *Images of Ourselves: Women with Disabilities Talking*. London: Routledge and Kegan Paul; Keith, Lois (ed.) (1994). *Mustn't Grumble. Writing by Disabled Women*. London: The Women's Press, 1994; and Wates, Michele, and Jane Rowen (eds.) (1999). *Bigger than the Sky. Disabled Women on Parenting*. London: The Women's Press are examples of collections of British women's disability life writing; see also Thomas (1999a), 18-24, 49-55, 76-78, 86-97 and Thomas, Carol (1999). "Parents and families: disabled women's stories about their childhood experiences." *Growing Up With Disability*. Eds. Carol Robinson and Kirsten Stalker. London: Jessica Kingsley, 85-96.

18 The recent special issue of *Life Writing* from 2016 on disability and illness memoirs is a case in point because most articles focus on American examples.

19 Asch/Fine (1988), 3.

20 *Ibid.*, 3. See also Garland-Thomson, Rosemarie (2010). "Integrating Disability, Transforming Feminist Theory." *The Disability Studies Reader*. Ed. Lennard J. Davis. New York: Routledge, 358.

21 Asch/Fine (1988), 3.

22 Garland-Thomson, Rosemarie, and Barbara Waxman Fiduccia (1999). "Introduction: Who Are Disabled Women and Girls?" *Women and Girls with Disabilities: Defining the Issues. An Overview*. Eds. Barbara Waxman Fiduccia and Leslie R. Wolfe. Washington: Center for Women Policy Studies, 3. See also Deegan, Mary Jo, and Nancy Brooks (eds.) (1985). *Women and Disability: The Double Handicap*. New Brunswick: Transaction Books; Garland-Thomson, Rosemarie (2001). *Re-shaping, Re-thinking, Re-*

defining: Feminist Disability Studies. Barbara Waxman Fiduccia Papers on Women and Girls with Disabilities. Washington: Center for Women Policy Studies.

23 Garland-Thomson/Waxman-Fiduccia (1999), 3. See also Swain, John, and Sally French (2008). "Affirming Identity." *Disability on Equal Terms.* Eds. John Swain and Sally French. Los Angeles, London, et al.: Sage, 76. On the abuse of disabled girls and boys see Higgins, Martina (2008). "The Narratives of Disabled Survivors of Childhood Sexual Abuse." *Disability on Equal Terms.* Eds. John Swain and Sally French. Los Angeles, London, et al.: Sage, 52-61. Recently, the British government has published a report on the significance of gender difference regarding disabled persons' experiences of domestic violence: "While men are at risk of, and do experience, domestic abuse, women experience more repeated physical violence, more severe violence, much more sexual violence, more coercive control, more injuries and more fear of their partner", see *Disability and domestic abuse. Risk, impact and response* (2015). London: Public Health England, 8. Web. <https://www.gov.uk/government/uploads/system/uploads/attachment_data/file/480942/Disability_and_domestic_abuse_topic_overview_FINAL.pdf>.

24 Begum, Nasa (1994). "Snow White." *Mustn't Grumble. Writing by Disabled Women.* Ed. Lois Keith. London: The Women's Press, 46-51; Polio, Suna (1994). "Being Sam's Mum." *Mustn't Grumble. Writing by Disabled Women.* Ed. Lois Keith. London: The Women's Press, 77-83.

25 Mintz (2005), 131.

26 Gilmore, Leigh (1994). *Autobiographics: A Feminist Theory of Women's Self-Representation.* Ithaca: Cornell University Press, 12.

27 Thomas (1999a), 66; Morris, Jenny (1993). "Feminism and Disability." *Feminist Review* 43, 57-70; Morris, Jenny (1998). "Feminism, Gender and Disability." Paper presented at a Seminar in Sydney, Australia www.repositoriocdpd.net:8080/bitstream/handle/123456789/673/Inf_Morris J_FeminismGenderDisability_1998.pdf?sequence=1.

28 Garland-Thomson (2010). See also Wendell, Susan (1989). "Towards a feminist theory of disability." *Hypathia* 4, 104-124.

29 Mintz (2007), 1.

30 Mintz (2005), 133, 139.

31 *Ibid.*, 133.

32 Mintz (2007), 6-7.

33 Keith (1994a), 5. See also Keith, Lois (1994). "This Week I've Been Rushed Off My Wheels." *Mustn't Grumble. Writing by Disabled Women.* Ed. Lois Keith London: The Women's Press, 62.

34 Keith (1994a), 2-3.

35 See Ann Macfarlane's poem "Watershed", which describes how the author witnessed the murder of a disabled girl who lived in the same institution for

disabled children as herself; see Macfarlane, Ann (1994). "Watershed." *Mustn't Grumble. Writing by Disabled Women*. Ed. Lois Keith. London: The Women's Press, 161-162.

36 Mintz (2007), 6.

37 On the affect system as the primary motivational system in human beings that is closely related to but distinct from the cognitive system and innately linked with the drive system see Tomkins (1995a), 34, 37, 63.

38 Paul John Eakin has argued that autobiographical identity formation neither presupposes a concept of continuous identity nor a fully intact memory which generates coherent linear narratives (Eakin 2008, 9-14). However, his concept of narrative identity emphasises the intellectual, cognitive aspects of memory as the basis of identity formation (*Ibid.*, 15). This focus is strongly visible in his analysis of Antonio Damasio's theory in which the discussion of feeling is reduced to the "feeling of knowledge", the feeling of "core consciousness" and the feeling of a single, unified cognitive experience (*Ibid.*, 75-76). The autobiographical texts in Keith's collection, however, emphasise the close connection between personal memories, affects and identity formation. In many cases, the personal experience of affects seems to be condition for a later recollection of scenes from the past and their inclusion in the narratives where they can evoke affective and emotional responses from authors and readers alike. Recently, Rosalía Baena has focused on the role of emotions in disability narratives and has emphasised their relevance in processes of storytelling but she has not drawn on Silvan Tomkins's cybernetic theory of affects, see Baena, Rosalía (2012). "The Epistemology of Difference: Narrative Emotions in Personal Stories of Disability." *The Emotions and Cultural Analysis*. Ed. Ana Marta Gonzalez. New York: Routledge, 99-114. On a call for a stronger focus on inspiration as a significant emotion in disability studies see Chrisman, Wendy L. (2011). "A Reflection on Inspiration: A Recuperative Call for Emotion in Disability Studies." *Journal of Literary and Cultural Disability Studies* 5.2, 173-184.

39 Keith (1994a), 9-10.

40 Couser (2009), 16.

41 Shakespeare, Tom (1996). "Power and prejudice: issues of gender, sexuality and disability." *Disability and society. Emerging issues and insights*. Ed. Len Barton. Harlow: Longman, 191-214.

42 Mintz (2007), 221 n. 6.

43 For a longer discussion of Keith's volume see Coogan, Thomas (2008). "The Disabled Body: Style, Identity and Life Writing." Unpublished dissertation submitted at the University of Leicester. Web. <https://lra.le.ac.uk/bitstream/2381/3958/1/2008coogantaphd.pdf>.

44 Price/Shildrick (2002), 66-67.

[45] See Keith (1994a), 5. I disagree with Coogan who argues that Keith's collection is informed by a separatist ideological approach to disability (Coogan 2008, 219).

[46] Keith (1994a), 1, 3.

[47] *Ibid.*, 5.

[48] *Ibid.*, 6.

[49] In her poem, Jaihn Makayute expresses openly that she does not regard her disability as a condition to be proud of: Makayute, Jaihn (1994). "Freedom Fighter." *Mustn't Grumble. Writing by Disabled Women.* Ed. Lois Keith. London: The Women's Press, 187-188. See also Coogan (2008), 237.

[50] *Ibid.*, 5, 7.

[51] *Ibid.* 8-9. See Keith's expression of anger about inaccessible facilities (Keith 1994b), 64-65, 69-70.

[52] *Ibid.*

[53] On the reparative responses to anger see Tomkins, Silvan (1995). "Anger." *Shame and Its Sisters. A Silvan Tomkins Reader.* Ed. Eve Kosofsky Sedgwick and Adam Frank. Durham/London: Duke University Press, 218-219.

[54] Rushworth, Roz (1994). "Mustn't Grumble." *Mustn't Grumble. Writing by Disabled Women.* Ed. Lois Keith. London: The Women's Press, 40.

[55] *Ibid.*, 40.

[56] *Ibid.*, 38.

[57] *Ibid.* 39.

[58] Smith, Sidonie, and Julia Watson (2010). *Reading Autobiography. A Guide for Interpreting Life Narratives.* 2nd ed. Minneapolis: The University of Minnesota Press, 72-73.

[59] Eakin (2008), x, 76-78. Eakin writes: "our life stories are not merely *about* us but in an inescapable and profound way *are* us […]. […] narrative is not merely about self, but is rather in some profound way a constituent part of self" (*Ibid.*, x, 2).

[60] *Ibid.*, 2.

[61] Rushworth (1994), 40.

[62] *Ibid.* 40.

[63] Couser (2009), 14.

[64] French/Swain (2008), 7-8. On legal decisions that declared disabled lives to be lives that are not worth living see Morris, Jenny (1991). *Pride Against Prejudice. Transforming Attitudes to Disability.* London: The Women's Press, 39-63. On the conditions that make disabled people's lives worth living see Sutton (2015a) and Sutton (2015b).

[65] Thomas (1999a), 14-15.

[66] Couser (1997), 183-185. In many ways, the texts in Keith's collection anticipate John Swain and Sally French's affirmative model of disability which

counteracts the dominant tragic and predominantly personal model of disability (Swain/French [2008], 65, 68; French/Swain [2008], 8).

67 Mason, Pam (1994). "Agoraphobia: Letting Go." *Mustn't Grumble. Writing by Disabled Women*. Ed. Lois Keith. London: The Women's Press, 112.

68 On the metaphorical paradigm which associates disability with immorality and demonic possession see Couser (2009), 21-23.

69 *Ibid.*, 106.

70 *Ibid.*, 109.

71 *Ibid.*, 112.

72 Einat Avrahami has shown that authors of illness autobiographies express a high awareness about the contingency and changeability of the self- and body images of they create, see Avrahami, Einat (2007). *The Invading Body: Reading Illness Autobiographies*. Richmond: University of Virginia Press, 15.

73 *Ibid.*, 111.

74 *Ibid.*, 112.

75 Sedgwick, Eve Kosofsky, and Adam Frank (1995). "Shame in the Cybernetic Fold: Reading Silvan Tomkins." *Shame and Its Sisters. A Silvan Tomkins Reader*. Eds. Eve Kosofsky Sedgwick and Adam Frank. Durham and London: Duke University Press, 22; Sedgwick, Eve Kosofsky (2003). *Touching Feeling. Affect, Pedagogy, Performativity*. Durham and London: Duke University Press, 36; Tomkins, Silvan (1995). "Shame-Humiliation and Contempt-Disgust." *Shame and Its Sisters. A Silvan Tomkins Reader*. Eds. Eve Kosofsky Sedgwick and Adam Frank. Durham/London: Duke University Press, 138-139.

76 Tomkins (1995b), 138.

77 O'Connor, Marian: "Ellie O'Sullivan." *The Guardian* 25 November 1999: n. pag. Web. <https://www.theguardian.com/news/1999/nov/25/guardian-obitua ries3>.

78 O'Sullivan (1994), 13-14. See also "Appendix." *Mustn't Grumble. Writing by Disabled Women*. Ed. Lois Keith. London: The Women's Press, 199-214, 208-210.

79 *Ibid.*, 14.

80 *Ibid.*, 17.

81 Bindel, Julie (2011): "Nasa Begum Obituary." *The Guardian* 22 June 2011: n. pag. Web. <https://www.theguardian.com/society/2011/jun/22/nasa-begum-obituary>.

82 Begum (1994), 46, 50.

83 *Ibid.*

84 *Ibid.*, 46-48.

85 *Ibid.*, 50.

[86] *Ibid.*

[87] *Ibid.*

[88] Duffy, Mary (1994). "Making Choices." *Mustn't Grumble. Writing by Disabled Women*. Ed. Lois Keith. London: The Women's Press, 25-31, 25, ll. 7-8, 9, 12, 14, 15, 20.

[89] *Ibid.*, 26 ll. 5-9, 13-16, 19-22, 25.

[90] *Ibid.* 30, ll. 9-13.

[91] *Ibid.* 30, ll. 17-21.

[92] *Ibid.* 30, ll. 19-20.

[93] *Ibid.*, 30, ll. 1-3, 11-14.

[94] *Ibid.* 31, ll. 1-3.

[95] *Ibid.* 31 ll. 7-15.

[96] *Ibid.* 31, ll. 16-24.

[97] The video is included in a documentation by Sharon Snyder and David Mitchell: Snyder, Sharon, and David Mitchell: *Vital Signs: Crip Culture Talks Back*. Web. 1995. <https://www.youtube.com/watch?v=P23ov4QVHhI>.

[98] On a discussion of reparative oscillations between negative and positive affects that can generate novel self-images in psychotherapy see Sedgwick (2003), 128.

[99] On a discussion of Duffy's video see Garland-Thomson, Rosemarie (2005). "Dares to Stares: Disabled Women Performance Artists and the Dynamics of Staring." *Bodies in Commotion: Disability and Performance*. Eds. Carrie Sandahl and Philip Auslander. Ann Arbor: University of Michigan Press, 37.

[100] In the soliloquy, Duffy asks: "How come I always felt ashamed when answering those big staring eyes and gaping mouths?", inverting the process of stigmatization by turning the viewer into a grotesque figure (Snyder/Mitchell 1995).

[101] Rushworth (1994), 40; Begum (1994), 51.

[102] Hall (2014), 8; Swain/French (2008), 69, 70-71, 75.

Bibliography

"Appendix." (1994). *Mustn't Grumble. Writing by Disabled Women*. Ed. Lois Keith. London: The Women's Press, 199-214.

Asch, Adrienne, and Michelle Fine (1988). "Introduction: Beyond Pedestals." *Women with Disabilities. Essays in Psychology, Culture, and Politics*. Eds. Michelle Fine and Adrienne Asch. Philadelphia: Temple University Press, 1-38.

Avrahami, Einat (2007). *The Invading Body: Reading Illness Autobiographies*. Richmond: University of Virginia Press.

Baena, Rosalía (2012). "The Epistemology of Difference: Narrative Emotions in Personal Stories of Disability." *The Emotions and Cultural Analysis*. Ed. Ana Marta Gonzalez. New York: Routledge, 99-114.

Begum, Nasa (1994). "Snow White." *Mustn't Grumble. Writing by Disabled Women*. Ed. Lois Keith. London: The Women's Press, 46-51.

Bindel, Julie (2011). "Nasa Begum Obituary." *The Guardian* 22 June 2011: n. pag. Web. 19 December 2016 <https://www.theguardian.com/society/2011/jun/22/nasa-begum-obituary>.

Campling, Jo (1981). *Images of Ourselves: Women with Disabilities Talking*. London: Routledge and Kegan Paul.

Chrisman, Wendy L. (2011). "A Reflection on Inspiration: A Recuperative Call for Emotion in Disability Studies." *Journal of Literary and Cultural Disability Studies* 5.2, 173-184.

Coogan, Thomas (2008). "The Disabled Body: Style, Identity and Life Writing." Unpublished dissertation submitted at the University of Leicester. Web. 19 December 2016 <https://lra.le.ac.uk/bitstream/2381/3958/1/2008coogantaphd.pdf>.

Couser, G. Thomas (1997). *Recovering Bodies. Illness, Disability, and Life Writing*. Madison: University of Wisconsin Press.

--- (2009). *Signifying Bodies. Disability in Contemporary Life Writing*. Ann Arbor: The University of Michigan Press.

Deegan, Mary Jo, and Nancy Brooks (eds.) (1995). *Women and Disability: The Double Handicap*. New Brunswick: Transaction Books.

Disability and domestic abuse. Risk, impact and response (2015). London: Public Health England. Web. 19 December 2016 <https://www.gov.uk/government/uploads/system/uploads/attachment_data/file/480942/Disability_and_domestic_abuse_topic_overview_FINAL.pdf>.

"Don't Call Me Crazy." BBC 3 broadcast 28 June – 12 July 2013. Web. 19 December 2016 <https://www.youtube.com/watch?v=NHms2hTDuL4>.

Duffy, Mary (1994). "Making Choices." *Mustn't Grumble. Writing by Disabled Women*. Ed. Lois Keith. London: The Women's Press, 25-31.

Eakin, Paul John (2008). *Living Autobiographically. How We Create Identity in Narrative*. Ithaca/London: Cornell University Press.

French, Sally, and John Swain (2008). "There but for Fortune." *Disability on Equal Terms*. Eds. John Swain and Sally French. Los Angeles, London, et al.: Sage, 7-20.

Garland-Thomson, Rosemarie (2001). *Re-shaping, Re-thinking, Re-defining: Feminist Disability Studies. Barbara Waxman Fiduccia Papers on Women and Girls with Disabilities*. Washington: Center for Women Policy Studies.

--- (2005). "Dares to Stares: Disabled Women Performance Artists and the Dynamics of Staring." *Bodies in Commotion: Disability and Performance.* Eds. Carrie Sandahl and Philip Auslander. Ann Arbor: University of Michigan Press, 30-41.

--- (2010). "Integrating Disability, Transforming Feminist Theory." *The Disability Studies Reader.* Ed. Lennard J. Davis. New York: Routledge, 353-373.

---, and Barbara Waxman Fiduccia (1999). "Introduction: Who Are Disabled Women and Girls?" *Women and Girls with Disabilities: Defining the Issues. An Overview.* Eds. Barbara Waxman Fiduccia and Leslie R. Wolfe. Washington: Center for Women Policy Studies.

Gilmore, Leigh (1994). *Autobiographics: A Feminist Theory of Women's Self-Representation.* Ithaca: Cornell University Press.

Hall, Alice (2014). *Literature and Disability.* London/New York: Routledge.

Helloim nikita (2016). "My Mental Health Story." 14 April 2016. Web. 19. December 2016 <https://www.youtube.com/watch?v=hKnI7n22Nx0>.

Higgins, Martina (2008). "The Narratives of Disabled Survivors of Childhood Sexual Abuse." *Disability on Equal Terms.* Eds. John Swain and Sally French. Los Angeles, London, et al.: Sage, 52-61.

Keith, Lois (1994a). "Introduction." *Mustn't Grumble. Writing by Disabled Women.* Ed. Lois Keith. London: The Women's Press, 1-9.

--- (1994b). "This Week I've Been Rushed Off My Wheels." *Mustn't Grumble. Writing by Disabled Women.* Ed. Lois Keith London: The Women's Press, 61-72.

Kordi, Gohar (1994). "I Was Touched." *Mustn't Grumble. Writing by Disabled Women.* Ed. Lois Keith. London: The Women's Press, 122-128.

Macfarlane, Ann (1994). "Watershed." *Mustn't Grumble. Writing by Disabled Women.* Ed. Lois Keith. London: The Women's Press, 161-162.

Makayute, Jaihn (1994). "Freedom Fighter." *Mustn't Grumble. Writing by Disabled Women.* Ed. Lois Keith. London: The Women's Press, 187-188.

Mason, Pam (1994). "Agoraphobia: Letting Go." *Mustn't Grumble. Writing by Disabled Women.* Ed. Lois Keith. London: The Women's Press, 106-112.

Mercer, Sophie (2015). "Living With Depression, My Story." 12 February 2015. Web. 19 December 2016 <https://www.youtube.com/watch?v=dO-153uksq4&t=200s>.

Mintz, Susannah B. (2005). "Dear (Embodied) Reader: Life Writing and Disability." *Women's Life Writing and Imagined Communities.* Ed. Cynthia Huff. New York: Routledge, 131-152.

--- (2007). *Unruly Bodies. Life Writing by Women with Disabilities.* Chapel Hill: University of North Carolina Press.

Morris, Jenny (1991). *Pride Against Prejudice. Transforming Attitudes to Disability*. London: The Women's Press.

--- (1993). "Feminism and Disability." *Feminist Review*, 43, 57-70.

--- (1998). "Feminism, Gender and Disability." Paper presented at a Seminar in Sydney, Australia <www.repositoriocdpd.net:8080/bitstream/handle/123456789/673/Inf_MorrisJ_FeminismGenderDisability_1998.pdf?sequence=1>.

O'Connor, Marian (1999). "Ellie O'Sullivan." *The Guardian* 25 November 1999: n. pag. Web. 19 December 2016 <https://www.theguardian.com/news/1999/nov/25/guardianobituaries3>.

Office for Disability Issues (2011). *Equality Act 2010. Guidance*. London: Office for Disability Issues.

O'Sullivan, Ellie (1994). "The Visit." *Mustn't Grumble. Writing by Disabled Women*. Ed. Lois Keith. London: The Women's Press, 13-17.

Pink, Janice (1994). "What Happened To You?" *Mustn't Grumble. Writing by Disabled Women*. Ed. Lois Keith. London: The Women's Press, 74-76.

Polio, Suna (1994). "Being Sam's Mum." *Mustn't Grumble. Writing by Disabled Women*. Ed. Lois Keith. London: The Women's Press, 77-83.

Price, Janet, and Margrit Shildrick (2002). "Bodies Together: Touch, Ethics, and Disability." *Disability/Postmodernity: Embodying Disability Theory*. Eds. Mairian Corker and Tom Shakespeare. London, New York: Continuum, 63-75.

Rushworth, Roz (1994). "Mustn't Grumble." *Mustn't Grumble. Writing by Disabled Women*. Ed. Lois Keith. London: The Women's Press, 38-40.

Sedgwick, Eve Kosofsky (2003). *Touching Feeling. Affect, Pedagogy, Performativity*. Durham and London: Duke University Press.

---, and Adam Frank (1995). "Shame in the Cybernetic Fold: Reading Silvan Tomkins." *Shame and Its Sisters. A Silvan Tomkins Reader*. Eds. Eve Kosofsky Sedgwick and Adam Frank. Durham and London: Duke University Press, 1-28.

Shakespeare, Tom (1996). "Power and prejudice: issues of gender, sexuality and disability." *Disability and society. Emerging issues and insights*. Ed. Len Barton. Harlow: Longman, 191-214.

Smith, Sidonie, and Julia Watson (2010). *Reading Autobiography. A Guide for Interpreting Life Narratives*. 2nd ed. Minneapolis: The University of Minnesota Press.

Snyder, Sharon, and David Mitchell (1995). *Vital Signs: Crip Culture Talks Back*. Web. 19 December 2016 <https://www.youtube.com/watch?v=P23ov4QVHhI>.

Sutton, Jan (2015a). "Jan's story: I began to feel like a human being again." Save the Human Rights Act. 30 April 2015. Web. 19 December 2016

<https://savetheact.uk/jans-story-i-began-to-feel-like-a-human-being-again/>.

--- (2015b). "Life after the ILF: We are all valuable enough to have a reasonable quality of life." 12 July 2015. Jan Sutton's blog. Web. 19 December 2016 <http://jansutton.blogspot.de/>.

Swain, John and Sally French (2008). "Affirming Identity." *Disability on Equal Terms*. Eds. John Swain and Sally French. Los Angeles, London, et al.: Sage, 65-78.

Thomas, Carol (1999a). *Female Forms: experiencing and understanding disability*. Buckingham: Open University Press.

--- (1999b). "Parents and families: disabled women's stories about their childhood experiences." *Growing Up With Disability*. Eds. Carol Robinson and Kirsten Stalker. London: Jessica Kingsley, 85-96.

Time to Change (2016). Web. 19 December 2016 <https://www.time-to-change.org.uk/personal-stories>.

Tomkins, Silvan (1995a). "What Are Affects?" *Shame and Its Sisters. A Silvan Tomkins Reader*. Eds. Eve Kosofsky Sedgwick and Adam Frank. Durham/London: Duke University Press, 33-74.

--- (1995b). "Shame-Humiliation and Contempt-Disgust." *Shame and Its Sisters. A Silvan Tomkins Reader*. Eds. Eve Kosofsky Sedgwick and Adam Frank. Durham/London: Duke University Press 133-178.

--- (1995c). "Anger." *Shame and Its Sisters. A Silvan Tomkins Reader*. Eds. Eve Kosofsky Sedgwick and Adam Frank. Durham/London: Duke University Press, 197-233.

Wates, Michele, and Rowen Jade (eds.) (1999). *Bigger than the Sky. Disabled Women on Parenting*. London: The Women's Press.

Wendell, Susan (1989). "Towards a feminist theory of disability." *Hypathia* 4, 104-124.

Cyprian Piskurek (Dortmund)

I Support Therefore I Am: British Football Fan Autobiographies

Taking a look at the United Kingdom's best seller lists, the genre of (auto)biography seems to be as popular as never before. In this section, the subgenre of the sports star biography has also proved extremely successful, and – as one would expect concerning the nation's most popular sport – within this field footballers' life stories, of which around 20% are biographies, take the lion's share. Although readers are entitled to question whether some of these autobiographies have not been scripted by ghost writers and fully qualify as such, it comes as no surprise that the life stories of players like Wayne Rooney and Steven Gerrard, or managers like Sir Alex Ferguson and José Mourinho, have sold hundreds of thousands of copies. This essay will, however, focus on an only circumstantially related phenomenon that has developed over the past twenty years on the margins of this genre: the football fan autobiography.

While the inflationary output of memoirs by more or less well-known 'stars' may have already jeopardised the long-held conviction that autobiographies represent life narratives of noteworthy and publicly important people, the new phenomenon of fan life writing has turned this conception around. The authors of fan memoirs are people who have not put down in writing how they came to be politicians, film stars or artists, but people who chose a supposedly profane cultural practice, the lifelong support of a football team, as the framework to narrate life stories that are not necessarily extraordinary. At first glance one might think that these authors aim at their proverbial fifteen minutes of fame, but these texts also fill Raymond Williams's ground-breaking verdict that "culture is ordinary"[1] with life: if the blurring of the once elitist privilege of autobiography[2] had become more and more visible with the postmodern advent of autobiographies by Big Brother or talent show participants, then the publication of fan autobiographies seems a consistent next level.

1. The Altered Perception of Football Fandom

That football fans would self-consciously construct a version of themselves that is defined by their being football fans is relatively new; although football had been firmly established as the most popular game in Britain for more than a hundred years, Rogan Taylor assessed in 1992 that "Football supporters in general were in a position where they needed to gain the 'respect' of wider society".[3] From a factual perspective this might be understandable, as "sports are irrelevant to practically every important matter in society";[4] *watching* sports and devoting time, money and energy to this might seem even more extravagant than practising. However, this perception gradually changed in the 1990s, since when the relationship between sport and its fans

> has been most notably affected by the interrelated processes of increased involvement of big businesses in the running and organization of sport, the importance and influence of the mass media, processes of globalization, and more generally the changing nature of audiences in late-capitalist society.[5]

Fandom was no longer regarded as just a passive form of consumption and incorporation, but it was acknowledged that the cultural practices of fans held a potential for agency and resistance. Being a fan was thus increasingly seen as speaking "a generally understood language through which one's identity is communicated",[6] and football fans themselves gained some form of awareness that their fandom was not necessarily limited to the Saturday activity of going to the stadium, but would in many instances permeate followers' everyday lives and thus prove constitutive of their social identities. This new-found consciousness of self was a prerequisite for the urge to represent these selves in writing.

Alongside this new self-awareness, another reason for the genesis of football fan autobiographies is certainly the general interest in football, which has increased massively over the past twenty-five years. Football had always been one of the most popular pastimes in the United Kingdom, and the moniker 'the people's game' clearly attests to that. But while one loved watching football one did hardly write about the practice of watching until the early 1990s. When the FIFA World Cup 1990 in Italy presented in its televised form a colourful and carnivalesque alternative to the bleak and violent state of British football in the 1980s, this paved the way for a reformed public perception of the game. With large-scale stadium renovations and with the breakaway of the twenty-two top clubs in the new Premier League, professional football established itself as a modern and shiny product. Consequently, lucrative sponsoring and television deals helped the league to become the richest in the world, with spiralling wages and ticket prices. This gentrified version of a sports that was hitherto firmly rooted in a working-class following increasingly attracted new supporters (or customers, as the managing directors liked to call them), and this new demographics meant a move towards the mainstream of society.

This development also brought about the evolution of literary representations of the game. There had been sporadic examples of football in novels, as in J.B. Priestley's *The Good Companions* or Robin Jenkins's *The Thistle and the Grail* and occasional non-fiction accounts of the football world that went beyond sports journalism, like Arthur Hopcraft's *The Football Man*. But this was nothing compared to the wave of texts that would flood the country in the 1990s and 2000s, and that commentators would subsume under the heading New Football Writing. This genre was characterised by an emphasis on the seminal role of fans as part of the game, and these portrayals of fandom stood in marked opposition to the stigmatisation of fans as predominantly violent hooligans in previous decades. The work that started this new interest in football writing and which became a role model that many later works would aspire to emulate was Nick Hornby's debut *Fever Pitch*, released in 1992. Hornby's autobiographical text was revolutionary in its focus on fandom – something that no one writing about British football had attempted before.

2. A Role Model for Autobiographical Fan Texts

Hornby's style of writing in *Fever Pitch* had certainly been influenced by the alternative football fanzine scene of the 1980s, from which periodical publications like *When Saturday Comes* originated that tried to reclaim the game from the opposing forces of hooliganism and commercialism. Hornby's debut also has an older predecessor in the form of U.S. author Frederick Exley's 1968 work *A Fan's Life*. Subtitled "a fictional memoir", this story about the narrator's lifelong infatuation with American Football, in particular the New York Giants, deliberately juggles with autobiography's ambiguous relationship to fiction. In a note to the reader that precedes the actual narrative, Exley pre-emptively claims that what follows is not necessarily autobiographical: "Though the events in this book bear similarity to those of that long malaise, my life, many of the characters and happenings are creations solely of the imagination."[7] This disclaimer might stem from legal precaution, especially in the light of the negative portrayal of the protagonist's estranged wife, which is "drawn freely from the imagination and adhere[s] only loosely to the pattern of my past life".[8] However, the unusual detail of Exley's disclaimer rather raises doubts about the fictional character of the book than washing them away. In asking "to be judged as a writer of fantasy",[9] Exley rather calls on readers to wonder whether he is a writer of thinly veiled autobiography. There are other hints within the text which intentionally corroborate this, like the name Ex, by which his friends call the narrator's father.

The actual memoir then presents episodes from the narrator's life that relate to his obsession with "my delight, my folly, my anodyne, my intellectual stimulation":[10] the New York Giants. His teaching job, his friendships, his marriage and his relationship with his kids are interpreted within the framework of his fandom for the American Football team. This is a strategy which Hornby applies almost twenty-five years later in *Fever Pitch*. Here it is (English) football and North London club Arsenal F.C., but the relationship between an individual life and the devotion to a sports team is the driving force behind the narrative. Hornby's book shies away from an explicit disclaimer whether *Fever Pitch* is autobiographical or not, but neither does it claim to be fiction. A good way into the text there are hints that the narrator's first name is Nick and that his surname is Hornby, but the ease with which the text was transformed into a fictional film years later (with Hornby writing the script) shows the fragility of such labels. The book, whose first edition was subtitled "A Fan's Life", was, however, advertised as non-fiction, and few readers would have got the impression that this was all part of the author's imagination. In terms of narratology, some commentators have insisted, though, that *Fever Pitch* is closer to fiction than to autobiography.[11] As a consequence, the relationship between Nick Hornby the author, Nick Hornby the narrator and Nick Hornby the protagonist remains as problematic as in many examples of 1960s New Journalism in the tradition of Norman Mailer or Gay Talese.

This complex relation between author, narrator and protagonist, which we readily accept for fictional texts, is superficially deemed to be absent in autobiography: since the author claims to narrate his own life story based on biographical truth, the autobiographer seems to speak more directly to readers than any of the three instances in fiction – that is the illusory pretension of autobiographies. However, critics have long since postulated that biographical truth cannot exist, or can at least not be represented, as the text form relies on subjective selection and interpretation: "Every autobiography is a work of art [...]; it does not show us the individual seen from outside in his visible actions but the person in his inner privacy, not as he was, not as he is, but as he believes and wishes himself to be and to have been."[12] This dilemma of representation that every writer of autobiography faces is "governed by the technical demands of self-portraiture",[13] even if this suggests the impossibility to reconcile the real referent with his or her life story. Such an argument would then culminate in "the claim that the public persona behind the first-personal pronoun might have no necessary connection with the autobiographer, as long as the story coheres with enough widely known facts".[14] *Fever Pitch*, which with its spotlight on selected matches and episodes in the protagonist's life stylises itself as almost fiction, could then be seen as a text that self-consciously problematises the fallacies of the genre and plays with the pretended boundary between fiction and the non-fictional autobiography.

Fever Pitch tells a life story, and its almost completely linear chronology follows the established conventions of autobiography. The narrative begins with the protagonist's childhood, follows him through adolescence and young adulthood and then concludes in maturity. This might seem ironic, given Hornby's age (mid-30s) when he published the book, but in terms of his fandom, what he interprets as maturity and a form of closure is reached at a rather early biological age. The focus is on the formation and development of the self, and it is especially in times of crisis that the defining moments of this self-formation occur. The decisive aspect, both in formal and in narrative terms, is that two parallel stories are narrated and related to one another, because the narrator's personal life is intertwined with the fate of his beloved Arsenal. This becomes obvious in the titles of the book's short chapters, each of which is complemented by a subtitle referencing a specific Arsenal match.[15] The chapter about the 1972 power cuts, "Social History" is thus narrated alongside "Arsenal v Derby, 29.2.72",[16] and his first meeting with his father's new wife and stepson, "A New Family" becomes "Arsenal v Wolves, 15.8.72".[17] This conveys a clear message that football is not only an integral part of the narrator's life, but it is the principle that structures his memory and his perception of how he has arrived at the state of selfhood from which he writes. Decisive life events are thus not related in their own right, but only gain their place in the narrative by their reference to a football match. On the other hand, football is not just an unimportant addendum to the expected milestones within an autobiography, but a goal by Charlie Nicholas stands on equal footing with the end of a relationship or the decision to see a therapist. Arsenal's first cup win that Hornby witnesses or his move to a different standing section at Highbury are thus privileged as rites of passage over the obtaining of a university degree, while other matches just trigger the memory of a non-football event. At first glance, it might even seem as if the football matches are used as a mnemonic tool in order to master the unstructured realm of memory; however, the detail with which football matches or rituals are retold suggests that non-football events might equally serve as stepping stones for the remembrance of all things Arsenal. Commenting on this interaction between the two life spheres in his memory, the protagonist muses: "The first time I was best man at a wedding? We lost 1-0 to Spurs in the FA Cup third round, and I listened to the account of Pat Jennings' tragic mistake in a windy Cornish car park".[18] And a little later he presents the following analysis of the way his memory works:

> These scores and scorers and occasions are of a piece: Pat's slip against Tottenham was not, of course, as important as Steve's wedding, but to me the two events have now become intrinsic and complementary parts of some new and different whole.[19]

Even if Hornby narrates life events that are not about football at first glance, he regards all of them in relation to his permanent involvement with the game. In a disarming moment of self-diagnosis the narrator of

Fever Pitch analyses that it is impossible to have a conversation with him that does not revolve around football; he claims that he may try, but in his head he will immediately connect all utterances to matches, seasons, individual players or managers: "I now accept that football has no relevance to the Falklands conflict, the Rushdie affair, the Gulf War, childbirth, the ozone layer, the poll tax, etc., etc., and I would like to take this opportunity to apologise to anyone who has had to listen to my pathetically strained analogies."[20] At such an early point in the narrative this serves as a disclaimer how the perception of the narrator's life is permeated by football and how it centres on his fandom, because despite the aforementioned apology *Fever Pitch* is all about analogies between football and the narrator's life story. This ties in with Philippe Lejeune's oft-quoted definition that autobiography is a "retrospective prose narrative produced by a real person concerning his own existence, focusing on his individual life, in particular on the development of his personality".[21] The ground-breaking achievement of Hornby's book is the claim that this development of the narrator's personality is dominated by the fate of Arsenal F.C., instead of parents, tutors, peer groups or other guiding principles. *Fever Pitch* makes this quite explicit by emphasising that Arsenal takes over an anchor point for the young protagonist's development of his self that his divorced parents cannot provide. While Hornby's estranged father takes the young boy to his first match, thus fulfilling a conservative English father-son ritual, the illusion that this will bring Hornby sr. and Hornby jr. closer together does not last long. Soon the young boy starts going to matches on his own and both the absence of the father and the femininity of his fatherless household are postulated as reasons for the appeal of the stadium's "overwhelming *maleness*".[22] Arsenal is able to absorb Hornby so quickly because it provides a degree of stability that the young boy is lacking at home. Thus, the football crowd takes over the role of constructing notions of gender and self.

3. 'Fever Pitch' and Its Aftermath

Hornby's text caused a landslide in the production of fan texts, both fictional and non-fictional; this was certainly helped by the newfound mainstream appeal of football mentioned above, but also by the success of the 'confessional' genre which showed male authors' possible ways "to unburden themselves in print in the 1990s".[23] The coming out of the low cultural closet which Hornby had so cleverly achieved inspired a lot of writers, or even led to people taking up writing at all. The German website blutgraetsche.de, which has been defunct since the year 2005, implemented a section that translated into "Hornby's heirs" (*Hornbys Erben*) where subscribers to the site could publish their own episodes about football seasons and how they affected their respective lives. Books were published by authors like Colin Shindler, whose *Manchester United Ruined My Life* (1998) even quotes *Fever Pitch* as an inspiration,[24] Alan Edge's *Faith of Our Fathers* (1997) or Mark Hodkinson's *Believe in the Sign* (2007). Several other books that assessed the state of the game in the 1990s would at least devote substantial episodes to autobiographical accounts and the making of the respective writer as a fan; examples would be Nick Varley's *Parklife* (1999), Jim White's *You'll Win Nothing with Kids* (2007) or Colin Irwin's *Sing When You're Winning* (2006). In the same vein as Hornby's text (and as conventional autobiographies), these exclusively male narratives would start with the narrator's introduction to the game, ideally as young boys and taken by their fathers, chart the emancipation from older peers by attending matches on their own, follow the protagonists into maturity and often disillusionment with the ways of modern football, and in some cases even come full circle as these narrators introduce their own children to football. None of these texts focuses solely on match days, but the life that the narrators lead outside of the game is related alongside their development as fans; the teams might change – from Liverpool F.C. (Edge) to Rochdale at the other end of the spectrum (Hodkinson) – but the general stance towards football fandom as a meaningful and long-neglected cultural practice would be found in all of these examples.

In other words, the interpretation of fandom as the ordering principle of a (post)modern life is central, and this seems consistent and logical. Older models of autobiographies also singled out such principles which guided the narrative development of the life represented: Saint Augustine's autobiography interprets his life in terms of his spiritual development, Sigmund Freud's autobiography relates his way in the medical profession, and Bill Clinton's life story obviously tries to explore how he became a politician and statesman. It is with hindsight that the autobiographer defines within each discursive framework how his development of self gains narrative significance. While in earlier examples this equalled the extraordinariness of such well-known personalities, Hornby and his successors focus on the ordinariness of what has defined them: the everyday practice of football fandom.

In addition to their focus on individual life stories and the relevance of football fandom for the development of forms of selfhood, these autobiographies fulfil a political function as well: in emphasising their personal development alongside the development of a general history of English football, these narratives articulate severe discontents with the route that modern football has taken. The years 1989 to 1992 can be regarded as a watershed in the recent history of football in the British Isles because certain developments during these years paved the way for a pivotal restructuring of hierarchies in professional football. In April 1989, the stadium catastrophe at Sheffield Wednesday's Hillsborough ground cost 96 lives when Liverpool supporters were crushed against fences and trampled to death before an FA Cup semi-final. Tragically, this was the third major disaster affecting English football within a relatively short time span, after two other catastrophes in May 1985: the Bradford stadium fire, in which 56 people died, and the disaster at Brussels' Heysel stadium, in which Liverpool supporters were involved and which caused the death of 39 mostly Italian fans. These stadium catastrophes showed that the crumbling grounds or policing practices needed drastic improvement.

In the wake of Hillsborough, Lord Justice Taylor was thus called on to investigate the state of British football and issued two documents which are widely known as the Taylor Report. Taylor suggested turning all grounds in the top divisions into all-seater stadiums in order to promote more orderly crowds, and he also called for close-circuit television to prevent incidents of hooliganism. Contrary to Taylor's warnings, these costly renovations were partly financed by supporters because clubs raised their ticket prices drastically. This also coincided with the colourful presentation of the World Cup 1990 in Italy, which painted an alternative vision of what football on television could look like: this stood in marked contrast to the hooligan-ridden pictures of empty terraces in 1980s England. Moreover, the top clubs in England had for some time voiced their dissatisfaction with the democratic distribution of television money among the 92 clubs in the top four divisions. In the wake of the Taylor Report and Italia '90 this led to the breakaway of the top division from the socialist principles of the Football League. In turn, the new Premier League was set up in 1992 and managed to negotiate a lucrative television deal. All these developments led to a reorganisation of English football: hooligans were driven from the stadium, but large groups of traditional working-class supporters as well. The Premier League developed into a shiny global product, but the ensuing 'hyper-commodification' of the game alienated many supporters of old. Nick Hornby's *Fever Pitch* ironically also came to be seen as a collaborator in this move of football into the mainstream. Hornby's text was certainly praised for giving football fans a voice and showing new forms of expressing fandom, but on the other hand the "literaturisation of soccer"[25] also signified the appropriation of traditional working-class practices by the learned elites.

New Football Writing has in many instances shown a tendency to comment on these developments by establishing a more or less strict binary opposition between a more authentic and democratic pre-Taylor past and a corrupted and commodified post-Taylor present. Authors like Irwin evoke sensual recollections of smells and tastes of old football – Bovril and Wagon Wheels[26] – in order to contrast this with the sanitised *nouveau riche* prawn sandwiches that are on offer in the expensive executive boxes. Such romanticised versions of football in the 1960s or 1970s can be found in most of these examples; as nostalgia signifies not just a misty-eyed version of the past but just as much a present lack which can be remedied by nostalgic recollections, these texts contribute to discourses of resistance against the neoliberal excesses in modern football. It is telling that fan autobiographies position themselves within this discourse: as no fan autobiography has been written yet that begins after 1992, the crucial *rites de passage* date back into the 'golden age' of fandom in the 1960s or 1970s.

Hornby's or Hodkinson's, Irwin's or Shindler's socialisation via football thus took place in a rougher, more masculine and more proletarian setting than contemporary football would be able to provide. This is crucial for the narrated life stories of these fans because the whole course of their passage through a fan's life is measured against the certainties of their fan childhood. It is a common pattern that autobiographies fall back on these certainties and stabilities of a young age because of the reassuring structure this provides. The inevitable orientation to the autobiographer's past highlights the passage of time and life writing attempts to counteract the ephemerality of time by the illusion that remembering might capture that which is irrecoverably lost. Autobiographies therefore employ "nostalgia which transfers desire to the past, which makes the past the locus of a longed-for but irretrievable unity".[27] With regard to fan autobiographies, this is a form of collective nostalgia which might explain why a group of football fans sees the necessity to narrate their fan lives after the seminal changes of the 1990s: the very real contemporary structures and constraints around fandom urge the authors into a form of symbolic resistance by narrating those experiences that they feel have been taken away from them, and that coming generations will not be able to experience in the same way.

4. Writing Hooligans

This need to recreate a lost past is just as crucial for a subgenre that has developed within New Football Writing, and that is the hooligan autobiography. Here, former organised hooligans who were involved in major football riots of the 1970s and 1980s retell the stories of their battles and how they came to make their way within the strict hierarchies of hooligan culture. Early examples, like Colin Ward's *Steaming In. Journal of a Football Fan* appeared in the late 1980s, but it was not until New Football Writing had made its mark that a wave of similar texts was published from the late 1990s onwards. Steve Redhead has identified 91 such books released between the years 1987 and 2010,[28] and there are small publishing houses like Milo Books or John Blake Publishing that have specialised in such memoirs of violence. These texts, which carry titles like *Booted and Suited*, *Want Some Aggro?*, or *Bring Out Your Riot Gear – Hearts Are Here. Gorgie Aggro, 1981-1986* follow a "helplessly predictable"[29] formula: a former hooligan who is now in his forties or fifties narrates how he came to be attracted to violence at football matches, how he came to be accepted by the hard men on the terraces and made his way up within the hierarchy, and how his group then stood their ground in the legendary battles with opposing firms. While the fact that the narrators are all 'retired' and hooliganism is allegedly a thing of the past suggests that these are confessions of people who have turned their back on violence, the retelling of these fights also displaces the battles from the football grounds onto book pages; the "'hit and tell'"[30] aspect of these books, which is meant to establish one's own group as tougher and better than its former rivals, offers itself as a strategy to those who have become either too old to fight, or who have been driven away from organised violence by the discourses of regulated football in the Premier League era.

It is nonetheless more than telling that the accounts of former battles are integrated into a coherent life story, which is meant to provide an explanatory framework for why the books' subjects turned to violence. This type of literature is "unashamedly partisan and often boastful, recounting up to 40 years of aggressive male football fandom",[31] and these books overflow with class markers that stylise the young boys' neighbourhoods as working-class breeding grounds for tough forms of masculinity. The disadvantaging that these writers present as a recurring motif in their lives functions as an important mode of characterisation: at the lower end of the social hierarchy, bullied by aggressive fathers and peers, the protagonists did not falter and learned to fight back. In fact, the hooligan autobiography as a subgenre represents another form of regained agency: hooligans, whose subculture had been ostracised by society and who had become the modern folk devils of the 1970s and 1980s thus challenged the privilege of who would interpret their cultural practices. Cass Pennant writes in one of the most successful of these books: "Spurred on by the inaccuracies in accounts of the exploits of West Ham's InterCity Firm in various publications, I decided to use my unique position as a former member of the I.C.F. to set the record straight."[32] These inaccuracies, in the hooligans' eyes, are produced by "boffins from universities around the country [who] were all too quick to jump on the hooligan bandwagon", publishing "nonsensical myths about football behaviour".[33]

Of course, these authors – in a similar way as nonviolent writers of New Football Writing – benefit from changes in the publishing industry. It has become much easier to find small specialist houses or self-publish one's work, often as books-on-demand or e-books. Nonetheless, one should not underestimate the symbolic resistance that the adoption of the elitist genre of autobiography represents for a subculture as stigmatised as hooliganism. These are texts that often diverge from traditional models of autobiography, as some of them aim to narrate not just an individual life story but that of a close-knit group as well, which is why the respective hooligan crew is frequently mentioned in the title. However, these texts certainly focus on the individual account of the narrator, even if the narration emphasises his dissolution into the group. Compared to Nick Hornby and other non-violent fan autobiographies, the hooligan texts refer much less frequently to the actual game of football but rather highlight group rituals and confrontations with other fans on their travels to and from the stadium. Despite these differences, football fandom functions in both sets of texts as more than just a cultural practice. It is the central marker of identity for the protagonists and serves as a projection screen for the development of their selves. Football is vital for the way the protagonists negotiate and re-define their affiliations with class or with peer groups, and mostly – especially in hooligan autobiographies – this is interpreted against the background of conservative models of masculinity. Cass Pennant's autobiography, for example, is the one text that goes beyond the foreseeable pattern of such narratives when the story relates how a coloured son of immigrants made his way within the racist hooligan structures.

Even the fan autobiographies by Hornby and the likes have to be interpreted in the discursive framework of football hooliganism. Since spectator violence in the 1970s and 1980s had brought football and its spectatorship into disregard and turned football fans into social pariahs, New Football Writing and the alternative fanzine scene saw it as their obligation to challenge the unholy alliance between fandom and violence by adding critical voices from within fan cultures. When Prime Minister Margaret Thatcher had succeeded in stigmatising football fans per se as criminal and mindless thugs, non-violent fans had to make themselves heard in order to call these automatic labelling reflexes into question. In this regard, fan life writing gained even more significance, as "autobiographical self-narration becomes an avenue for challenging stigma by telling stories – stories that might redefine a self that has been publicly mortified". [34] In other words, although Hornby playfully pathologises his obsessive fandom these fan narratives also serve as an attempt at explaining and rescuing fandom's reputation from readymade and socially dominant verdicts. Autobiographies by hooligans complicate this thesis because they work in two directions: on the one hand, these narratives are at least partly marketed as confessions by retired or even reformed hooligans, which means that their having left violence behind makes these stories – to some extent – socially acceptable. On the other hand, the glorification of past misbehaviour fortifies and reestablishes essentialist assumptions about football fandom and hooliganism. The stigma of deviance is thus rather celebrated than thwarted.

5. Conclusion: Reading Fan Autobiographies

A discussion of fan autobiographies would be incomplete without raising questions about the audience of these texts. If Redhead has identified more than 90 hooligan autobiographies and, in the wake of *Fever Pitch*, dozens of 'regular' fans have published similar autobiographies, there must be a considerable market for this topic. However, Nick Hornby's fan memoir remains the only critically acclaimed success in this regard. This is certainly due to the general quality of the writing of an author who would afterwards consolidate his reputation with bestselling fiction books, and also to the innovation that the choice of topic meant back in 1992. But Hornby's text about his life with Arsenal would hardly have succeeded if it had not struck a chord with football fans in general. One of the timeless qualities of *Fever Pitch* is the fact that fans of other teams still felt interpellated by the book because they might not care about Charlie George or Arsenal's 1989 team, but the text spoke on so many levels to those supporting other colours: football fans could recognise themselves in the rituals and the devotion, in the sensual and the senseless of fandom that Hornby described.[35] And even fans in other countries, or members of later fan generations would laud the book for constructing a much more meaningful portrayal of the species of the football fan than was available before; when German second division team Union Berlin renovated its stadium a few years ago, a quotation from *Fever Pitch*[36] was painted onto a wall behind the turnstiles in order to greet visiting fans with one of Hornby's universal truths about football fandom.

Hornby's successors would, however, share the fate that the groundwork of lifting fandom onto a new, socially acceptable level had already been laid by *Fever Pitch.* Texts like Shindler's *Manchester United Ruined My Life* would continue the route that *Fever Pitch* had suggested, but they would basically remain just another version of the original text with a focus on another club and another fan – yet, the basic pattern would still hold. And for the wave of hooligan autobiographies one would expect that a book about a West Ham United firm would not win much credit with Millwall fans, and that the principle of football rivalries as such would limit each book's potential audience; some of the comments that can be found on amazon.com for these books prove that the partisanship of club affiliation makes it impossible to neutrally assess the text at hand for many people who follow the genre. And even if hooligan memoirs represent an extreme version of New Football Writing, this limitation that each author's colours seem to place on potential readers rings true for many fan autobiographies as well. It seems as if those who, by their indubitable devotion to a certain club, have earned the credentials to write a fan autobiography have by this very devotion already alienated those who follow different colours – which is one of the paradoxes of football writing.

In conclusion, the autobiographical writings of football fans signal a clear break from much more prominent celebrity life stories. Especially in the world of sport, where autobiographies call on public fantasy about sporting stars, it marks a democratising process if the focus of life writing can also be shifted onto fans. This ties in with the still rather recent general recognition that fandom is significant – for both fans and those studying fans. The ordinariness of fan stories, however, bears the potential of a much more equal relationship between text and reader, as these narratives call on readers' own experiences. If "the autobiographical relationship depends on the narrator's winning and keeping the reader's trust in the plausibility of the narrated experience and the credibility of the narrator",[37] then the fan autobiography can activate potential readers' experiences in a way that the detached life stories of celebrities can often only aspire to. Moreover, in referring to the more or less universal cultural practices of a group, fan autobiographies in their multiplicity as a genre can articulate political discontents about the state of fandom in a more authoritative way than individual life stories are able to. In all of these cases, the connection between experience and identity is deemed so essential that the autobiographical mode seems ideally suited to articulate the altered perception of fandom's significance.

Notes

1 Williams's 1958 essay "Culture is ordinary" provided a programmatic ethos for the emerging discipline of British Cultural Studies; interestingly enough, the essay begins with an autobiographical account that introduces readers to the ordinariness of the culture that surrounded the young Welshman.

2 Cf. Smith, Sidonie, and Julia Watson (2010). *Reading Autobiography. A Guide for Interpreting Life Narratives*. 2nd ed. Minneapolis and London: University of Minnesota Press, 3.

3 Taylor, Rogan (1992). *Football and its Fans. Supporters and their relations with the game, 1885-1985*. Leicester, London and New York: Leicester University Press, 179.

4 Cashmore, Ellis (2010). *Making Sense of Sports*, 5th edition. Abingdon and New York: Routledge, 479.

5 Crawford, Garry (2004). *Consuming Sport. Fans, sport and culture*. London – New York: Routledge, 7.

6 Sandvoss, Cornel (2005). *Fans. The Mirror of Consumption*. Cambridge and Malden: Polity, 3.

7 Exley, Frederick (1968). *A Fan's Life: a fictional memoir*. New York: Random House, n.pg.

8 *Ibid.*

9 *Ibid.*

10 *Ibid.*, 2.

11 Cf. Bentley, Nick (2008). *Contemporary British Fiction*. Edinburgh: Edinburgh University Press, 118.

12 Gusdorf, Georges (1980). "Conditions and Limits of Autobiography." Trans. James Olney. *Autobiography: Essays Theoretical and Critical*. Ed. James Olney. Princeton: Princeton University Press, 45.

13 de Man, Paul (1979). "Autobiography as De-facement." *Modern Language Notes* 94.5, 920.

14 Cowley, Christopher (2015). "Introduction: What Is a Philosophy of Autobiography?" *The Philosophy of Autobiography*. Ed. Christopher Cowley. Chicago and London: University of Chicago Press, 7.

15 Several Cambridge United games, whom Hornby adopts as a second team during his university career, form the exception.

16 Cf. Hornby, Nick (1992). *Fever Pitch*. London: Gollancz, 59.

17 *Ibid.*, 67.

18 *Ibid.*, 73.

19 *Ibid.*, 74.

20 *Ibid.*, 11.

21 Cf. Lejeune, Philippe (1982). "The autobiographical contract." *French Literary Theory Today*. Ed. Tzvetan Todorov. Cambridge et al.: Cambridge University Press, 193.

22 Hornby (1992), 19, italics in original.

23 Redhead, Steve (1997). *Post-Fandom and the Millennial Blues. The Transformation of Soccer Culture*. London: Routledge, 90.

24 Cf. Shindler, Colin (2012). *Manchester United Ruined My Life* ([1]1998). London: Headline, 5.

25 Redhead (1997), 88.

26 Cf. Irwin, Colin (2006). *Sing when you're Winning. Football Fans, Terrace Songs and a Search for the Soul of Soccer*. London: Deutsch, 20, 283-285.

27 Anderson, Linda (2004). *Autobiography*. Abingdon and New York: Routledge, 72.

28 Cf. Redhead, Steve (2010). "Little Hooliganz: The Inside Story of Glamorous Lads, Football Hooligans and Post-Subculturalism." *Entertainment and Sports Law Journal* 8.2. Web. N. pag. <https://www2.warwick.ac.uk/fac/soc/law/elj/eslj/issues/volume8/number2/redhead/> 10 January 2016, 12, Appendix 1. Some of the 91 titles listed by Redhead are not autobiographies, though, but were written by journalists after interviewing former hooligans.

29 Dart, Jon (2008). "Confessional tales from former football hooligans: a nostalgic, narcissistic wallow in football violence." *Soccer & Society* 9.1, 45.

30 Redhead, Steve (2004). "Hit and Tell: a Review Essay on the Soccer Hooligan Memoir." *Soccer & Society* 5.3, 394.

31 Redhead (2010), 4.

32 Pennant, Cass (2002). *Congratulations. You have just met the I.C.F.*, London: John Blake, 16.

33 Pennant, Cass and Martin King (2005). *Terrace Legends*, London: John Blake, 4.

34 Yar, Majid (2014). *Crime, Deviance and Doping. Fallen Sports Stars, Autobiography and the Management of Stigma*. Basingstoke and New York: Palgrave Macmillan, vii.

35 Cf. Ochsner, Andrea (2009). *Lad Trouble. Masculinity and Identity in the British Male Confessional Novel of the 1990s*. Bielefeld: Transcript, 164.

36 "Ich verliebte mich in den Fußball, wie ich mich später in Frauen verlieben sollte: plötzlich, unerklärlich, unkritisch und ohne einen Gedanken an den Schmerz und die Zerrissenheit zu verschwenden, die damit verbunden sein würden." "I fell in love with football as I was later to fall in love with women: suddenly, inexplicably, uncritically, giving no thought to the pain or disruption it would bring with it." (Hornby [1992], 15).

37 Smith and Watson (2010), 34.

Bibliography

Anderson, Linda (2004). *Autobiography*. Abingdon and New York: Routledge.

Bentley, Nick (2008). *Contemporary British Fiction*. Edinburgh: Edinburgh University Press.

Cashmore, Ellis (2010). *Making Sense of Sports*. 5th edition. Abingdon and New York: Routledge.

Cowley, Christopher (2015). "Introduction: What Is a Philosophy of Autobiography?" *The Philosophy of Autobiography*. Ed. Christopher Cowley. Chicago and London: University of Chicago Press, 1-21.

Crawford, Garry (2004). *Consuming Sport. Fans, sport and culture*. London – New York: Routledge.

Dart, Jon (2008). "Confessional tales from former football hooligans: a nostalgic, narcissistic wallow in football violence." *Soccer & Society* 9.1, 42-55.

de Man, Paul (1979). "Autobiography as De-facement." *Modern Language Notes* 94.5, 919-930.

Edge, Alan (1997). *Faith of Our Fathers. Football as a Religion*. Edinburgh: Mainstream.

Exley, Frederick (1968). *A Fan's Life: a fictional memoir*. New York: Random House.

Gusdorf, Georges (1980). "Conditions and Limits of Autobiography." Trans. James Olney. *Autobiography: Essays Theoretical and Critical*. Ed. James Olney. Princeton: Princeton University Press, 28-48.

Hodkinson, Mark (2007). *Believe in the Sign*. Hebden Bridge: Pomona.

Hornby, Nick (1992). *Fever Pitch*. London: Gollancz.

Irwin, Colin (2006). *Sing when you're Wining. Football Fans, Terrace Songs and a Search for the Soul of Soccer*. London: Deutsch.

Lejeune, Philippe (1982). "The autobiographical contract." *French Literary Theory Today*. Ed. Tzvetan Todorov. Cambridge et al.: Cambridge University Press. 192-222.

Ochsner, Andrea (2009). *Lad Trouble. Masculinity and Identity in the British Male Confessional Novel of the 1990s*. Bielefeld: Transcript.

Pennant, Cass (2002). *Congratulations. You have just met the I.C.F.*, London: John Blake.

Pennant, Cass and Martin King (2005). *Terrace Legends*, London: John Blake.

Redhead, Steve (1997). *Post-Fandom and the Millennial Blues. The Transformation of Soccer Culture*. London: Routledge.

--- (2004). "Hit and Tell: a Review Essay on the Soccer Hooligan Memoir." *Soccer & Society* 5.3, 392-403.

--- (2010). "Little Hooliganz: The Inside Story of Glamorous Lads, Football Hooligans and Post-Subculturalism." *Entertainment and Sports Law*

Journal 8.2. Web. N. pag. <https://www2.warwick.ac.uk/fac/soc/law/elj/eslj/issues/volume8/number2/redhead/> 10 January 2016.

Sandvoss, Cornel (2005). *Fans. The Mirror of Consumption.* Cambridge and Malden: Polity.

Shindler, Colin (2012). *Manchester United Ruined My Life* ([1]1998). London: Headline.

Smith, Sidonie, and Julia Watson (2010). *Reading Autobiography. A Guide for Interpreting Life Narratives.* 2nd ed. Minneapolis and London: University of Minnesota Press

Taylor, Rogan (1992). *Football and its Fans. Supporters and their relations with the game, 1885-1985.* Leicester, London and New York: Leicester University Press.

Varley, Nick (2000), *Parklife. A search for the heart of football*, London et al.: Penguin.

Ward, Colin (2004). *Steaming In. Journal of a Football Fan* ([1]1989). London et al.: Pocket Books.

White, Jim (2007), *You'll Win Nothing With Kids. Fathers, Sons and Football*, London: Little, Brown.

Williams, Raymond (1993), "Culture is ordinary ([1]1958)." *Studying Culture: an introductory reader.* Eds. Ann Gray and Jim McGuigan. London and New York: Arnold, 5-14.

Yar, Majid (2014). *Crime, Deviance and Doping. Fallen Sports Stars, Autobiography and the Management of Stigma.* Basingstoke and New York: Palgrave Macmillan.

Gabriele Linke (Rostock)

Between Ethnography and Ecology: Autobiographical Narratives from Rural Scotland since the Second World War

1. Introduction

The edge of the sea, the croft in the hills, the Highland farm and the edge of the wilderness are the places that have featured centrally in much of the published autobiographical writing from rural Scotland since the 1960s. If we read the cues in the titles, this scenery appears to have been populated by characters such as the hired lad, crofter, island wife, island nurse and the shepherd, who are the narrators whose self-images informed the titles of their life stories. Both the places and the people evoke images of a rural idyll firmly rooted in narratives of the romantic Highland experience and the pastoral tradition. This is the first impression that arises from a survey of the autobiographies that were published or re-published in recent years (cf. bibliography), and it does not come as a surprise because autobiographers, like other writers, tend to write themselves into a certain tradition by making use of existing narrative patterns and genre elements which are then creatively modified, adapted and combined. Numerous social discourses in and on the non-urban parts of Scotland, especially the popular discourses produced by the tourism industry, tap into the Highland myth of heather-clad hills and glens, burns and lochs, abundant wildlife, sparse human settlement and, generally, unspoilt nature, with the odd local character fitting smoothly into the scene.

But will autobiographical narratives, which by definition represent the writer's attempt to give a truthful account of his or her own life as subjectively remembered and reconstructed,[1] be limited to a version of the romantic idyll of the Highlands and islands as promised by their titles? Hardly, because titles do not only – somehow – represent the contents of a book but also place it in a complex and compartmentalised literary marketplace that requires the classification of a book so that it may reach its prospective readers. Broad classifications such as 'non-fiction', 'autobiography' and 'Scottish' are usually suggested by all kinds of paratexts such as subtitles, reviews and introductions as well as the shelf labels in the bookstores. However, a closer inspection of the peculiar narrative plottings and the historically specific emplacements of each life story reveals a considerable diversity of both personal experiences and modes of writing.

In this paper it will be argued that, beside each author's own course of life, changes in the ways of rural life – that is, ethnographic observations – as well as increasingly explicit reflections on the relations between humans and nature – that is, ecological ones – are major features of recent autobiographical narratives set in rural Scotland. The argument will follow ideological twists and turns in the public discourses on rural Scotland since the Second World War, starting with observations on the rapid change in farming due to mechanisation and attempts to preserve the memory of the old ways of farming and the folk life that was an inseparable part of it. In the 1950s, there was the beginning of a movement (back) towards crofting as a response to Cold War anxieties and an expression of the ecological stirrings that have become ever stronger since the 1960s. Autobiographers have increasingly reflected not only on work on a farm or croft but also on their relationship with the Scottish wilderness, and with nature in general, especially the weather. Alongside these shifts, new types of narrators have entered the field. While up to the 1950s, autobiographical writers on this subject tended to be native to rural Scotland,[2] recording its traditional way of life, the Scottish Highlands and islands have since then attracted a growing number of incomers, some of which found their experience worth writing about.

Before these lines of argument can be developed in detail, the concepts of ethnographic and ecological life writing will be given some consideration, followed by a survey on the texts that will be entered into the line of argument. A more detailed analysis of selected examples of strongly ethnographic and strongly ecological life narratives will illustrate the complexity of the issues with which these two discursive strands are interwoven, but also the shifts of emphasis and focus that can be detected in these narratives.

2. Ethnographic and Ecological Life Writing: Some Reflections on Genre

The basis of this study is formed by autobiographical texts, which are, according to Philippe Lejeune, "retrospective prose narratives written by a real person concerning his own existence", in which the narrator puts the focus on the story of his individual life.[3] Lejeune's "autobiographical pact" between writer and reader signals a shared understanding that autobiographical texts as a genre are anchored in a world of reference beyond the text.[4] I am here referring to Lejeune's definition of autobiography, a complex and coherent written narrative, because it captures the core of autobiographical texts in general and is also applicable to autobiographical subgenres such as childhood memoir and the more hybrid texts discussed in my study. The focus of a narrative, for example, may not be consistently on the author's own life, but other criteria established by Lejeune do apply. When the more general terms 'life writing' and 'life narrative' are used occasionally, this is done for stylistic reasons and refers to autobiographical forms of life writing, not biographical ones.

However, scholars in the field have agreed that the boundaries of the genre to, for example, fiction are unstable and that, despite autobiography's claim to facticity, the constructive character of memory and the process of remembering renders subjective any personal narrative reconstruction of past experiences. Furthermore, any autobiographer's motivation for writing down, or having persons record, their memories may influence the selection of the details of the story, from places and people to anecdotes and photos. Emplotment, emplacement and, thus, autobiographical subgenres may also be shaped by such motivations.

Since any individual life is embedded in the natural and built environment as well as social practices, autobiographers must select experiences, choose a focus, a central plot and place(s) and model their own story. Because the focus of this paper is on rural Scotland, the two sides of the emplacement of life narratives, that is, the natural and the social environments, will be at the centre of the analysis.

When autobiographers record their observations on social practices such as local customs and structures of communal life, they assume the role of an ethnographer. The understanding of the term auto-ethnography as it is used here diverges from its academic definition as a "qualitative, self-focused, and context-conscious method" employed by ethnographic researchers who render their own lived experiences and the "social phenomena involving self" the subject of interpretation.[5] The authors of the autobiographical texts considered here have not been researchers who were academically trained in ethnographic methods with a clear project in mind. Rather than being "narratives of field work experiences",[6] their life writing, I argue, becomes ethnographic in that they devote time and space to the description of social phenomena such as family and kinship relations, parenting, grief, customs and rituals, which are common subjects of ethnographic work. However, the ethnographic elements in autobiographical writing are usually not "thick descriptions" in the sense that Clifford Geertz suggests as a means to interpret cultures.[7] Since autobiographers tend to describe social phenomena only as part of memorable experiences and as observations that may be of interest to readers, neither their observations nor their own role are subjected to academic scrutiny. Thus it may be more appropriate to categorise the autobiographical texts considered here as autobiographies with ethnographic elements or ethnographic autobiographies, that is, "life narratives of ethnographic interest".[8]

In some cases, however, the recording of memories of life in rural communities does become the dominant purpose of autobiographical narratives. This happens in particular in times of socio-cultural change when a specific way of life is rapidly disappearing and social scientists, historians, anthropologists and the like set out to record life narratives of ethnographic interest in an attempt to preserve and acknowledge people's vanishing ways of life. In the second half of the 20th century, such efforts aimed, for example, at working-class life in the tenements of Edinburgh and Glasgow before the slum clearances of the 1950s and 1960s[9] but also covered the lives of the rural population.[10] In Billy Kay's project *Odyssey*[11] as in several other cases, the intention was to chronicle the experiences of working people who would not usually have written them down. These publications share their interest in the lives of common, and often marginalised, people with postcolonial ethnographic-autobiographical projects that served to give the (former) subalterns a voice and acknowledge their ways of life.[12]

While some autobiographies foreground the narrators' locatedness in social networks and cultural practices as well as their roles as observers and chroniclers, others are more concerned with their relations to nature and non-human life, giving up the "anthropocentric premise of traditional life writing" and opening the text to include the human interrelatedness with the non-human environment, acknowledging the "non-autonomy" of the self.[13] In such writing, the world is not limited to society but includes the ecosphere.[14] This kind of ecological life writing taps into a variety of long-established textual traditions, including writing about the pastoral, the wilderness and relations with animals, but also the picturesque aesthetic – issues that, according to Greg Garrard, establish the subject of ecocriticism.[15] Although the ecological or eco-autobiographies considered here are not necessarily ecocritical in that they criticise the human impact on the environment, there will occasionally be references to the destructive impact of human activity on the environment because it is almost impossible to write about the physical environment without commenting on damages and noticing losses.

Agricultural activities such as crofting and farming assume a particularly contested place in writings about the non-human environment. As Garrard points out, agriculture can be seen as "both the cause and symptom of an ancient alienation from the earth" because the farm is supposed to bring fruit out of the struggle against nature and the mastery of it, and not as nature's gift.[16] More recently, however, in a time of high urbanisation, farming and crofting have increasingly been re-interpreted as a way of life close to nature, and supposedly in harmony with it. Similarly, the boundaries between wilderness and cultivated land seem to be perceived as much fuzzier than the binary opposition of wilderness v. cultivated land suggests, and wild and domestic animals mix on the croft. It will be subject to debate to what extent an autobiographical text by a crofter can dissolve such boundaries and restore a rural idyll.

3. Autobiographical Narratives from Rural Scotland: Survey and Selection

The autobiographies selected were published between 1960 and 2015, covering life in rural Scotland from the Second World War to the early 21st century, with some harking back to childhood and youth before the war. One group of texts comprises those that describe the changing working lives of agricultural labourers, the 'hired lads'. David Kerr Cameron's *The Cornkister Days: A Portrait of the Land and Its Rituals* (2008 [1984]), set in the North-East Lowlands of Scotland, is only partially autobiographical but draws on a variety of other texts, literary and historical, to give a detailed description of farming and life in farming towns, following changes in technology and society from the 1930s to the 1980s. His piece on his childhood memories, "The Cottar's Bairn" (1996), also harks back to the 1930s and 1940s. The narrative of *The Hired Lad* (2010 [1993]) by Iain Campbell Thomson starts in 1947 and represents only a segment of his life, that is, his years as a young "itinerant farm worker" (ix) in Stirlingshire until he was offered the opportunity to go to college on a scholarship.

Iain R. Thomson's *Isolation Shepherd* (2010 [1983]) covers a similarly short period from 1956 up to the early 1960s when Loch Monar was included in the hydro-electric power scheme for Scotland and flooded. During those years, he and his family lived in remote Glen Strathfarrar tending sheep and running a croft.

Narratives of crofting life have also been written by crofters' wives. The autobiography establishing this tradition is probably Katharine Stewart's *A Croft in the Hills*, first published in 1960, with the ninth reprint in 2014. It is the story of an English couple who buy a croft at Abriachan and live there for several years. Since then, more women who, with their families, left England for crofting in Scotland have recorded their experiences and observations, always bringing the curiosity and keen eye of the outsider to the crofting community. A similar but more recent narrative of a family leaving England for a Scottish island is Judy Fairbairns' *Island Wife: Living on the Edge of the Wild*, first published in 2013.

Although Mary J. MacLeod, an English nurse, does not turn into a crofter's wife, she is, like Fairbairns and Stewart, fed up with life in the South of England so that she and her husband easily fall in love with a croft house on a Hebridean island and move there in 1969 to stay for most of the 1970s. In 2012, she publishes her memories of this time and her observations on the Hebridean way of life under the title *The Island Nurse*.

Life on the Outer Hebrides is also subject of Christina Hall's *To the Edge of the Sea: Schooldays of a Crofter's Child* (1999). Her perspective is quite different because she writes about island life as an insider and covers her childhood on the Outer Hebrides and later her secondary schooling in a convent and school in Fort William. Writing about the 1950s, she also records island traditions and reflects on changes effected by post-war policies and the advent of tourism.

Finally, John Lister-Kaye's *Song of the Rolling Earth: A Highland Odyssey*, first published in 2003, with more than ten reprints by 2014, will be discussed. Lister-Kaye spent his childhood in England but moved to the Highlands in the early 1970s, making a living and earning a reputation as a natural history guide and nature writer. In 1976, he founded Aigas Field Centre, which has offered environmental education to groups[17] from all over the world ever since. He is the author of several books that combine natural and local history, nature observation and autobiographical elements. His life writing is strongly ecological and, at times, ecocritical.

This list of autobiographical texts certainly does not claim to be comprehensive but it may, however, allow glimpses at both the variety and the recurring themes of life writing about rural Scotland. A group of texts that has not been considered here are travellers' autobiographies such as Duncan Williamson's *The Horsieman* and Jess Smith's *Jessie's Journey*. Although travellers sometimes worked on farms and spent much time travelling country roads, their focus is not primarily on rural life, which is why they will not be discussed here.

4. Ethnographic Autobiography: Commemorating Farming Life before Industrialisation – a Lament?

Life in rural communities and the character of agricultural labour have been fundamentally affected by industrialisation and the use of machines in particular. The transformation started in the nineteenth century but accelerated after the Second World War. In autobiographical narratives about the mid-twentieth century, change is a recurring theme, as, for example, in Iain Campbell Thomson's life narrative:

> My story is set in the years immediately following the Second World War, when farm mechanisation, particularly in the south of the country, was gathering momentum. However, many farms in Scotland, where fields were small, the terrain difficult and cash for investment in short supply, were slow to change, and [...] I chronicle events on just such a small mixed farm in Stirlingshire [...].[18]

Thomson's "love affair with the land" (ix) began in his years as an itinerant farm worker. Looking for a job, he went to the hiring fair in Glasgow's horse market and was hired immediately by the Stirlingshire farmer with whom he spent the next few years till he received a grant to go to college. On the farm, he lived in a bothy, a "squalid accommodation for unmarried farmtoun workers"[19] without any mod cons, but reflecting on his own remembering, he finds that "the passage of time lends enchantment to one's memories" (*Ibid.*). Although the joy of working with horses and the smell of "the sweat drifting back from a fine pair of Clydesdales" dominate his memories of that time, he also has memories of his "hands painfully chapped with the cold and the endless days walking behind harrows" (*Ibid.*). In his "Postscript" (164-166), he reminisces on the drudgery of ploughing in winter and the different forms of ploughs; furthermore, he summarises the principles of farming, the rotation of land use, the seasons of agricultural work and the work done manually, concluding with his hope that his story will have enlightened younger readers and been shared with older readers remembering "a time when the cart horse was a daily companion in a hard but satisfying way of life" (166). For himself, however, he claims that, when tractors and combines appeared, "[t]here was little for it but to learn new skills and join the revolution", although "the basics of farming don't change" (*Ibid.*).

Thomson is fully aware that he sometimes reached for the "rose-tinted spectacles" (*Ibid.*), as the anecdotes he relates about his time as a hired lad are mainly happy, often funny and always involve much social interaction. He describes activities such as the Gartmore and Dalmary ploughing competition, potato picking, hand-milking, harvest time, haystacking, new horses, pranks played on people, entertainments such as visits to pub, cinema, ice cream parlour and dances in the schoolroom, negotiating wages, courtship and the daily life on a farm, including food, clothes and routines. Therefore, his narrative is strongly auto-ethnographic in that he is describing social phenomena involving the self, but preserving the memory of a bygone way of life. Agricultural work as portrayed by Thomson is a social affair always involving the collaboration of people, with animals, and horses in particular, playing a significant albeit decreasing role.

For him, memories of his happy years as a footloose and fancy-free young lad coincide with memories of his learning the many facets of farming skills before the onset of large-scale mechanisation, resulting in the glorification of both youth and traditional farm work. Thomson also gets to know intimately rural life at that time, and especially the – hierarchical – social order, as he remembers his first invitation to the farmer's parlour as the crossing of a social barrier (107) and his realisation that the barrier of class lay between him and farmers' daughters.[20]

A different, more elegiac tone sounds through David Kerr Cameron's *The Cornkister Days*. Cameron, as a child in the 1930s and youngster in the 1940s, witnessed the old farming traditions in the North-East Lowlands of Scotland. In his opening sentence, "[t]hey are gone from the land, those men I once knew", he bemoans the disappearance of the last generation of pre-mechanisation agricultural labourers, which he further describes as follows:

> Theirs was the society of the Clydesdale horse and the hired man. It was a society of folk dominated by hard work and the sixmonthly Sacrament Sunday though, for all that, the man who travelled the stallion round the spring touns crept quietly into the maidservant's bed and was not made unwelcome.[21]

Cameron, like Thomson, links this era to the horse and the hired man and emphasises hard work as well as sociability and sometimes relatively free contact between the two sexes. However, he also acknowledges even more than Thomson that it was a class society where the hired man, the cottar and the tenant farmer were at the mercy of the laird. It has to be pointed out, though, that Cameron, although speaking from his own experience in his childhood and youth, writes social history rather than an autobiographical account of country life because after the Second World War, he became a journalist. Attempting a detailed description of the rural way of life before mechanisation, he thus draws on literature, ballads and other sources.

While Thomson adds a postscript to his narrative, Cameron concludes with "Laments for a Lost Landscape" (284-298), in which he mourns the vanishing of the men of the land and of the old folk culture and rituals that marked the seasons and traditions. He considers the Second World War to be the watershed after which agri-business and agri-technology took over and the old ways of "working *with* nature" gave way to "working *on* nature", which he obviously resents as "it may in the end be unwise" (297). The relationship with the land plays a role here as in Thomson's narrative and indicates that ethnographic observation may also be directed at the relationship of a society with its non-human environment. Their concern about the consequences of industrial agriculture gives Thomson's and Cameron's texts an almost ecocritical slant.

Cameron's "The Cottar's Bairn", published after *The Cornkister Days*, is a more strongly autobiographical piece about his childhood, in which he re-works the main themes of his earlier writing in a much more personal way: the hard-working men, the distinctive characters, the importance of horses, the rituals, the close-knit communities, the sociability and deep humanity of people in the farm touns, and the precarious life and frequent moving, or "flitting", of the families of hired men. In his childhood memories, he also locates himself in history, calling himself a child "born to straddle two cultures, the old and the new" and "the last generation to know the ballad as well as the plough".[22] This self-description appears to summarise the motivation of his generation for their ethnographic writing on farming life: Having known the old ways and seen them disappear, they feel the obligation to preserve their heritage and record what they, in their youth, experienced as a rich and fulfilling way of life that was doomed to disappear.

The third male autobiographer who writes about crofting life in the 1950s is Iain R. Thomson, who remembers his years as a shepherd on a remote croft in Glen Strathfarrar. His story covers the history of the glen and its families, the seasons of work on the croft, the vagaries of the weather, his dealings with domestic and wild animals, and hunting and fishing expeditions, but it usually provides anecdotes and descriptions of animals and activities rather than reflections.

It is only in his "Epilogue" that he meditates on changes in the way of life, naming 1960 as the watershed year for Glen Strathfarrar because it marks the beginning of "physical change and altered human attitudes" as well as the departure from "an essentially class-based Victorian life style" with the advent of "a supposed egalitarianism in matters of countryside access and land usage".[23] Thomson, like the other authors, emphasises that traditionally, people had to work with the elements, not against them, but that the coming of hydro-electricity despoiled the glen and expressed the new attitude that the "taming of the glen" was an achievement (221). In contrast to others, however, he finds that fewer and fewer families want to live in a remote environment and more and more are satisfied by TV documentaries on the wilderness. Finally, he demands that humans approach the natural environment not with planning and science but with care, "affection and environmental morality" (226), thus closing on an ecocritical stance.

5. The Shifting Meanings of Crofting: Between Ethnography and Ecology

The crofters' autobiographical texts discussed here have been written by women, except for the one by Iain R. Thomson. Christina Hall's memories of her "schooldays as a crofter's child" show the characteristics of a childhood memoir such as strong sensory impressions and a focus on family and schooling, but it falls neither in the paradisiacal nor the unhappy childhood category.[24] Rather, its strength lies in the detailed description of the social environment, including many elements of an auto-ethnography of Hebridean life after the Second World War. Like the previously discussed texts, Hall's testifies to the awareness that the way of life experienced by the young author has vanished.

Hall addresses many aspects of Hebridean life in the post-war years such as life on the croft, home entertainments and storytelling, schooling and the inevitable corporal punishment (about which she has "no hang-ups"),[25] food, transportation and the crofters' work, including ritual activities and customs such as Hogmanay celebrations and first footing, seasonal peat cutting and Games Day. Furthermore, she writes about "being farmed off to the aunties at an early age" (35), that is, being given away to live with two maiden aunts on another island (first

Benbecula, then Barra) for all of her elementary school years, presenting it as a normal decision by parents to grant their child good educational chances – one of the aunts was a teacher and headmistress – but also to relieve the crammed conditions in the small croft house of a family with six children.

One episode may illustrate Hall's ethnographic approach. At the age of nine, one day she runs away from her aunts only to travel home to attend a cousin's wedding. Over several pages, Hall describes the three-day event of a traditional Hebridean wedding, from the wedding eve ('The Day of the Chickens') through the wedding day to the 'house wedding' for the helpers, and with much detail about the wedding as a "social minefield", the miracle of catering, the presents, etc., not to forget the obligatory fight (36-41). Hall concludes her description with, "[s]o that is how Highland weddings have been reported" and compares it with her own three-day wedding, but also points out that "[n]ow things are different", that either young people live together without formalities, or they get married on the mainland or have an island wedding at a local hotel and restaurant so that food-related customs such as the chicken day have disappeared (41). Like the world of agricultural work, the world of local customs has been transformed since the post-war years.

Hall confirms the importance of her ethnographic memories, emphasising, "I'm so glad I was there, so early in my life, to see it done in the old way" (*Ibid.*). Similar to farm work, the social customs were generally communal activities, with particular functions for different groups of people, broad participation, etc., which is also expressed clearly in the case of funerals, which Hall describes in, again, some detail (67-69). Later on, when she is at school in Fort William, crofting life enters her world through the letters from her father, but here and there, she also slips in a critical comment on the changes, observing, for example, that "[n]ow, on the island most of the milk, bread and coal come from the shops, while acres of arable land lie fallow and cows are conspicuous by their rarity, as are peat stacks" (91). The subgenre of the childhood memoir lends itself perfectly to Hall's auto-ethnographic project, the relevance of which seems to arise from her distance to childhood and her awareness as an adult that she witnessed an era of island life that has vanished but the memories of which need to be passed on.

In Hall's, a Hebridean islander's, text, her ethnographic interest is paramount and reflections on nature are rare, usually just marking the place of some activity as in the case of her arrival in Barra with her aunts (29). In contrast, the autobiographical texts by those female authors who were born and raised in England but later settled in rural Scotland express a stronger concern with the natural environment, beside more or less complex observations on life in the crofting communities. Katharine Stewart, in her introduction to the first edition of *A Croft in the Hills* in 1960, explicitly reflects on her and her husband's decision to live on a croft:

> And I believe that each small stand taken against the shrill wind of disenchantment which is blowing across the world has more positive human value than many of the assertions being made by science today. [...] When you have lived for a few years in the bare uplands, where life has been precarious from the start, you [...] become so deeply involved in the true drama of being that mere attitudes and pursuit of possessions are discarded as absurd. [...] And, after all, human steadfastness is the only ultimate weapon fit to guarantee survival in a real sense. That is why I thought it worthwhile to record the process by which three small human beings, completely re-enchanted with their world, found the strength to walk without fear among the astonishing beauty of its wilderness.[26]

This introduction illustrates not only the outsider's usual fascination with the "beauty of [the] wilderness" but also the impact of the spirit of the time, which was marred by the fears of the Cold War, particularly the threat of the extinction of humankind by a nuclear war, which she later mentions explicitly (34). But Stewart's "shrill wind of disenchantment" certainly also means the rising consumerism and the changing character of work brought about by technological innovation and automation. In a wide sense, her approach is ecocritical, contemplating the destructive forces at work in the world and deciding to counterbalance these forces individually with a deliberate movement back to nature and a simple life, which is, for her, the place of escape from the late modern world. Stewart presents the longing for a return to a natural – today it would also be called organic – way of life as the central theme and vision running through her early years and vividly describes the first glimpses of their later home: a glen with croft houses dotted here and therc, well-cultivated fields, a school and tiny post office, a small loch, a shapely hill, and the house with a garden and arable land (4).

Although good relations and mutual support with the neighbours play a role throughout Stewart's story and she mentions ceilidhs (44-45) and many neighbourly visits, her main interest lies in the description of their new organic life. She praises this life because the whole family is in it together and there are "no watertight compartments", as everybody works and helps where and when it is needed (32). With regard to food, they become partly self-sufficient although they never get beyond subsistence farming. Besides describing work and family life on the croft through the seasons, she lays out her philosophy, as, for example, their belief that, when you learn to understand the earth and "work along the rhythm of it", it will "repay you in ways beyond your reckoning" (34). They see their crofting as "a quiet merging into the landscape" rather than an act of mastery. Memories of nature observation are frequent – of birds, plants, mosses and the weather, but again and again, Stewart also gives way to her urge to defend their way of life because she feels that in industrialised society, "the validity of the crofter's way of life may be in doubt" (120), his productivity questioned and he himself may be considered unambitious or anti-social. Stewart holds against these doubts that "the family unit, the neighbourly unit, the man-and-beast unit [fit] securely into the pattern of hill and field and sky" (94), and that the crofter is not a slave to machines and money but extremely free and autonomous (121).

Like other writers, however, she observes changes because the hills are "still too near to 'civilising' influences" so that, while the older generation is dying out, the younger generation are adopting contemporary habits and no longer "think long thoughts, or assess things in terms of human values" (160). Repeatedly, she extols the teachings of crofting life, that is, to work with patience and "with the rhythm of the unfathomable, never against it", to recognise the point of submission, and to celebrate the simple things (161). Thereby she develops an environmental philosophy that includes a strong community aspect but, above all, also a critique of industrialisation and the ensuing alienation of people from each other, from the land and the forces of nature. Against these destructive forces, she posits a crofting life that relinquishes the claim to mastery of nature in favour of an organic symbiosis between humans and nature. That way, Stewart's account of crofting in the late 1950s can be read as an early ecocritical text and a logical response to post-war modernisation, anticipating, and being part of, the environment- and community-oriented discourses of the 1960s. Writing an "End Piece" twenty years later, she asserts that her story is "no lament" but rather a portrait of her family as a forerunner of the later growing demand for a small house and simple rural life (164).

The two other narratives by English women who moved to a Scottish croft or an island are set in later decades – Mary J. MacLeod's story of her time as a district nurse on a Hebridean island in the early 1970s, and Judy Fairbairns' life on an island estate starts in the early 1980s. MacLeod, as an island nurse, pays much attention to the living conditions, the characters and the social customs she encounters when on her round on the island. She goes to the island for reasons similar to Stewart's, that is, because she and her husband had been disillusioned with life in England and followed their dream of something "better than [their] frenetic lifestyle in the south of England: something gentler, uncluttered".[27] She also envisions a pastoral childhood for her children. In contrast to Stewart, however, the MacLeods do not consider crofting because she and her husband do not want the poverty that usually resulted from it. Although the MacLeods are prepared to live without luxuries, they hold certain expectations of life, "a decent standard for the boys, a comfortable home and enough for some of the finer things of life" (23). They find a comfortable house that does not require crofting and work as an electrician and a district nurse.

From the beginning, MacLeod combines her admiration of the rough climate and wild nature with avid observations on island habits, starting with the traditional procedures of selling a crofter's house on the island to outsiders (24-32), but also recounting ceilidhs, storytelling, weddings, funerals and severe drinking on Hogmanay. It comes as no surprise, though, that her accounts of customs are much more superficial than Hall's and her attention is caught primarily by outward appearances. She occasionally exoticises the islanders, as she describes, for example, the women at a wedding, remembering:

> I turned my attention to the footwear, which was equally diverse. I saw good stout lace-ups, winkle-pickers, patent leather courts, platform soles and fancy buckled affairs circa 1910. It was like watching a pageant. (125)

"Watching a pageant" may be read as a metaphor of her position on the island as she watches island life with the eyes of an onlooker who is interested in it but whose participation is limited. She also relates several stories that reveal the human drama and sometimes squalid living conditions on the islands, as for example the story of Biddy, a woman who was locked in and chained by her brother for years (106-118), or of the end of stubborn old Neilly, who had cancer but refused care (308-310). Most involvement in the community results from MacLeod's job as a nurse as she is called to provide medical assistance in the many emergencies in the hills, with the boats and ships, and on the crofts, many of which require the effort of the whole community, which does not fail to impress the nurse. In her "Epilogue", MacLeod recalls the colours and smells, the sights and sounds of the island and the "dear, unique people" of her "Hebridean sanctuary" (346). MacLeod's autobiographical text, however, dwells more on the human dramas the nurse encounters than on nature and details of customs.

6. Eco-autobiographical Writings

Judy Fairbairns' rather recent autobiography *Island Wife*, with the subtitle "living on the edge of the wild", follows a different agenda. The main narrative revolves around her life as a mother of five, a wife and hotelier, losing herself and, through personal and marriage crises, finding herself again as an artist. Into this narrative of female development from self-sacrifice to self-assertion and emancipation, she weaves her encounters with wildlife as well as her husband's various pursuits as a crofter, hunter, expert on whales and marine biologist.

The starting point of their move from England to the island estate she calls Tapsalteerie is similar to other incomers' in that Fairbairns claims that she and her husband had developed a dislike of life in the South, of English commercialism and the many rules that were stifling individuality, and dreamed of a pastoral life on the land, with pure water, steep mountains and their children running fast and free,[28] in a rural idyll where "[t]here are no dangers, no fast roads, no hum of traffic, and there is no crime" (53). She also constructs Scotland in contrast to England:

> In the flat lands we came from, Nature is kept on a tight leash. She is fenced in and fed chemicals for her own good and timed and planned

> and organised until she explodes with a powerful and dangerous rage. Here, we can't but listen to her, humbled by her strength and grace. (63)

Statements like the above quotation are not only eco-autobiographical but also ecocritical, criticising the effects of an (English!) industrial agriculture that strives for mastery of nature and exploits the land until destruction, and juxtaposing this approach with an attitude that is marked by respect for nature. This vision of a return to a more natural way of life on an island comes true but turns out to have some downsides because money is short, the estate in a state of neglect, and Fairbairns gets worn out by the drudgery of running the hotel and raising five children with little help from others. Nevertheless, scattered throughout the book, there are scenes of intense observation of nature, of conscious seeing and listening, of expressing marvel as well as respect in sight of wild animals' peaceful play (179-180; 225), the noises of the rutting season (176) or the first signs of spring (240).

Her husband's life is, however, closer to "the edge of the wild", as he tends the farm animals, goes hunting, offers sea-fishing trips and finally becomes the Whale Man, an expert on whales' habits and marine biology, running the first whale-watching business in the UK. In Fairbairns' accounts of her husband's development into a whale expert, she retells his story of the genuine connection between a whale and him[29] and his intuitive understanding of whales. In various episodes, she recalls how her husband's advice and wisdom is sought when there are whales in trouble, and how he responds with deep respect as well as an attitude of non-interference (215; 289-293), which also marks narratives of her own encounters with nature, as she suggests meeting nature with submission rather than mastery. The spirit of environmental conservation informs her writing at two levels, that is, in her own role as an observer and through her husband's professional life as the Whale Man. There is, however, little ecocriticism.

Auto-ethnographic elements also occur in Fairbairns' narrative when, for example, she describes the local concept of time or the procedures surrounding the valuation of livestock (72-77). Learning the local ways and being admitted into the community are almost compulsory parts of incomers' autobiographical writing about rural Scotland; Fairbairns, however, closes with a description of her and her husband's daily walks, their watching the deer and listening to the birds (348), thereby closing the circle that started with their dreams of a life close to nature.

An autobiographical text that has a much stronger focus on the environment and also includes explicit criticism of environmental pollution is John Lister-Kaye's *Song of the Rolling Earth.* He claims that his book is about his "home in a Highland glen and the wildness of the mountains and forests, which frame our daily lives", mentioning the people, geology, flora, fauna and climate as components of home that shaped his highly personal experiences.[30] Like other incomers from England, he constructs Scotland in contrast to England, as "essentially different from the manicured pastoral greenness of [his] English childhood", but he goes beyond this:

> In the Highlands in the 1960s, many people still lived side by side with nature and they were embraced by it within the normal rotation of their everyday lives, as still happens in Africa or the underdeveloped world where interaction with wildlife and wild country is the norm rather than the exception. (3)

His perception of respect and submission to rather than mastery of nature as the Highland way becomes all the more interesting as he links it with (African) underdevelopment, assigning it a more archaic, primitive though positively natural status, explicitly othering and exoticising this way of life. From his retrospective point of view, however, he is able to see that as a youth, he was in love with "what [he] perceived to be the natural world" (*Ibid.*) and that this perception was deceptive because the land turned out to be full of "historical grief and contemporary contradictions" (2). Musing about his dissatisfaction with his own research, he returns to the example of native peoples such as the Bushmen and Aboriginals, the Sami and Inuit, establishing them as models of a life in direct association with their natural environment and possessors of a knowledge of their environment that is intuitive, comprehensive and appreciative. This re-appreciation of indigenous, non-western ways of knowing is closely related not only to the postcolonial but also to the ecological and ecocritical debates that have gained public attention since the 1970s.

His narrative is not plot-driven like Fairbairns' but rather meanders between extensive descriptions of encounters with nature, anecdotes from his obsession with nature in his childhood and youth, experiences outside of Scotland, excursions into Scottish history and natural history, family anecdotes, and so on. His autobiographical narrative shows characteristics of a male exemplary life, the life of a naturalist, mentioning his discovery that he was, among his peers, "unusual" with his childhood knowledge of nature and natural history (14), elaborating on his schooling and education, and relating how during his traineeship in Port Talbot, a South Wales steel town, he experienced the pollution of air and sea, which awakened his environmental consciousness:

> The process was unstoppable: progress equals profit equals industry equals pollution, so help me God. [...] Lifeless Margam [Marshes] and the yellow scum were where we were all heading. For the first time I think I began to understand the ways of the white man.[31]

Not only does he recount the formative experience of the severe environmental pollution caused by industry, he also immediately connects it with "the ways of the white man", that is, western industrial capitalism and the destruction of nature inherent in it from the beginning. When he is confronted with the damages caused by the first major oil spill after the wreckage of the tanker 'Torrey Canyon' near Cornwall in 1967 (24-35), this experience becomes a turning point in his life, making him escape to a new role to "swerve away from the abyss", seeking "atonement that would assuage the collective guilt of consumer association – help [him] wash the blood from [his] hands" (35). Here as in other episodes, his writing is clearly ecocritical, but these critical reflections usually refer to incidents outside of Scotland. He emphasises the innovative kind of business venture his Aigas Field Centre represents and repeatedly philosophises on the negative effects of modernity and western science, and on "Western man's" alienation from his origin, propagating an unmediated dialogue with nature as the route to happiness, holiness, love, joy and spirit (44-47).

Although auto-ethnographic elements are rare in Lister-Kaye's book, they have their place as an indispensable part of Highland life, and thus he writes about crofting, its meaning and history as well as the drudgery involved, the small returns and the sometimes low standard of living, and, finally, the crofters' self-reliance, independence and happiness, their sense of belonging and community, again comparing this "*primitive*" life style with Australian and American indigenous peoples' lives (186-200). It must be pointed out, though, that he does not give details of customs such as ceilidhs and funerals in crofting communities the way Hall does but rather uses the occasion to reflect on the Scottish natives' "tribal" and "primeval" relationship to the land and to nature (204), employing anthropological or ethnological concepts and confirming the semi-academic tone he assumes in much of his writing, often including, for example, the Latin names of plants and animals. His references to both anthropology and biology are certainly based on his work in the Aigas Field Centre, and his eagerness to proliferate "insight", explicitly expressed in the epilogue (332), has clearly shaped his whole writing.

7. Concluding Remarks

The discussion of nine different texts by eight authors has brought to light both, differences and recurring themes. Recurring themes are the various activities of traditional farming and crofting and the insight that the crofter has to work with nature rather than strive for control and mastery of it. Several autobiographers who are incomers from England construct rural life, especially crofting, in the Scottish Highlands and islands in contrast to England, sketching England as the place where social and economic pressures and consumerism rule, nature is controlled, and agriculture aims at maximising turnout – all in all, where mastery of nature is the goal. Crofting is then seen as a return to a respectful approach to the land, and crofters as people ready to submit to the forces of nature. In this context, it appears that English incomers assign a recuperative power to crofting and rural Scotland, very similar to the mythology of the American West, where those tired of civilisation went as pioneers.

Besides serving as a positive alternative to industrial England, crofting and the working crofting community are evaluated along a temporal axis, as a traditional way of life which has been weakened or wiped out either by modernisation and the hydro-electric power scheme for Scotland, or by the unsustainability of this kind of subsistence farming. In this connection, the 'ecological epilogue' is employed strikingly frequently by autobiographers, who look back from the time of writing to the changes that have occurred since the narrated time, which is in many cases the post-war era. As the texts are autobiographical, it can be assumed that the authors, with their knowledge and experience decades later, re-assess and re-interpret their experiences with rural life in their youth, often assigning them, with hindsight, an ecological dimension by observing, for example, that the character of agricultural work has changed and the old way of working with rather than against the forces of nature has gone. With the old ways of working, some of these ecological epilogues claim, the people and their way of living have perished.

This shows that for many authors, reflection on nature and environment is closely connected with human activities, be they farm work, neighbourliness or customs, and the borderline between ecological and ethnographic elements of a narrative can sometimes hardly be drawn, as for example with descriptions of sheep shearing.

With regard to auto-ethnographic elements, it turns out that incomers' narratives usually only mention customs such as ceilidhs while native Scottish authors such as Christina Hall describe the various activities at, for example, a wedding in much more detail. In the texts considered here, gender seems to account for some differences. While in the narratives from a male perspective, agricultural work with its joys and dangers appears to be the main topic, often interspersed with some local history, women's narratives give more space to family and social relations, including customs.

Furthermore, I would argue that the critical inspection of the texts has shown that the preservation of memories of a traditional way of living has been a major purpose for authors writing about the immediate post-war years, complemented by 'ecological epilogues'. More contemporary narratives such as Fairbairns' and Lister-Kaye's, though, tell of a professional involvement with nature, which, in the few texts considered here, tends to be a predominantly male domain. Finally, it must be conceded that many other texts as well as topics – the rural class system, farming, stalking and poaching, etc. – are still waiting to be explored.

Notes

1 For a discussion on the nature of truth in autobiographical writing, see Smith, Sidonie, and Julia Watson (2010). *Reading Autobiography*. 2nd ed. Minneapolis: University of Minnesota Press, 11, 15-16.

2 Over the centuries, there have, of course, been incomers, and travel writers in particular, who recorded the peculiarities of rural life, a popular example of which are the various travelogues on life on St. Kilda, starting with Martin Martin's *Description of the Western Isles of Scotland* of 1716.

3 Lejeune, Philippe (2016). "The Autobiographical Pact." *The Routledge Autobiography Studies Reader.* Eds. Ricia Anne Chansky and Emily Hipchen. Abingdon: Routledge, 34.

4 Lejeune, Philippe (1989). *On Autobiography.* Ed. by Paul Eakin, transl. by K. Leary. Minneapolis: University of Minnesota Press, 11-18.

5 Ngunjiri, Faith Wambura, Kathy-Ann C. Hernandez and Heewon Chang (2016). "Living Autoethnography: Connecting Life and Research." *The Routledge Autobiography Studies Reader.* Eds. Ricia Anne Chansky and Emily Hipchen, 240.

6 Jolly, Margaretta (2001). *Encyclopedia of Life Writing A-K.* Chicago: Fitzroy Dearborn, 311.

7 Geertz, Clifford (1973). *The Interpretation of Cultures.* New York, NY: Basic Books.

8 Deborah Reed-Danahay, cited in Smith, Sidonie, and Julia Watson (2010), 259.

9 See, for example, the Springburn Oral History Project 1986/7, the results of which were published in Faley, Jean (1990). *Up Oor Close: Memories of Domestic Life in Glasgow Tenements, 1910-1945.* Oxford: White Cockade.

10 For example, MacDougall, Ian (2000). *Bondagers: Eight Scots Women Farm Workers.* East Linton: Tuckwell.

11 Kay, Billy (ed.) (1996 [1980 & 1982]). *The Complete Odyssey: Voices from Scotland's Recent Past.* Edinburgh: Polygon.

12 Cf. Smith/Watson (2010), 258-9.

13 Zapf, Hubert (2016). "Cultural Ecology, Literature, and Life Writing." *The Routledge Autobiography Studies Reader.* Eds. Ricia Anne Chansky and Emily Hipchen, 247-254, 247; 248.

14 Garrard, Greg (2012). *Ecocriticism.* London: Routledge, xix.

15 *Ibid.*

16 *Ibid.* 67-9.

17 Lister-Kaye, John (2014 [2003]). *Song of the Rolling Earth: A Highland Odyssey.* London: Abacus, 39-43.

18 Thomson, Iain Campbell (2010 [1993]). *The Hired Lad.* Edinburgh: Birlinn, vii.

19 Cameron, David Kerr (2008 [1984]). *The Cornkister Days: A Portrait of the Land and Its Rituals.* Edinburgh: Birlinn, 300.

20 *Ibid.*, 70.

21 Lister-Kaye (2014 [2003]), 1-2.

[22] Cameron, David Kerr (1996). "The Cottar's Bairn." *Roots in a Northern Landscape: Celebrations of Childhood in the North East of Scotland.* Ed. Gordon W. Lawrence. Edinburgh: Scottish Cultural Press, 18.

[23] Thomson, Iain R. (2007 [1983]). *Isolation Shepherd.* Edinburgh: Birlinn, 217.

[24] Sanders, Valerie (2001). "Childhood and Life Writing." *Encyclopedia of Life Writing A-K.* Ed. Margaretta Jolly. Chicago: Fitzroy Dearborn, 203-204.

[25] Hall, Christina (2005 [1999]). *To the Edge of the Sea: Schooldays of a Crofter's Child.* Edinburgh: Birlinn, 31.

[26] Stewart, Katharine (2012 [1960]). *A Croft in the Hills.* Edinburgh: Birlinn, vii-viii.

[27] MacLeod, Mary J. (2012). *The Island Nurse.* Edinburgh: Mainstream, 12.

[28] Fairbairns, Judy (2013). *Island Wife. Living on the Edge of the Wild.* London: Two Roads, 49-53.

[29] *Ibid.*, 118.

[30] Lister-Kaye, John (2014 [2003]). *Song of the Rolling Earth: A Highland Odyssey.* London: Abacus, "Preface" (n. pag.).

[31] *Ibid.*, 20.

Bibliography

Cameron, David Kerr (2008 [1984]). *The Cornkister Days: A Portrait of the Land and Its Rituals.* Edinburgh: Birlinn.

Cameron, David Kerr (1996). "The Cottar's Bairn." *Roots in a Northern Landscape: Celebrations of Childhood in the North East of Scotland.* Ed. Gordon W. Lawrence. Edinburgh: Scottish Cultural Press, 1-21.

Fairbairns, Judy (2013). *Island Wife. Living on the Edge of the Wild.* London: Two Roads.

Faley, Jean (1990). *Up Oor Close: Memories of Domestic Life in Glasgow Tenements, 1910-1945.* Oxford: White Cockade.

Garrard, Greg (2012). *Ecocriticism.* London: Routledge.

Geertz, Clifford (1973). *The Interpretation of Cultures.* New York, NY: Basic Books.

Hall, Christina (2005 [1999]). *To the Edge of the Sea: Schooldays of a Crofter's Child.* Edinburgh: Birlinn.

Jolly, Margaretta (2001). *Encyclopedia of Life Writing A-K.* Chicago: Fitzroy Dearborn.

Kay, Billy (ed.) (1996 [1980 & 1982]): *The Complete Odyssey: Voices from Scotland's Recent Past.* Edinburgh: Polygon.

Lejeune, Philippe (1989). *On Autobiography*. Ed. Paul Eakin, transl. by K. Leary. Minneapolis: University of Minnesota Press.

Lejeune, Philippe (2016). "The Autobiographical Pact". *The Routledge Autobiography Studies Reader*. Eds. Ricia Anne Chansky and Emily Hipchen. Abingdon: Routledge, 34-48.

Lister-Kaye, John (2014 [2003]). *Song of the Rolling Earth: A Highland Odyssey*. London: Abacus.

MacDougall, Ian (2000). *Bondagers: Eight Scots Women Farm Workers*. East Linton: Tuckwell.

MacLeod, Mary J. (2012). *The Island Nurse*. Edinburgh: Mainstream.

Martin, Martin (1719 [1716]). *A Description of the Western Islands of Scotland [...]*. 2nd ed. London: A. Bell et al. Eighteenth Century Collections Online.

Ngunjiri, Faith Wambura, Kathy-Ann C. Hernandez and Heewon Chang (2016). "Living Autoethnography: Connecting Life and Research." *The Routledge Autobiography Studies Reader*. Eds. Ricia Anne Chansky and Emily Hipchen. Abingdon: Routledge, 240-246.

Sanders, Valerie (2001). "Childhood and Life Writing." *Encyclopedia of Life Writing A-K*. Ed. Margaretta Jolly. Chicago: Fitzroy Dearborn, 203-204.

Smith, Jess (2004). *Jessie's Journey: Autobiography of a Traveller Girl*. Edinburgh: Mercat.

Smith, Sidonie, and Julia Watson (2010). *Reading Autobiography*. 2nd ed. Minneapolis: University of Minnesota Press.

Stewart, Katharine (2012 [1960]). *A Croft in the Hills*. Edinburgh: Birlinn.

Thomson, Iain Campbell (2010 [1993]). *The Hired Lad*. Edinburgh: Birlinn.

Thomson, Iain R. (2007 [1983]). *Isolation Shepherd*. Edinburgh: Birlinn.

Williamson, Duncan (2008 [1994]). *The Horsieman: Memories of a Traveller 1928-58*. Edinburgh: Birlinn.

Zapf, Hubert (2016). "Cultural Ecology, Literature, and Life Writing". *The Routledge Autobiography Studies Reader*. Eds. Ricia Anne Chansky and Emily Hipchen. Abingdon: Routledge, 247-254.

Contributors' Addresses

James Fenwick
Cinema and Television History Research Centre, De Montfort University, Leicester, LE1 9BH, E-Mail: james.fenwick@dmu.ac.uk

Dr. Sarah Herbe
Fachbereich Anglistik und Amerikanistik, Universität Salzburg, Erzabt-Klotz-Str.1, 5020 Salzburg, E-Mail: sarah.herbe@sbg.ac.at

Simone Herrmann
E-Mail: s.herrmann87@gmx.net

Prof. Dr. Gabriele Linke
Institut für Anglistik/Amerikanistik, Universität Rostock, August-Bebel-Straße 28, 18055 Rostock, E-Mail: gabriele.linke@uni-rostock.de

Dr. Markus Oppolzer
Fachbereich Anglistik und Amerikanistik, Universität Salzburg, Erzabt-Klotz-Str.1, 5020 Salzburg, E-Mail: markus.oppolzer@sbg.ac.at

Cyprian Piskurek
Institut für Anglistik und Amerikanistik, TU Dortmund, Emil-Figge-Str. 50, 44221 Dortmund, E-Mail: cyprian.piskurek@uni-dortmund.de

PD Dr. Katrin Röder
Institut für Anglistik/Amerikanistik, Universität Potsdam, Am Neuen Palais 10, 14469 Potsdam, E-Mail: kroeder@uni-potsdam.de

Prof. Dr. Ralf Schneider
Fakultät für Linguistik und Literaturwissenschaft, Literatur und Kultur Großbritanniens, Universität Bielefeld, Universitätsstraße 25, 33615 Bielefeld, E-Mail: ralf.schneider@uni-bielefeld.de